THE GORAK
ENLIGHTENMENT

The Path to OM

Jayraj Salgaokar is the editor, publisher, co-founder, and managing director of *Kalnirnay*, the world's largest-selling multilingual publication, published in nine languages. He writes regularly in *Loksatta*, *Maharashtra Times*, and other leading Marathi newspapers. He is a visiting lecturer on newspaper printing technology and internet in various colleges and media schools. His interests include reading, spirituality, and mountaineering.

Shree Gorakhnath

An Artist's Imagination

SPIRITUAL MASTERS

THE GORAKHNATH ENLIGHTENMENT

The Path to OM

'Yoga & Tantra,
Buddha & Siddha,
Shakti & Tara'

Jayraj Salgaokar

HarperCollins *Publishers* India

Indus Source Books
Indian Spirit, Universal Wisdom

First published in 2016 by Indus Source Books
This edition co-published in India in 2018 by
HarperCollins *Publishers* India
Building No 10, Tower A, 4th Floor, DLF Cyber City, Phase II,
Gurugram – 122002
www.harpercollins.co.in
and
Indus Source Books
PO Box 6194
Malabar Hill PO
Mumbai 400 006
www.indussource.com

1 2 3 4 5 6 7 8 9 10

Copyright © Jayraj Salgaokar 2016, 2018

Research Associate : Deesha Kriplani

P-ISBN: 978-93-5302-484-0
E-ISBN: 978-93-5302-485-7

Dedicated to the memory of

Smt. Durga Bhagwat, Shri Dharamvir Bharati,

& Yogacharya B.K.S. Iyyengar,

all of whom were the initial inspirations for this book.

Contents

Disclaimer

This book attempts to trace the intimate connections between the esoteric origins and the paths of Hatha Yoga and Buddhist Tantra, and tries to make it more accessible and easy-to-read for the general public. It is an amalgam and a concise compilation of the expert works of various authors. It gives an overview of the different gods and goddesses, masters and students, and schools and philosophies that define their constitution and essence. However, for those seeking more expert and detailed literature, the books and reference material mentioned in the bibliography are highly recommended.

This book is a research work with reference to, and relying upon the contents of, a variety of folklore and folk stories. Any attempt on the part of any reader to connect this material to personal life, or to use it for any experiments without proper guidance of an expert in the respective field, will be at the risk and cost of such reader.

Introduction

O m. The first sound of the universe. The sound that marks the beginning of all time and of all creation. It defines the eternal cosmic truth as it is said that this sound awakens our spirit to live in love and light and experience a never-ending bliss. It is for this reason that this word is the first syllable of every religious mantra and sacred chant.

Om filled up the space of darkness that was our world. Gradually, as the word grew stronger like a heartbeat, the whole universe turned into a mighty ocean with strong currents that flowed passionately. From them arose a golden glowing egg called the *Hiranyagarbha* (Golden womb). This eggshell contained Brahma—the Creator of the Universe who divided the shell into *Prithvi* (earth) and the *Swarga* (the heavens), and filled it with air to keep it apart. He added high mountains, great rivers, and drew six elements of sight, smell, touch, taste, hearing, and thought from himself and combined them to create all living beings—humans, animals, fishes, birds, insects— and filled the cosmos with pure pulsating life that could procreate.

From that moment till today, our world has undergone a massive metamorphosis. We are no longer defined by divine essence but by materialism, our achievements, social standing in society, caste, class and financial status. These, in turn, have built up our egos, pride or *ahankar,* and delusions of grandeur. We are beings who have forgotten our divinity, our purity, our source and our goal—which is to merge with the *Parmatma*, and return to Om.

Om is the sound of being and nothingness. But chanting Om is not the only way we can reach our true potential or complete our spiritual self. It is a long process that requires discipline and a defined path of self-realisation. This path is called yoga, the path that helps the practitioner to attain the highest goal called moksha or nirvana—eternal freedom from the cycles of birth and death.

Mysticism and yoga are among the many gifts that the rich cultural land of India has given to the world. Life-changing and beneficial to all spheres of life, the practice of yoga has reached the length and breadth of the planet. People around the globe have made Sanskrit chants of "Om" and the daily practice of yogic asanas (postures) an integral part of their lifestyle and spiritualism. It is beyond any religion or cult. It is universal.

The word "yogi" defines someone who has chosen to part with the material world and all its material pleasures and attachments. He looks to gain spiritual fulfilment, to blend body and mind with the soul, and finally achieve a union of the soul with the Brahman or *Parmatma*, the Final Truth. (This is according to one of the philosophical systems called Vedanta. There are many other traditions where the concept of the final truth differs from Vedanta).

While yoga is accessible to all, the path to become a true yogi is known only to a few. An esoteric practice, it requires years of learning, dedication, willpower, and thirst for the connection with the universal consciousness and spiritual marriage with the Divine. Only those who seek this path with complete sincerity and patience are truly successful, but only to some extent. When they finally reach there they realise that they are the Brahman.

This mystic science owes everything to two esoteric cults—the Siddhas and the Buddhas. While the Siddhas originated on Indian soil and the Buddhas are deeply established in India and Nepal, the philosophies, paths and deities of these two cults are intimately connected. (The Siddhas belong to the Hindu as well as the Buddhist Tantric traditions. The two should not be equated. According to the Buddhist tradition, the Siddhas aim at becoming the Buddha. There are male and female Siddhas—yogis and yoginis—in the Buddhist tradition, having the same goal and capability.)

Pious and passionate, a blend of these two paths can escalate an individual's consciousness and help him/her realise his/her complete potential. Many names, forms and legends portray the gods and goddesses of these cults in myriad ways across centuries since antiquity. From Adinath to Matsyendranath each section explores the anomalies and similarities of these two cults bound together by the heterogeneous spiritual thread of Gorakhnath.

Born in different centuries, in different castes and countries, people worship the Siddhas from Adinath to Matsyendranath. Reincarnated in different forms across centuries, these deities and their teachings give mortals respite from suffering and samsara and show them the right direction towards their spiritual path where there is only bliss and peace. This book attempts to outline this journey that will ultimately help us return to our true nature, of purity, innocence, and simplicity.

Yoga masters call this state *Sahaj* (simple, natural, *sahajyana*). Buddhists call it Voidness or *Shunya* (zero). Osho calls it No-mind. Gorakhnath calls it Death of the ego . . . Finally it all merges into a single sound . . . Om. . . . Om. . . . Om.

~ **Deesha Kriplani**

Foreword

$\mathcal{I}$ have gone through the manuscript of the proposed book *The Gorakhnath Enlightenment,* by Shri Jayraj Salgaokar. The book consists of three parts: Part 1: Yogic and Tantric Gods and Goddesses, Part 2: Gorakhnath: The Thread that Binds Shaivism and Vajrayana Buddhism, and Part 3: The Siddhas and the Buddhist Tradition. The purpose of the book as the disclaimer says, is to trace the intimate connections between the esoteric origins and paths of Hatha Yoga and Buddhist Tantra, and it is meant for the general public. It is based on various sources, and mostly authentic works. The bibliography at the end of the book evinces the vast and systematic reading the author has done for this book.

The title itself is further explained with three more sub-titles: Yoga and Tantra, Shakti and Tara, and Siddha and the Buddhist Tradition. These three subtitles presumably correspond to the three parts of the book. The author, in these three parts, makes an overview of different religious and esoteric traditions, and tries to show Gorakhnath as the link between the Shaivites and Tantric Buddhists, whose teacher, Matsyendranath, was the chief facilitator of the Siddha cult in Nepal. In general, the presentation is lucid, and authenticated by many quotations and references.

The general presentation is good and the conclusion made by the author acceptable, in connection with the usage of certain terms, common to Hindu and Buddhist traditions. It is necessary, I think, to take into consideration some basic facts. There are similarities in the names of gods and goddesses of Hinduism and Tantric Buddhism. Here, I would not use the words God and/or Goddess with the capital letter "G" as they are deities. The word "God" is used in the sense of *Īśvara* as in Vedānta, but it may still have the Christian connotations. The similar names may point out to a common original source or a partial borrowing from one tradition by the other, but the theoretical differences still have to be taken into account. The Goddess Tārā is common to both, Hindu and Buddhist religious traditions, but there are differences in the development of the concept of her being a deity. The goddesses in Vajrayāna are sometimes described in similar ways as they are in Hinduism. This can be the element of influence of Hinduism, or of some Hindu Tantric sect. Yet, it is to be noted that a goddess in Vajrayāna is mostly a consort of the respective manifestation of the Buddha, and in the Tantric symbolism of Vajrayāna, it is not "Shakti". Śakti is an active principle, while the female deity in Vajrayāna is a consort of the Buddha, and is passive. It is the union of the two principles that is to be realised. This is similar to the Shaivite concept but not the same. Therefore, Shakti and Tārā are not "Identical identities" (1.4). Some scholars of former generations, such as Benoytosh Bhattacharya, have used the term Śakti for a Buddhist goddess. The proper terms are Prajñā or Vidyā. In Vajrayāna, she is sometimes described in similar terms that point to her active role, but it is not a common way of description. As regards Ganeśa, he is not regarded to be as important as in Hinduism.

Jñāneśvara's association with the Nātha cult (2.5) is known and accepted. However, I believe, he does not elaborate on the Tantric theory and practices of the cult. There were fake gurus popularising Tantric practices even in that period who were condemned by the right Tantric teachers, at least those belonging to Vajrayāna. I think, Jñāneśvara showed the non-Tantric path but remained silent on the Tantric practices.

Further, although the Tibetan tradition believes that Nāgārjuna, the teacher of the Madhyamaka doctrine, and the Alchemist, are one and the same, I, like many modern scholars, do not think this is correct. While discussing the question of a number of historical figures of the same name (3.4), or while describing the alchemy of Nāgārjuna (3.9), the position taken by the author in this respect needs to be made clear.

While describing the "Tantric Roots of the Siddhas" (3.5), the author quotes David Frawley. The recent identification of the Indus civilisation with Saraswati civilisation by some Indian scholars, is still a controversial issue. It is not proper to call that civilisation, with all its phases, as "Vedic", until there are convincing evidences.

In the sub-section "Historical Roots of Tantric Buddhism" of Section 3.5, it is stated: "With time there were many disagreements between the Buddhists and thus, two separate schools came into being—the Tenets of the Elders called Hinayana, and the Tenets of the Radicalists, called Mahayana." An accurate statement would be: "There was a schism that resulted into the emergence of two schools, the Sthaviravada, "The school of the orthodox ones – the Elders", and the Mahāsanghika, "The school of a Big Group". There were further eighteen or twenty different schools or sects (nikāya) that were called Hīnayāna by the later Mahāyānists. The Sthaviravāda or Theravāda was one of them. The Mahāyāna came into being after that schism, and emerged from the Mahāsanghikas.

There are certain misconceptions popularised by former eminent scholars. The sub-sections of Section 3.5, namely, "Types of Tantra", "The Outer Tantras" and "The Inner Tantras" are based on the Tibetan sources translated into English. For example, Kazi Dawa-Samdup, in his book *Shrichakrasambhara Tantra,* divides the Vajrayāna into four—Kriyā, Caryā, Yoga, and Anuttara Yoga. This division occurs in the Tibetan tradition and does not have the exact parallels in the Indian tradition of Vajrayāna found in Sanskrit scriptures. M.M.H.P. Shastri uses the term Kālachakrayāna. This is not correct. It is a text; Kālachakratantra is a Sanskrit text with Tibetan and Mongolian translations, and belongs to Vajrayāna. There are no sub-cults such as Kālachakrayāna. The concept of Śūnyatā is not peculiar to the Vajrayāna; it is developed in the Madhyamaka doctrine of Nāgārjuna, which is the foundation of Vajrayāna. There are two ways of sādhanā in Mahāyāna: the Paramitāyāna and the Vajrayāna. Both the ways have the same doctrinal basis.

The statements made about the ultimate reality in the Upanisads and those found in Buddhist texts can be similar. However, the aim was not the same. The concept of *Sahaj* (3.7) is peculiar to Tantric traditions. Buddhism did develop a theistic tendency; however, it did not come closer to the Upanisadic concept of Brahman. Brahman, as the Supreme Being, did not establish itself in Vajrayāna. Brahman is the eternal, ultimate principle. No sect of Buddhism maintains that. The concept of Moksa in the Hindu spiritual system (3.8) and that of Mahāsukha in Vajrayāna are not the same; and the concept of Ātman has been refuted by all the tenets of Buddhism. Therefore, it is not proper to say that the concept of Ātman is linked with what Gautam Buddha says about liberation.

As the author points out, Hinduism and Buddhism have many similarities (3.11). Sometimes the names and terms of yogic practices differ as he says, but sometimes they are common to both the traditions. For instance, terms such as Pratyāhāra, Dhāranā, Samādhi and so on, are common to Patañjali's Astānga-Yoga, and the six-limbed yoga in Vajrayāna. However, the interpretations and the ways of practice differ. While many concepts, terms and practices of Shaivism and Vajrayāna are similar, there exist doctrinal differences. Therefore, it is not correct to say that "the essence and foundations of these is the same" (3.11).

The list of the eighty-four Siddhas with their names is mostly common to these traditions. It is difficult to say to which tradition they originally belong. However, their teachings are interpreted according to the respective traditions. Incidentally, the number "eighty-four" (3.11) has a variety of significance; the significance in different traditions differs. It is not a good idea to mix all those concepts connected with the number "eighty-four", those occurring in connection with the 84000 Dharmaskandhas in the Pāli, other Buddhist scriptures, and other non-Buddhist texts.

In short, I would suggest that it is not proper to mix the concepts belonging to different traditions, and assume that they are one and the same. It is possible that the author does not aim at showing the unity of different traditions and that he wants to show the similarities.

As regards the reference to the Vedic ritual of Soma-sacrifice, it is necessary to state the nature of the Soma juice. The Soma juice was an elixir and was not consumed to rejuvenate the body. True, there is a mantra that says: "We have drunk Soma and have become immortal (ápāma sómam amŕtā abhūmâganma)". However, the significance is different. They offered the Soma juice to the deities and consumed it as the remainder of the oblation. They performed the sacrifice in the perfect manner, as a result of which they became (rather, were aspired to become) immortal. Nowhere in the Vedas is it prescribed that one should drink Soma to rejuvenate one's body; Soma has to be offered to the gods and cannot be taken outside the sacrifice! Secondly, the mostly accepted identification of Soma is with the Ephedra. Soma described in late texts, for example, in the *Suśruta Samhitā* of Āyurveda, appears to be different from that in the Vedas. The Vedic Soma gradually became difficult to obtain and was replaced by other local plants, resembling the Vedic Soma in appearance but not necessarily having the same medicinal properties, for example, the plant Rānśenī, in Maharashtra. I have elaborated this minor point just to show how a general statement, made with a certain assumption, can mislead the reader.

I am thankful to the author for giving me the opportunity to read his book. I must say that I read it with interest and am amazed at the commendable efforts the author has made.

~ **Shrikant Bahulkar**
shrikant.bahulkar@gmail.com

Note on Shrikant Bahulkar's Opinion

This book is a compilation of various commendable works. Certain theories like "Shakti & Tara: Identical Identities" may seem controversial. However, this book only explores the idea of such mysteries and doesn't claim to be the ultimate truth. Based on reading material, discussions and historical texts mentioned in the Preface, this book merely puts forth and deeply analyses the connections and differences between the two esoteric cults of the Nath Siddhas and the Buddhists. Hopefully, this book will also open a whole new avenue in the search for the ultimate truth, of how Gorakhnath remains the binding force across these two cults. This is perhaps the book's ultimate journey. Most of the suggestions made by Dr. Bahulkar have been carried out in the text.

Author's Note

ince childhood, the Nath Panth (cult) fascinated me. Growing up in a Marathi household, we always revered Sant Jnaneshvar for bringing dignity to the language by creating the *Jnaneshvari*—a commentary on the *Shrimad Bhagavad Geeta*. The *Geeta* before Jnaneshvar Mauli (an affectionate term for mother), was only accessible to those who knew Sanskrit—the elite Brahmins. The common man, until the *Jnaneshvari* was written, depended upon the interpretations presented by the Brahmins. The classical upper class at the time, that is the Brahmins, was fluent in Sanskrit and controlled both, religion and religious texts, as a result of their knowledge of the language. Jnaneshvar was born a Brahmin. He wrote the *Jnaneshvari* for the common folk who did not know Sanskrit.

The siblings—Nivruttinath, Jnananath (Jnaneshvar), Sopan, and their sister Mukta Bai—were orphaned at a young age. Their parents Vitthalpant and Rakhumabai had taken *sanyas*. *Sanyas* is the renouncement of all material and familial ties, to retire into a frugal life dedicated to prayer and meditation. When the couple realised the futility of life as sanyasis, they returned to their regular life. The orthodox Hindu society at the time did not approve of this decision, and did not grant them permission to lead a normal homely life. The couple was thus ostracised. The torture they faced at the hands of a society bound with rigid values forced the couple to take their own life, leaving behind these four young children.

Because they were children of an ostracised couple, no learned man was ready to take Jnaneshvar under his tutelage as a *shishya* (disciple). Circumstances forced Jnaneshvar to find a guru in his elder brother Nivruttinath. Nivruttinath belonged to the Nath Parampara (tradition) that goes right up to Adinath—the first Nath. The Nath cult rebelled against the obsolete, orthodox religion that prevailed at the time. Their objective was to reform society through the thoughts of the Nath Panth. Jnananath is the apex of the Nath Panth that was established by Adinath. The classical tradition of Nath Panth charts are shown on page nos. 90, 91 and 92 of this book. Here is a simplified chart of the Nath Parampara.

As I researched Jnaneshvar, the Nath Parampara of Adinath, Matsyendranath and Gorakhnath started to fascinate me. It was around this time that I came across a book written by George Weston Briggs called *Gorakhnath and the Kanphata Yogis* (1936). It was interesting to see the original perspective of an American scholar in relation to the Datta Sampraday i.e the Siddha Sampraday in the Nath cult. Briggs explores the Aghora Sampraday within the Datta Sampraday, and links it to the Bodhisattva doctrine, which is interesting.

The Aghora sect is perceived in a negative light due to its excess use and abuse by a handful of people wanting to make money and spread fear. "Aghora" literally means a person without any fear; a person who has conquered the fear of death. The *pratha* (tradition) is to make one sit on burning *chita* (funeral pyre), and save him at a critical moment. It is believed that this makes the *sadhak* fearless (a-ghora, no-ghora, no-fear) of death. If one conquers the fear of death, then there is no fear left to be conquered at all.

Coming back to Jnananath, he tamed and changed the left-hand paths of worship, as they were called. He introduced the concept of *namajapa* (chanting of the holy name) and Bhakti Yoga (meditation) to prayer. The thought he propagated was, that the only way to attain a peaceful mind was to chant the name of "Hari". He also promoted the practice and principle of yoga in chapter six (*adhyaya*) of the *Jnaneshvari*.

This was the genesis of the *Haripatha* (a simple hymn for

daily chanting), which was a book written keeping in mind the convenience of the *sadhaks*. Jnananath simplified the path of prayer. To quote him directly, "*Te Naam Sope Re Ram Krishna Govinda* ("The name is simple: Ram Krishna and Govinda"). The Warkari *Parampara* (tradition) is a peace loving cult that Jnananath initiated and the simplification of the methods and means of worship led to the tradition being followed on a mass level. Interestingly, even today, the Warkari Panth is widely followed. Every year, about two million Warkaris go on a long march (also called the Wari) to Pandharpur, to see Vithoba Mauli (mother). The distances of the Wari vary from 80 to 120 kilometers, depending upon the point of origin of the march. The groups are called Dindis, and the journey is spent singing and dancing to the bhajans, abhangas, and ovis (all forms of devotional poetry) of the Warkari tradition. The villages and towns that fall on the path of the Wari welcome the Dindis and take care of food, water, tents, medicines and toilets, for the Warkaris.

Shri Hari Vitthal is the probably the only Hindu god whose idol is depicted without any weapons. Most Hindu gods and goddesses are depicted with weapons in their hands. Shri Hari Vitthal's hands rest on his waist and he stands on a brick that was thrown to him by his disciple, Pundalik. As the story goes, Vitthal came to see Pundalik who was busy taking care of his ailing parents. He asked Shri Hari Vitthal to wait at the door step. Vitthal is depicted as the lord waiting patiently at the gates with

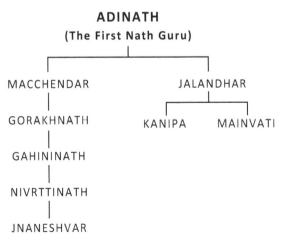

ADINATH
(The First Nath Guru)

MACCHENDAR   JALANDHAR

GORAKHNATH   KANIPA   MAINVATI

GAHININATH

NIVRTTINATH

JNANESHVAR

his hands on his waist. Jnaneshvar interpreted this story to spread a new thought with respect to religion across Maharashtra—a religion of peace and devotion. Eventually, this thought spread to all of India, from the north to the south. In Punjab and Tamil Nadu, Shri Hari Vitthal's bhajans are sung even today. The book by Sant Jnaneshvar is one of the most important documents of the Marathi language which is spoken by over hundred and thirty million people all over the world.

To understand Jnaneshvar, one needs to understand the Nath Panth right from Adinath to Jnananath. In this quest to understand the Nath Panth, I came across two important books, *The Alchemical Body: Siddha Traditions in Medieval India* (1936) by David Gordon White, and the above mentioned book, *Gorakhnath and the Kanphata Yogis* (1938). These two books played a vital role in pulling me deeper into Gorakhnath and his philosophy, as well as the Nath Panth. Much of the Nath Panth is documented in the form of folklore and folk music. For instance, Gorakhnath the great philosopher and writer has composed a *nirguni* bhajan "Shunya Gadh Shahara", famously performed by the celebrated Indian classical music singer Kumar Gandharva (available on the internet). The verse explores the similarities and the symbolism of the essence of *shunya* in Nath Panth, which is also the essence of the Buddhist thought of Shunyata, and of modern Existentialism (Albert Camus and Jean Paul Sartre). The Existential theory interprets Shunyata as an attempt to not feel anything at all. The idea is to believe in every second of one's being, and preserve every moment, so as to not feel Shunyata or emptiness. After all, what is the universe but a whole, blank space or void—Shunyata? J. Krishnamurthy also zeroes down on the principle of Shunyata in his philosophical thought. He thinks there is complete security only in nothingness—*shunya*. When Shunyata concentrates on a point, that emptiness becomes a black hole—the reason for the Big Bang that created the planet that we live on. Aryabhatta's greatest gift to the mathematical theory was *shunya*—zero. Everything begins from Shunyata and everything ends at Shunyata. The Shunyata principle of Gorakhnath and the Buddhist philosophy enlightened me for a splash of a moment, and that moment stretched to infinity.

At this point, I would like to share an interesting event that occurred while I was researching the Buddhist doctrine. While reading through references, I felt a strong urge to visit the Potala Palace. But how did one go there? Getting a visa for Tibet was next to impossible back in those days. Indians could get the Chinese visa for the Kailash yatra or for trade and commerce at the most. It was around this time that a few friends of mine from my college days had organised an expedition to Mount Everest called Tata Everest 1998. They had attempted Mt. Kanchenjunga a couple of years before that, but had failed miserably. This made their chances to raise donations very difficult. Finally, the Tata Group pledged rupees one crore. However, at the last moment, the Tatas agreed to pay only half the amount: rupees fifty lakh. The group needed to raise the rest of the amount. Through some of our influential contacts at the Mantralaya, we convinced the then Chief Minister of Maharashtra, Mr. Manohar Joshi, to provide the money needed for the expedition. Because of my background in media, I also supported and helped the group with their publicity. On a stray Saturday afternoon, my friend Rajendra Phadke, an avid mountaineer and an integral part of the Everest expedition, came home with one of the participants, Ratnesh Jhaveri. The girl who was in charge of media relations could not be a part of the expedition because of a domestic issue. This had rendered them with a free spot on the program. There was massive renovation under progress at home, and with some trepidation, I asked my wife Bharti if I could be a part of this expedition. She said yes! In my heart, I knew that had she said no, I would have still gone ahead. This was not an opportunity to be missed. My journey to the Everest base camp began.

We arrived in Kathmandu to start for the base camp on Monday. We rushed towards the base camp in three days instead of five because our team was expected to reach the peak soon. The Chinese army had just summitted Mount Everest and our team wasn't far behind. At that point, out of sheer intuition, I told our group leader Rajendra Phadke that our team would not reach the summit before Purnima (full moon night). He did not agree with me because my prediction went against every mountaineering norm.

The rush to reach the base camp didn't give us enough time to acclimatise and as a result, high altitude sickness set in for all four of us. A Chinese doctor examined us and instructed us to go to a lower altitude as our brain wasn't getting enough oxygen supply. We immediately decided to go to Kathmandu to lower the altitude but the doctor stopped us. "You're under the control of the Chinese government now. We decide where you go! You're going to Lhasa." I was probably the only one from the four of us, who started to dance in the high winds and extreme cold of the Tibetan side of Mount Everest. (Ours was the first Indian expedition to do a successful summit of the Everest from the Tibetan side.)

So, off we went to Lhasa. After visiting the Shiga-tse Monastery on the way, we reached Lhasa on the holy day of Buddha Purnima. I was very lucky to visit the second most important monastery led by Panchen Lama, who has been in the custody of the Chinese government since his childhood, on the most important day of the year for the Buddhist tradition. And the lucky streak continued as I also got to visit Potala Palace in Lhasa on the holy day of Buddha Purnima. Nobody in Lhasa seemed to be aware of the importance of the day, and the Chinese Government did not want to encourage any celebrations either. Looking back, it seemed impossible to achieve this by any standards. My friends left to go back to the base camp, and I decided to stay back in Lhasa. Over the next five days, I saw many shrines of importance, visited monasteries, and talked to a lot of monks. In short, I had a great time. On my way back, due to this unplanned detour, I had to buy my air tickets from Lhasa to Kathmandu. I had run out of money and the Chinese in Tibet were not accepting any credit cards. All alone, I asked my guide (possibly a government spy), if I'd have to pay any fees or taxes at the airport. The disgruntled guide said no. In hindsight, I realised that he was mad at me because there was no hope of a tip from a broke Indian traveller!

At the immigration counter, the Chinese officer took my passport, checked it, checked the visa, and said, "Hundred Dollars! Airport tax." I had hardly five hundred Indian rupees in my wallet. The man snatched my passport and asked a guard to make me stand against the wall. At this point, I was terrified. All the news reports of the torture that criminals faced in Chinese prisons came to mind. Out of nowhere, a man in khaki clothes, with a shoulder bag came by. He asked me what had happened and I told him my story in broken Nepali (I picked up the language in Darjeeling during my basic mountaineering course in my early 20s). What happened next was unbelievable. He took the five hundred rupees that I had, paid my tax of a hundred dollars in full, and allowed me to board the plane.

The appearance of a classical Buddha is a yogi with a *jholi* (shoulder bag) to collect alms. This was a miracle. Not an optical illusion.

Having got out of Lhasa, I thought my troubles were over. But I was wrong. When I landed in Nepal, the immigration officer told me that I had no visa. We had a group visa to enter Nepal from a single point. She said that since I had exited Nepal at Lhasa, I should go back to Lhasa and enter Nepal from there. "The flight leaves in the evening," she announced. It was a shock. Somehow with my broken Nepali and Bollywood stories, I managed to soften the lady immigration officer's heart. Half-an-hour later, I had cleared immigration and was on my way to my connecting flight to Bombay.

Stories like these do not happen as a matter of chance alone. There is a force beyond our understanding that leads us to our destiny when the time is right. There are many experiences at quite a few places that have shown me the way in life. Sometimes they've taken me higher, sometimes lower, but in the end, it was always a positive outcome. I believe the creation of this book is one such positive outcome. Information found its way to me, references presented themselves, and whenever I desired to read more about something, people have walked into my office with the exact book I was looking for. Whenever I desired research resources, experiences, questions or cross-references, they came to me in a magical manner. Jnananath was on my side all along the way. And I pray for him to remain by my side in the future.

Meeting Deesha Kriplani was again a great coincidence. Without her contribution, this book would not have taken shape. She came in with her friend who was to meet me at my office for some completely unrelated work. As we were talking, she took interest in the book because we were talking about the Hinglaj temple in Balochistan. Neither of us was fully aware of this at that moment, but when she later spoke to her mother, she found out that their Kuladevta (family deity) was Hinglaji (traditional architectural goddess). She was stunned and took a deeper interest in the book. She has truly put her heart into this project. No words can be enough to thank her. But I am sure that Guru Gorakh and Guru Nanakji inspired her to carry on the complicated research. My deepest gratitude to Shri Bheeshmaraj Bam and Dr. Bahulkar of the Bhandarkar Institute, Pune, Mr. Avdhoot Nadkarni of the Times of India, and Dr. Ravin Thatte, an expert on Jñāneśvari. My staff—Mrs. Rashmi Kulkarni, Mr. Rajan Sonar, Mr. Satyawan, and Ms. Harshali Patade have all been extremely helpful in completing the book. I remain grateful to them all.

I am also grateful to my upbringing where I was exposed to spirituality, initially by my late grandmother Smt Indirabai Salgaokar, and then by my late father. He introduced me to the saint-literature in Marathi (sant sahitya). I had the chance to meet and closely know a number of remarkable personalities from various fields who would come home to meet my father, who was a scholar of Sanskrit, Dharma Shastra (religious studies), and who had extensively researched both, astrology and astronomy. He possessed remarkable intuitive powers. He was a Ganapatya (devout follower of Lord Ganesha, the god of intelligence and remover of obstacles, and the son of Shiva-Shakti), but his knowledge of Nath Panth, Jnaneshvar and Marathi classical saint literature, was outstanding. He was blessed with an elephant-like memory. I owe him my deepest gratitude in creating this book, and in my life, in general. Some of my experiences and anecdotes are too strange for people to believe. But what I have experienced is the truth and not an illusion.

While writing this book, I have taken the liberty to go a bit far in analysing concepts, but this was inevitable. Linking the Nath Panth philosophy with Buddhism and the Bodhisattva is a bit of a leap. Orthodox and clinical scholars may frown upon the inclusion of the Dattatray (a Siddha cult) to explore similar practices. However, I have made this comparison on the basis of research and it is backed by references from various scholars such as Mr. Bam, or Mr. Avdhoot Nadkarni. The Pir Parampara of the Naths is well known. There are only four pirs in Maharashtra. The apex Peeth (seat) is at Pydhonie in Mumbai.

I have received invaluable blessings and guidance from Shri Yogi Bhainath Maharaj Mauli.

This is only the beginning of my personal quest for knowledge and learning, and it may continue over several lifetimes. It may even continue somewhere in another galaxy. All I know is that this journey has been on for ages, and that this lifetime is just a small part of it. I humbly offer this book to the reader with a small prayer to understand me, bear with me, and become a part of this journey from here to eternity.

There was a lot of risk involved in researching Buddhist Tantra, but with the blessing of Gorakhnath and Jnyananath, I managed to keep my sanity. And my firm belief that I am merely the means of my guru's will, prevented me from crossing the line. If one does these things for personal gain, greed, or out of vengeance against somebody, that line is easy to cross and then the jungle is an infinite space. Everything is for Aum Chaitanya Gorakhahanthaya Namaha, and for Jnanoba Mauli (mother).

॥ Hari Om Tat Sat ॥   ॥ Alakh Niranjan ॥   ॥ Om Mani Padme Hum ॥

~ **Jayraj Salgaokar**

In a Nutshell

"मग समाधि अव्यत्यथा। भोगावी वासना यया।
ते मुद्रा गोरक्षराया। दिधली मिनीं।।"
(श्री ज्ञानेश्वरी अध्याय १८वा ओवी १७५४ गीता प्रेस.)
(*Jnaneshvari* Chapter 18 Verse 1754: Geeta Press Edition.)

The mystical tradition of perpetual trance (samadhi) was gifted to Gorakhnath by his master (guru) Matsyendranath. The tradition is said to have perceptive experiences (bhoga) of a serene kind.

The above verse, towards the end of the *Jnaneshvari* explains the transition of Shaivaism to Vaishnavism that Jnaneshvar brought in. He did not have any disciple even though he belonged to the guru-*shishya* (master-disciple) *parampara* (tradition).

One wonders why? Possibly, he wanted to revolutionise the worship methods of the cult, by turning worshippers to the Bhakti Panth that focuses on the chanting of the *nama japa* (name).

His goal was to tame the Aghori Nath Panthis including some opportunists and con artists who were, at the time, trying to encash upon the wide popularity of the cult. Under the name of Nath Panth, many unethical rituals were being conducted, without much yogic knowledge. This led to contamination of the tenets of the yogic tradition and gave the faith a bad reputation.

Terms such as Gorakh Dhanda or Kanphata attained a derogatory status and were used in a negative sense by people at large. The above verse explains this transition to Vaishnavism and the root of it. This refers to the correct teachings of Guru Gorakhnath.

।। ॐ तत् सत्।।

।। Om Tat Sat~~

- Jayraj Salgaokar

About Shunyata

शून्य गढ शहर
Shunya Gadh Shahar
(Nirguni Bhajan: Gorakhnath)
The Essence of Gorakhnath's Philosophy
Sung by Pandit Kumar Gandharva (Available on internet)

शून्य गढ शहर घर बस्ती, कौन सोता कौन जागे है।
लाल हमरे हम लालन के, तन सोता ब्रह्म जागे है।।
जल बिच कमल, कमल बिच कलीयाँ, भंवर बास ना लेता है।
इस नगरिके दस दरवाजे, जोगी फेरी नित देता है।।
तन की कुंडी मनका सोटा, ग्यानकी रगड लगाता है।
पांच पचीस बसे घट भीतर, उनकू घोट पीलाता है।।
अगन कुंड से तपसी तापे, तपसी तापसा करता है।
पांचो चेला फिरे अकेला, अलख अलख कर जपता है।।
एक अप्सरा सामे उभी जी, दुजी सूरमा हो सारे है।
तिसरी रंभा सेज बिछावे, परण्या नही है कुंवारा है।।
परण्या पहिले पुत्तूर जाया, मातपिता मन भाया है।
शरण मच्छिंदर गोरख बोले, एक अखंडी ध्याया है।।

Shunya Gadh Shahar, shhar ghar basti, kaun sota kaun jage hai!
Laal hamare hum laalan ke, tan sotaa brahma jaage hai ||

Jal bich kamal, kamalbich kaliya, bhavar baas na letaa hai |
Is nagari ke das darwaaje, jogi pheri nit deta hai ||
Tan ki kundi manka sota, gyanki ragad lagaataa hai |
panch pachis base ghat bhitar, unku ghot pilata hai||
Agan kund se tapasi taape, tapasi taapsaa karataa hai|
pancho chela phire akela, alakh alakh kar japtaa hai||
Ek apsara saamne ubhi ji, duji surma ho saare hai |
tisari rambha sej bichave, parnyaa nahi hai kuvaaraa hai||
Parnya pahile puttur jaya, maat pitaa man bhaayaa hai|
sharan machindar gorakh bole, ek akhandi dhyaya hai||

I first heard this bhajan from my dear friend, renowned vocalist and performer of Indian classical music and also a foremost disciple of Pandit Kumar Gandharva, Shri. Satyashil Deshpande.

"Shunya gadh shahar, Shahar ghar basti!"

This bhajan, with music composed by Kumar Gandharva, touched my soul. Then I heard it again in one of his own concerts. Later, after great effort, I finally acquired a recording of this song. The lyrics of this bhajan are written by the doyen of the Nath Panth, Gorakhnath. My spiritual guru Shri. A.L. Bhagwat belongs to the Nath Panth. He used to worship the Navnaths at our residence on every Varuthini Ekadashi. He performed this puja at our house for ten consecutive years. And we have kept this tradition alive for thirty years now since he passed away. We perform this puja at our house, or at the residence of some other devotee, every year on the said auspicious day. One thing that I like about this puja is that in this worship, one mentally surrenders his home to the Naths and stays in his own house as a guest. There has also been a practice of arranging a bhajan concert in the evening, on the same day. Many stalwart singers and musicians have performed at our residence. On these occasions, all the performers are requested to sing this bhajan, and if it is unknown to them, we play the original tape after the concert. Of course, it was a great treat to hear it in Kumarji's own voice. Almost always, this is followed with a discussion on the meaning of this Nirguni bhajan.

Today, almost every song can be heard on YouTube and we have the facility to hear any bhajan, whenever we want. Even the lyrics and its meanings are available on the internet. There are many Nath disciples whose Nirguni bhajans are popular. And all the bhajans composed by Kumarji are beautiful and great to experience. Their poetry and philosophy, both have spiritual and literary depth par excellence. Kumarji's life-partner late Vasundharatai, his daughter, and his son, have sung these bhajans intensely at performances. The contributions of Matsyendranth, Gorakhnath and other Siddha yogis in the Nath Sampraday towards the understanding of Indian spirituality, is unbeatable. Around the ninth and tenth centuries, the Nath principles had made a great impact throughout India and the neighbouring countries. It was a time when various paths and religions began to have rifts. At such a time, the principles of the Nath Panth became acceptable to many paths and religions. Thus, Nath yogis became gurus to many. Overall, it can be seen that the Nath Panth has made a great impression on the Indian spiritual mind. Adinath Shiva and Bhagwan Dattatraya are said to be the founders of this path.

Indian spirituality and the path of devotion have now reached all over the world. These Nirguni bhajans are available on YouTube for everyone to enjoy and have been sung by Kumarji's own disciples, Shri Pralhad Tipaniya, who is popular for singing Kabir bhajans, Shrimati Shabanam Veermani, who has received a doctorate for her research on Kabir's poetry, Dr. Krishnakumar, Shri Vijay Sardeshmukh, Pandit Satyasheel Deshpande, Rahul Deshpande, and many other great musicians. Many have interpreted the meaning according to their understanding. In fact, understanding the philosophy described in a Nirguni bhajan is quite difficult. Even the symbolism used in the poetry to explain the meaning can be understood only by one who has studied the literature written by saints. The Nath Panth, like the *Bhagavad Geeta*, has accepted Karma Yoga, Jnyan Yoga and Bhakti Yoga. In Indian spirituality, *sagun* and *nirgun* are not considered as opposites. The stage of Advaita that can be achieved by Nirgun meditation, can be achieved by idol worship, which is even easier. Bhajans and kirtans are an important part of this *Sagun Bhakti*. But the Nath Panth proved that even Nirgun Bhakti can be professed very powerfully through a bhajan. The powerful words of poet-saints like Gorakhnath and Kabir have a tremendous impact. It is indeed a great boon to the followers of Bhakti Yoga that Kumarji selected these great works and composed them into beautiful sculptures of songs, which became very popular. These bhajans have given me immense joy at all times. Their meaning is quite complex and the number of bhajans I like is quite high. Therefore, I have decided to write about my favorite bhajan after pondering in depth and having many discussions. It is of course, a free translation of the meaning I appreciate the most.

The philosophy of Gorakhnath has been beautifully summarised in this bhajan. The story is an allegory of the spiritual journey of man. Gorakhnath is on a pilgrimage with his favourite disciple. As dusk arrives, they decide to spend the night in a fort. But by the time they reach the fort, it is quite dark. The fort is huge with a city situated inside it. But the temple in which they decide to stay, and also the houses around, do not show any signs of human activity. All the people seem to be in deep sleep. The disciple asks the guru how it is that everyone seems to be sleeping. Why is even a single soul not awake? What if an enemy attacks? How will they fight? The guru answers, "Well, both of us are awake, isn't it? It is the same with our bodies. The Brahma inside is always awake and the body is always in deep sleep."

It is a beautiful city and the guru and his disciple are felicitated and well-cared for. They are also requested to stay for a few more days. They have come to a lake for a bath. Pointing to some lotuses the guru says to his disciple, "Look how the lotuses are blooming and inviting the bee to taste the nectar. There are many lotus buds which will also bloom tomorrow. So the bee can have the nectar even tomorrow. But the bee is never tempted to settle there. Because he too, like us, is a wandering monk. Likewise, we should not be tempted to stay in this luxurious city. Our body is like this city, it has ten doors. 'Ten doors' implies the ten senses that we have. The enemy can attack through any door. 'Enemies' here mean the temptations and the hurdles which hinder our worship. So the yogi has to be alert at all times. All the doors have to be well-guarded."

There are other yogis who are staying in the temple. Preparations for the cannabis begin in the evening. The guru tells the disciple that our mind should be like the pestle and the body like the mortar underneath, so that the mind continuously analyses and assimilates the knowledge, and only then can true knowledge come to light. The five elements are present in our bodies in a subtle form. They are divided into twenty-five subtler forms by which our bodies are formed. There is a part of our intellect and mind in each cell of our body. When the true knowledge which we assimilate is accepted by us totally, it enters the body cells and then the truth is fully gained.

At night, a yogi is seen meditating in front of a light. The guru explains to his disciple that the yogi is meditating in front of the sacred fire. He is burning all his desires by awakening his inner radiance. He has five disciples which are his mind, intellect, ego, heart (*chitta*) and his speech. All of them are free to roam but they are told to chant "Alakh Alakh" continuously. Whatever is seen is not necessarily the truth. One has to reach the subtle truth behind every aspect. This is true in case of the senses too. "Alakh"means not to depend on the senses. Every time, whatever is seen or appears, is because there is a subtle truth that is working underneath the appearance. One has to keep on trying to figure it out with the help of meditation and deep contemplation.

The guru and the disciple are wandering and a beautiful lady comes and stands before the guru. She is mesmerised by the brilliance that his meditation has brought upon him. The disciple is tempted for a moment, but gains back control due to his guru's presence. Another beautifully adorned lady signals to them with her eyes, while a third young lady who looks as beautiful as Rambha, sets the bed and calls them closer. The disciple asks the guru, "When you were surrounded by such temptations, what did you do?" The guru answers that such situations were plenty, but he never got tempted. He further added, "I kept my celibacy intact. I do not have the need for the company of women, because I have got a son like you without even getting married. You are truly blessed by your father and mother i.e. Ishwar and Parvati, hence you have come to this path. In the same way even I am blessed. That is why I am blessed with a father like guru, Bhagwan Matsyendranath who supports me fully. I worship the Brahma and meditate ceaselessly abiding by his advice."

In the Nath Panth, it is said that a bond of father and son is created after the *diksha* (initiation) between guru and disciple takes place. In many of Gorakhnath's writings, he calls himself "Machhindra ka Puta". Ishwar and Parvati are said to be the father and mother of the world. It is also said that one finds himself drawn towards spiritual pursuit only due their blessings.

।।Alakh Niranjan।।

– Bhishmaraj Bam

Sant Jnaneshvar
An Artist's Imagination

I

Yogic and Tantric Gods and Goddesses

1.1 Adinath: The Founder of the Nath (Master) Sampradaya, the First Guru of the Siddhas (The Proven Ones)

One of the most powerful gods of the holy Hindu trinity, Lord Shiva, has many fascinating forms and awe-inspiring avatars. Each and every facet of this powerful god is mystical, magnificent and motivates mortals to rise, reach their highest potential and gain freedom from the shackles of life and death.

His philosophy of destruction, his music, his earth-shaking Tandava Nritya, his omnipresent Third Eye, the snake skin clothing, the human skull garland around his chest and the snake around his neck with the mighty Ganga flowing out of his crown, all describe his larger-than-life persona. He can digest any poison or drink (his favourite being *bhang*—a drink mixed with cannabis), his unique musical instrument *damaru*, his wife Sati (reincarnated into Parvati, Kali), his sons Ganesh (elephant-headed god) and Kartikeya (god with six heads), his vehicle Nandi, the ash of human body on his forehead and arms, and his residence either at the holy mountain Kailash in the Himalayas or at a crematorium, everything is beyond imagination like a sci-fi hero who comes to life, or has been existing since the beginning of time.

"Shiva" means auspicious, and just chanting his name with all your being is said to wash away sins—such is his power and so pure is his soul. It is he alone who had the strength to endure the mighty Ganges, and the sacred waters of this holy river flow through his matted hair. (01)

His mantra is *Om Namah Shivaya*.

A five-syllable mantra, it is a potent uttering for warding off negativity and forms the crux of many yogic and Tantric practices. In simple words, it means, "I bow to Shiva". Since "Shiva" means auspicious and pure, every time we chant this mantra, we acknowledge and bow to the purity of our own self, our soul, and get closer to the divinity within us. It deeply cleanses the mind and chanting it 108 times is especially practised to gain blessings, empowerment, and enlightenment. (02)

Sacred scriptures describe Shiva's exalted intuitiveness, his sixth sense, how his Third Eye watches all the goings-on of the world, even though he meditates on Mount Kailash with his hypnotic eyes half closed in contemplation. Part of the Trimurti or Hindu Trinity, along with Brahma (the Creator) and Vishnu (the Preserver), Shiva is considered to be the Destroyer or the Transformer. He is also called Bholenath which means the innocent master or, "The Lord who is Easily Pleased", and who easily forgives even the gravest sins of those with the substance and willpower to change. As *Neelkanth*, the "Blue-Throated One", who drank all the poison of the ocean, he became the saviour of all mankind. It is because of his resilience and passionate persona, that he is also called Mahadeva (the God of Gods or the Great God) because he is beyond the cycles of birth and death, and helps humans reach immortality. Folklore describing his blessings and powers is plentiful.

Trimurti or Hindu Trinity

His forms are both quiet and angry. In his quiet, sombre form he is described as a yogi, an ascetic meditating alone on Mount Kailash. He is also described as a householder with his consort Parvati (Kali, Shakti), residing with his two children Kartikeya and Ganesh. He is Natraj (the King of Dance) who expresses his anger, his passion, and his ecstasy. When he dances the *Lasya* he is gentle and benevolent, spreading joy and beauty everywhere; but when he dances the Tandav he is fierce, angry, violent, and on a mission to destroy the stagnant views of the world and its people. These two opposing aspects are in tandem with his persona which destroys and then transforms with compassion, and it is these self-realised devotees whom he protects and nurtures.

He is also called Maha-Kaal. Kaal is time, and it also means death. He controls death. His wife is called Mahakali. He goes to war rarely, to help the creator God Vishnu fight against evil; generally he commissions his wife Kali or Durga to fight the enemy. If and only if she cannot handle the situation, which is a rarity, does he takes charge. He opens his Third Eye to burn the enemy and the enemy territory, plays his percussion instrument—the *damaru*, and dances his wild dance—the Tandav that shakes the whole earth. He is the Mahayogi.

Lord Vishnu

He is also called "Adinath" or "first guru" and founder of the Siddha cult. In this context, the word can be interpreted as powerful ruler or lord, and it's this reverential name that Lord Shiva is known by among the yogis.

Nath yogis often address Adinath as *Alakh Niranjan* which is a title that commands great respect and faith. Of Sanskrit origin, *Alakshya* is the original word, of which *Alakh* is a regional form. It means invisible, indiscernible or unseen; basically something that is not easily perceived by the human eye or senses.

Niranjan means pure, untainted or void of passion. Together, *Alakh Niranjan* implies a pure omnipresent yogic consciousness.

He is also called "Adi Guru" or "first guru" of the Nath Sampradaya, and even identified as "Yogeshvara", which means Lord of the Yogis, which only reflects his dominion over mystic sciences, spirits and souls. In a broader sense, Adinath can also be taken to mean "The lord of the whole creation".

A lot of legends related to Adinath or Lord Shiva are passed on by the Nath yogis through the oral tradition and among these the most important one is the story of Matsyendranath who was mysteriously blessed and initiated by Lord Shiva, and who gained first-hand knowledge of the "Doctrine of Immortality" or *Amar Katha (*story*)* and *Tatva (*principle*)* which encompasses the deeper nuances of yoga and Tantra.

1.2 Matsyendranath and Avalokiteshvara: Parallel Powers and Philosophies

It is stated in folklore that Lord Avalokiteshvara Padmapani Bodhisattva was taught by Lord Shiva the intrinsic knowledge of yoga. One day, by the banks of the Kshira Samudra (Ocean of Milk), Goddess Parvati asked Lord Shiva to share his learning of the "Doctrine of Immortality" of yoga and Tantra with her alone. While listening to the many nuances, the soothing sounds of the ocean waves coerced the goddess to fall asleep. But Lord Shiva's instructions did not go unheard. Secretly disguised in the form of a fish was Lokeshvar or Avalokiteshvara, hearing every precious word. He thus became the first disciple and Siddha to receive his teachings directly from the greatest yogi Lord Shiva, who named him Matsyendranath (also known as Macchendranath)—"Lord of the Fishes".

Interestingly, the name Matsyendranath has three names conjoined as one—*"Matsya"* which means fish or born into fish, *"Indra"* the lord of lightning (*vajra*), and *"Nath"'* which means master, lord or guru. His legends are also very popular in the northeast regions of India, especially in Nepal and Tibet where he has many followers flocking to his shrines and singing his praises.

His mantra is *Om Siddha Yogi Matsyendra Nathaya Namaha* (I pray from my soul, Om siddhi Matsyendranath).

Matsyendranath was the founder of the Nath tradition and

the Siddhas that empower yogis with grand powers and spiritual attainment. He is also the main link for the merging of Pashupata Shaivism with later Buddhism in Nepal. He is renowned as a Tantric practitioner and also known for possessing some unusual magical powers. This particular Tantra is called the Bhairav Tantra in Shaivate Hinduism, or Haruka Tantra in Vajrayana Buddhism.

In Tibet, Matsyendranath is also called Luipa or "fish gut eater". The root of this word is considered to be "Lohita" in old Bengali, which means a type of fish. Luipa is thus synonymous with Minapa and Macchendra/Matsyendra. Luhipa, Lohipa, Luyipa, Loyipa, are other variants of this name and are used by devotees during their prayers around the world.

Another legend describing Matsyendranath or Luipa's journey into Vajrayana can be traced back to the land of Sri Lanka. Luipa was a king who renounced the throne of his wealthy father's kingdom and chose the path of enlightenment. Like Sakyamuni, he too escaped in the night with a single attendant to become a yogi, took a *krsnasara* (deer-skin) as a mat, a throne, and a shawl.

Luipa was handsome and charming, and begged for alms quite easily. He wandered through the length and breadth of India and arrived at Vajrasana, where Shakyamuni Buddha had achieved enlightenment. He attached himself to the hospitable and wise dakinis, who transmitted their feminine insights to him. From Vajrasana he then travelled to Pataliputra, the king's capital on the river Ganges, where he lived on the alms he begged for, and slept in a cremation ground. One day while he was begging in the bazaar he came near a brothel and his karma invited this fateful encounter as this courtesan was a dakini incarnated as a courtesan. The dakini gazed at him deeply and after reading the nature of his mind said, "Your four psychic centres and their energies are quite pure, but there is a pea-sized obscuration of royal pride in your heart." She then poured some putrid food into his clay bowl and asked him to leave. Luipa threw the inedible food into the gutter. The dakini saw what he did and angrily shouted as he was leaving, "How can you attain nirvana if you're still concerned about the purity of your food?"

After listening to this, Luipa was mortified and realised that his critical and judgemental mind was still subtly active, and that was the obstacle to his attainment of Buddhahood. Thus, for him, some things were perceived more intrinsically desirable than others. Soon after this realisation, he went to the river Ganga and began a twelve year sadhana to destroy his rigid thought-patterns, prejudices and preconceptions. He thus began to eat the entrails of the fish that the fishermen disembowelled, "to transform the fish guts into the nectar of pure awareness by insight into the nature of things as emptiness." This is how the fisherwomen gave him the name Luipa or "eater of fish guts". This practice gave him his name along with power and realisation. Luipa became a renowned guru, and there is great mention of him in the legends of Darikapa and Dengipa.

Luipa is often said to be the master of the mother-Tantra and his gurus are the dakini gurus—mundane dakinis believed to be embodiments of the female principle of awareness. The "royal pride" that the courtesan or worldly dakini had mentioned, can be viewed as "racial, caste and social discrimination", and the putrid food she poured into his bowl can best be described as the path of dung eating. The basis of this method is to cultivate what is most foul and abhorrent. By doing this gradually, the consciousness is stimulated to the point of transcendence and the yogi familiarises himself/herself with whatever is most disgusting, and eventually it tastes no different from bread and butter. The result of this method is the "attainment of the awareness of sameness" which is at the core of all pride, discrimination and prejudice, and this process transmutes these moral qualities into emptiness. In simple words, the dakini's question meant that as long as an individual or yogi is unable to perceive the inherent reality of emptiness in every sensual stimulus, every state of mind, and every thought, he/she will remain in dualistic samsara, and continue to judge, criticise and discriminate. To attain the non-duality of nirvana, the yogi must find the awareness of sameness in what is most revolting, and realise the one taste of all which is pure pleasure.

When seen from the standards laid out by society in general, fish is the flesh of a sentient being and therefore seen as disgusting by the orthodox Brahmin. Moreover, left-over fish guts are considered to be fit only for dogs, the lowest life-form on the totem pole, and thus such a practice made Luipa unclean, untouchable, and unapproachable in the eyes of his former peers. A dung eater in usual circumstances would be humiliated, and if he destroys all these associations with his birth, privilege and wealth, he/she will be able to perceive real pride, i.e., divine pride, that is inherent in all sentient beings.

Luipa's timeline in history is often questioned, and even though he is identified with Minapa/Macchendranath, it is believed that Luipa has no significant Hindu associations, although his sadhana has a prominent *Shakta* ethos. However, though both these spiritual entities appear in different places and timelines in history, there are so many similarities in their powers, name and iconography, that they are often said to be one and the same.

Luipa is granted first place in the eighty-four legends. He is considered the first guru (adi-guru) of the Mahamudra Siddhas in time and status, just like Saraha who is considered to be the first founder of Vajrayana Buddhism, especially the tradition of the Mahamudra. It is believed that Saraha's reputation lies in his literary genius whereas Luipa's name evokes a sense of the Siddha's tremendous integrity and commitment. Both Saraha and Luipa are said to be the originators of the Samvara Tantra lineages, but it is Luipa who goes by the title of "Guhyapati" or the Master of Secrets as he received direct transmission from the dakini Vajra Varahi. Luipa is also a great example of Saraha's preachings, as seen through his *doha* songs, and his sadhana became the source of inspiration and example for some of the greatest names amongst the Mahasiddhas—Kambala, Ghantapa, Indrabhuti, Jalandhara, and Naropa among others, were all initiates into the Samvara-Tantra according to Luipa's method.

Matsyendranath's origin is also very intriguing. It is believed that Matsyendranath hailed from the region of Kamarupa in Assam and there is evidence for this—the shrine of Kamakhya has waves of the sea in a drawing under its windows, which are very symbolic of the god. He is also respected as the guardian deity of Nepal, and is said to preside and look after the destinies of its kingdom. It is also said that he rejuvenated Shaivism and established the worship of Lord Shiva in Nepal.

There is an important legend related to the rain (monsoon) in Nepal and it is said that Matsyendranath was brought from Kapotal Parbat (near Kamarupa) in Assam, to Nepal, to bestow its lands with rain and save it from a twelve-year long drought, which occurred because of his student Gorakhnath. According to the story, because he wasn't received with respect, Gorakhnath sat on a mount in the south of Devi Patan and meditated there for twelve years to block the rain in order to avenge the insult. The king of Bhatgaon, along with an acharya (a priest-teacher), went on a pilgrimage to seek his teacher Matsyendranath who was residing in Kapotal Mountain and requested him to come to Nepal. To pay homage to his teacher, Gorakhnath finally left that spot and rain fell abundantly, and all was well once again. There are many folk tales and versions related to the same story. Another Nepali story speaks of how Gorakhnath imprisoned nine rain serpents with his siddhi (mystic Tantric powers) in a hillock, and sat upon them motionless for twelve years, thereby causing a drought. The king summoned a great teacher and consulted him, and after worship of Goddess Jagambara Gnanadakini who is a Shakti avatar, one of the nagas was released. The king then made a long and difficult pilgrimage to seek Matsyendranath who was meditating in Kapotal Mountain, and after a long time, he finally came out of his meditative state and sensed Gorakhnath's deed. He took the form of a bee and in an earthen pot went to Nepal, and the drought was lifted and rain fell.

Gorkhas, the well-known Nepalese mountain tribe, derive their name from Gorakhnath. Hence, an annual chariot festival or rathajatra is held in Patan, Nepal, in honour of Matsyendranath, to welcome the rains of the spring by pleasing the god. This festival also commences the religious year with much aplomb. A small idol of Matsyendranath, about three feet high, red in colour (called Rato Machhendranath, incarnation of the Tantric Lokeshvar), is the central part of this ceremony which is a long procession called Machhendranath Jatra, comprising many rituals that last for a month. The year also ends with a *ratha jatra* procession dedicated to Matsyendranath at Kathmandu, in which a white idol called "Karunamaya" is worshipped by the Nepalis for eight days. According to the legend associated with this festival, in the fifteenth century, while digging for potter's clay, some potters found a statue of Samu Matsyendranath. The reigning king, Gunakamadeva, repaired the image, and a temple was built to enshrine it. Pratap Malla, in the seventeenth century, established a chariot *(rath)* festival which the people celebrate till present times. Both the *rath* festivals have very strong Mahayani/Vajrayani Tantric influences. It is also important to note that Matsyendranath as the Rain God is important for both Hindus and Buddhists, and both these cultures honour him for blessings and overall well-being.

Legends tell of how Lord Matsyendranath can take any form and enter any body at will, and remain so, temporarily or permanently; just like Avalokiteshvara. Matsyendranath is identified with the Buddhist god Avalokiteshvara in Nepal. One tradition shows him entering the country from Assam, another from Ceylon. But both of these traditions could indicate non-Buddhist origins.

Lokeshvar or Avalokiteshvara is a Buddhist saint and also the fourth divine Boddhisattva, known as the "God of Compassion". He is a supreme deity in the East, especially prominent in Tibet. It's also debated that Lokeshvar belonged to a region outside the kingdom of Nepal, and came to the country on the command of Lord Buddha.

According to legend, he was created from a bright ray of light that emanated from Amitabh Buddha. Hence, luminosity and abundance of pure light are often associated with him. Avalokiteshvara's ability to see everything helps him reach out to all beings in all corners of the universe. His essence of light is thus symbolic of the compassion he brings to every soul he connects with. His mantra is said to be: *Om Mani Padme Hum*.

A six-syllable mantra, it is said that each syllable is associated with a cosmic realm, and regularly chanting it helps to purify the vices of that realm. Literally, the mantra means, "Om, the jewel in the lotus", with variable Hindu and Buddhist Tantric interpretations. According to the 14th Dalai Lama, it means "...independence on the practice of a path which is an indivisible union of method and wisdom, you can transform your impure body, speech, and mind into the pure exalted body, speech, and mind of a Buddha."

According to Patrul Rinpoche, author of *The Heart Treasure of the*

Enlightened Ones, the mantra is easy to say, yet quite powerful, because it contains the essence of the entire teaching. When you say the first syllable *Om* it is blessed to help you achieve perfection in the practice of generosity, *Ma* helps perfect the practice of pure ethics, and *Ni* helps achieve perfection in the practice of tolerance and patience.

Lord Buddha - Shakyamuni

Pa, the fourth syllable, helps to achieve perfection of perseverance, *Me* helps achieve perfection in the practice of concentration, and the final sixth syllable *Hum*, helps achieve perfection in the practice of wisdom.

Belonging to the Mahayana Doctrine, Avalokiteshvara's greatest merit is that he vowed to remain a boddhisattva and help other sentient beings seeking the path and did not become a Buddha or an enlightened soul who has gained nirvana (salvation). This attribute of compassion, generosity of spirit, and selfless pure will to help other beings towards enlightenment, has lent him a god's status. In many parts of the world, people worship him with great faith and fervour.

"Avalokiteshvara" is an amalgam of two words, "*Avalokita*" which means glance or look and "*Ishwara*" which means lord. His name thus means, "Lord of Compassionate Glances" or "Lord who is Seen Everywhere". Being greatly helpful, it is believed that he can take any form—animal, bird, insect, Brahman, god or spirit. He can rescue from murder, fire, or prison, bestow the childless with children, and do what he can to remove suffering of samsara from the lives of devotees, and bring them closer to the path of nirvana. He is helpful on all planes—physical, emotional, mental, and spiritual.

Interestingly, Buddhists also call Matsyendranath "Karunamaya Lokeshvar"which means "Lord of Compassion" just like the Boddhisattva Avalokiteshvara.

1.3 Shakti and Tara: The Soul Sisters

The gods would be incomplete without their goddesses, hence acknowledging and exalting the feminine energies is equally important to any kind of spiritual aspect as it is needed for balance of all energies.

Shakti is the dynamic feminine divine and the consort of Shiva in all her forms and incarnations of Sati, Parvati, and Kali. She is deeply worshipped in all her fiery, motherly, protective, nurturing and destructive forms. She embodies the creative life-force and the active aspect, and it is said that without her Shiva would just remain inactive, passive and lifeless, and the entire universe would come to a standstill. If he's the canvas, she's the painting; if he's the drum, she's the music; and if he's the flower, she is the fragrance. Their union is important for the entire universe and the union of their forces and energies within an individual (inner Shakti, in the form of Kundalini) is crucial for every individual to be truly enlightened. Shiva-Shakti are in this sense, inseparable and incomplete without each other.

Devotees of Shakti are called Shaktas and their school is called Shaktism. Their most important religious places and shrines are the Shakti Peeths. There is a very important historic legend that describes how these Peeths came into being. This epic incident changed the face of Hinduism, of India's spiritual make-up, and the Vedas at large.

King Daksha was the son of Brahma, who created him from his right thumb. Sati was one of his daughters (with wife Veerini), who married Lord Shiva. However, this was against his wishes and he didn't approve of his daughter's choice. He considered Shiva a barbarian who smeared ash on his body, wore skulls, and had matted hair, among other things, and he was repulsed by his appearance and general lifestyle of a yogi. On one great occasion, Daksha organised a great yagna (holy fire) and invited all the gods and goddesses, but did not invite Shiva. Offended, Sati reached the place of the yagna and was deeply hurt when her father ignored her and insulted her husband. In humiliation and in deep devotion to her partner, Sati jumped into the fire and died but her corpse did not burn fully. After he got to know this, Shiva plucked a lock of his own hair and invoked Veerbhadra and Bhadrakali, who reached the site of the incident and destroyed everything. Daksha's head was cut off by the men and he was later forgiven, and given a ram's head. Eventually, he completed the yagna but Shiva was grief-stricken and difficult to pacify. Heartbroken and pained, Shiva wandered the universe and danced the Tandav (the dance of destruction) with Sati's burnt corpse in his arms. Finally, Lord Shiva dismantled Sati's body using his powers and fifty-two parts of her body fell into different parts of India and its surrounding countries of Sri Lanka, Tibet (where her right hand fell and established the Dakshayani Shakti Peeth), Bangladesh, Nepal, Pakistan, and Baluchistan. Each of these places became a Shakti Peeth (holy shrine) where Sati's body's spirit, or cosmic energy and power connected to that limb, resides.

However, there are four Adi Shakti Peeths which are considered the most supreme and sacred among all these. The Kamakhya Temple in Assam (where her organs of regeneration fell), Taratarini Temple in Berhampur (where her breasts fell), Bimala Temple in Puri (where her feet, i.e., Pada Khanda fell) and Dakhina Kalika, in Kolkata, West Bengal (where four small toes from her right foot, i.e Mukha Khanda fell) are the most auspicious places of worship. At each of the fifty-two peeths, the goddess has a different name, grants different boons to devotees, and is also said to cure diseases or blocks related to the particular body part. (More on the Shakti Peeths is discussed in detail in a later chapter.)

Shakti energy is very malleable, ever-changing and also volatile. It is accessible to each person in a different form. A twentieth century book, *The Secret Doctrine* by H.P. Blavatsky, defines the many divisions of this Shakti. Here is a gist of it:

"Para Shakti" is the supreme force that exists throughout the manifest universe. Though scientists constantly try to measure light and heat, there's no definite way to measure spiritual heat or light. Thus in the human form, a person's aura (made up of electromagnetic vibrations) is a form of Para Shakti.

"Jnana Shakti" is the power of the intellect, memory, logic, reason, recognition and sensory data. Mystics also call the ability to recognise events that transcend time and space, along with a "sixth sense" of clairvoyance and clairaudience, as Jnana Shakti.

"Ichchha Shakti" is the power of will, the ability that fuels all our nerves, commands our body into action, tells our muscles what to do, makes us sing and dance, and drives us when we truly seek something. This Shakti is different from the solely cognitive ability of Jnana Shakti but it is still related to it. When Reiki healers send prana to their clients by placing their hands on their body (or via distance), they can do so as they are attuned to it and are motivated to do so through their Iccha Shakti.

"Kriya Shakti" is defined as a mystic power of manifestation that helps a person achieve extremely creative and radical results in almost anything. A synthesis of Kriya Shakti and Jnana Shakti

Tara

can help someone sing, create art, dance and in all artistic pursuits. It is important to note that Jnana Shakti, though mostly cognitive and intuitive, forms the basis of Kriya Shakti which in turn is the fuel or rein that steers creative expression to its ultimate goal to achieve results. This Shakti can also be used with other types of Shakti's to create or establish more radical conditions or changes in our life with regard to wealth and health.

"Kundalini Shakti" is an inherent power we are all born with. Coiled three and a half times like a serpent at the base of our spine, this Shakti can help an individual reach his highest potential, attain enlightenment, and achieve the highest state of spirituality. Activating this energy takes time and pious love for the Divine, and yogis spend their lives trying to reach this stage. It plays a vital role in deciding our karma and re-incarnation. (More on this Shakti is discussed in detail in a later chapter.)

"Mantra Shakti" is the power to invoke gods/goddesses, change circumstances, and even attract positive cosmic energies to our desired goals using certain spiritual incantations and chants. This Shakti is related to a part of all our yogic customs and prayers to the Divine and is crucial for all other Shaktis. For instance, for better memory (Jnana Shakti) students chant the Saraswati mantra, for better finances and property the Lakshmi mantra (which activates Kriya Shakti) is chanted, and so on and so forth. Though our destiny is dependent on our karma, Mantra Shakti to a great extent helps reduce adverse effects in our life if practised with sincerity and dedication.

Walking on the path of Goddess Shakti is crucial for every individual seeking salvation, and the Buddhist manifestation of her, Goddess Tara, nurtures the seekers like a devoted mother. Worshipped since ancient times all throughout the world but mainly in Tibet, Nepal, China, Japan, and also in Russia, she is the goddess of compassion, virtue, and mother's love.

A fully enlightened Buddha, it is difficult to grasp the entire essence of Tara in totality. At a relative level, ordinary minds can easily understand and appreciate her characteristics of limitless love, empathy and benevolence that she has for one and all. The story of her metamorphosis into a Buddha is a very interesting one. According to legend, there was once a princess, Yeshe Dawa, translated as "Moon of Primordial Wisdom", who was devoted to the Buddha of that era and who wanted to become a Bodhisattva by his grace. She wanted to take this vow to gain enlightenment, so that she could help all the beings who were suffering in samsara. However, the religious heads of that era held the notion that only those in a male body could become enlightened so they told her to pray for a male reincarnation. Princess Yeshe Dawa took an oath to carry out all her enlightened activities of the past, present and future, only through her god-given female form. Over time, she became a fully enlightened Buddha and was named Tara. It is important to note, that at ultimate levels of spirituality, the gender of male or female disappears, and these concepts are not differentiated against. This female form chosen by the Goddess Tara represents a very liberal, absolute, and benevolent mind, which we call the Great Mother.

There is another legend which describes Goddess Tara's emanations differently. According to this story, she was closely connected to the compassion of Bodhisattva Avalokiteshvara, also known as Chenrezig in Tibet. Since antiquity, he had been working selflessly to liberate and help all sentient beings from the suffering of samsara or human life. There came a time when he felt that every being in the world was liberated and blissful in the enlightened state called *Potala*, i.e., the pure land of Avalokiteshvara and Tara. But when he looked again, he realised that the six realms were still unchanged and beings were still suffering under miserable conditions and unending difficulties. Hurt and pained, he threw himself on the ground and shed tears of love and compassion. From the tear of his left eye, emanated Bodhisattva White Tara, and from the tear of the right eye, emanated Bodhisattva Green Tara. Together they told him,

"Don't worry! We two will help you."

It is difficult to comprehend or write about Tara's enlightened activities as there are so many! She is known for granting devotees many boons and blessings like longevity, prosperity, children, respite from diseases, and even stopping those at war. There are twenty-one emanations of her great being, which are praised and worshipped in many parts of the world. Primarily, Tara is the goddess who liberates sentient beings from eight great fears listed by Gautam Buddha. According to his teachings, fears transcend time. Thus, the fears people had in the ancient ages are the same as those faced today. Those who continuously practise and walk on her path are protected from all fears and can be free from their root causes.

Bodhisattva

The Tara Yantra is simple yet powerful. Its *bhupur* (outside square) is of a viridian leaf colour, which represents balance. This balance is needed to cross the ocean of samsara, and meditating on it produces the colour red. The Yantra's petals are of a rose-pink hue and denote shyness. Meditating on this makes one frank.

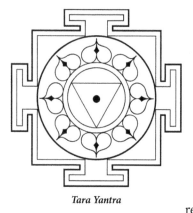

Tara Yantra

The upward pointing triangle is in vermilion which represents rage, and she is the goddess who helps us overcome all our fears. The vermilion triangle is set over the violet-purple hue of *akasha*, the centre of the fifth chakra that is also the seat of Saraswati (Goddess of Knowledge). Tara is connected with speech and Goddess Saraswati is said to reside on the tongue of the wise. Balance is integral to connect with Goddess Tara, and it is this virtue that helps the devotee float and travel across the oceans. A neutral green, it pacifies the violence produced by the vermilion shade, and meditating on the green *bhupur* helps to increase life/longevity.

Tara is also called "The Great Mother" or "The Wisdom Dakini", "Mother of Samsara and Nirvana", and "Mother of all Buddhas". She is so-called as she is the one who gives birth, nurtures, and helps us discover our own enlightened state of mind. She is everywhere and each living being can easily connect to her at any time as her power is beyond limits and boundaries of all kinds. It is essential that we keep our mind and heart open like "the ring of devotion", so that her "hook of compassion" can connect with us. Like Goddess Shakti, Goddess Tara too has many forms and emanations, which work on different levels to free us from suffering. For instance, Red Tara helps us activate our realisation and helps us deal with the egocentric and neurotic states that bring us down. With her help, we get untied from such suffocating confinements, liberate our souls, and reach out to others with more empathy.

In the words of some great Buddhist masters, "Go beyond dualities; relax; don't hope; don't grasp; let it go. Flow continually in the relaxing original state."

As the Wisdom Dakini, Tara helps us reflect on the true nature of our mind and the reality. Sometimes, our perceptions are limited by our six senses and outdated patterns of thinking. Society, caste, religion and many such norms bind our true nature, and we are trapped. To break away from such a pattern, a determined practice is needed. And for this, we need to develop what great masters call "The Dakini's Third Eye". This Third Eye is the wisdom mind, which mirrors our true self, helps us to see beyond dualities and frees us from all limitations. Everything is seen in totality, in an instant, and without any judgement. It is then that we return to our "Buddha" nature, which is true, pure, in perfect harmony with the world, and always experiencing peace and joy. In the great master Jigme Lingpa's words, "The entire universe is the Mandala of the Dakini". She is thus called "Mother of all the Buddhas", as she removes the many barriers of our pattern and habits which keep us away from the emptiness of our true nature. This state of emptiness or *shunya* is full of opportunities, change, movement, creativity and joy; without which the universe would be nothing. Thus, both the qualities of love and compassion, along with this experience of emptiness are the gift of the Mother and the ultimate Wisdom Dakini in each of us. (More on this *shunya* aspect is discussed in detail in a later chapter).

Tara's lineage can be traced to Kama and Terma, with the latter having the large version, the middle version, and the small version. The Terma lineage describes practices of Tara's emanations which are peaceful, semi-wrathful and wrathful. This system, however, got disrupted and even the texts with the knowledge of these practices disappeared. The lineage of each of these practices did continue with several masters, but some practitioners did not fully and appropriately honour the Wisdom Dakinis like Yeshe Tsogyal (student of Guru Padmasambhava). Despite such difficulties in the lineage, Tara remains one of the most revered and powerful deities of Tibetan Buddhism.

Although legends and folklore exalt these gods and goddesses in both, Hinduism and Tantric Buddhism, their teachings were taken ahead by one yogi whose influence and greatness gave yoga a clear direction and stronger roots in many parts of India, Nepal, and the world at large.

1.4 Tantric Goddesses: Guides, Guts and Glory
The prime feature of Tantra is worshipping the goddess in all her guts and glory. The feminine aspect is exalted in this path and worshipping the Divine Mother is not just about following a set of beliefs or dogmas, but involves developing our own higher self

through her grace and her wisdom. Traditional Tantra worships both, the male and female aspects, the god and goddesses together, so worshipping Shakti involves the worship of Shiva. Even worshipping their children Ganesh and Kartikeya is given importance, as also the other Hindu deities belonging to the pantheon.

Tantra views the feminine aspect as an embodiment of knowledge, wisdom, and energy of consciousness which is rooted in the qualities of receptivity, compassion and loving kindness. In all her various forms of beauty, the goddess possesses *samvit* (pure consciousness) of nature, and nature herself is the mirror of this beauty. The flowers, birds, mountains, forests, oceans, and sky are all like the music and dance of the goddess. The sexual beauty is an aspect of her personality, and Tantra only helps us discover this in our lives. The goddess is thus much more than her sexuality and this is just a metaphor for her qualities. Ultimately, she is the bliss of being, and we need to realise this joy within our hearts to be fully content. The ancient scriptures of the Hindu tradition—the Vedas—represent the three realms of speech, mind, and breath called the *Trayi Vidya* (the three wisdoms) which is similar in essence to the Greek idea of the Three Graces. Truly worshipping the goddess needs knowledge as that is her true form and this needs to be an inner worship that requires meditation.

Meditation on the goddess is a kind of "self-inquiry" that is constantly striving to acquire more knowledge. She is the embodiment of mystery, of all that is hidden, of secrets, subtlety, and sensitivity that have to be discovered. She is the inner guiding power within each of us, and she is the teaching as well as the comprehension. She is the muse who inspires, the high priestess with the truths, and the powerful force who is delightful and transformative. She is the unfamiliar, the unknown and the allure of all that we seek, and to find her we must first lose ourselves. When we surrender to her, we go beyond the realm of the known and enter the domain of time-space into the secrets of time and eternity.

The goddess embodies wisdom at all levels and her "Ten Wisdom Forms" or "*Dasha Mahavidya*" also known as "Ten Wisdom Goddesses" possess this diverse power in myriad forms. *Dasha Mahavidya* in a larger context represents the "Ten Great Streams of Knowledge" which mirror the workings of the universe and our inner psyche once the maya (illusion) blinding the realities from our sight is broken down. The insights these goddesses provide are full of knowledge, free from ill-will and attachment, and may not always be pleasant in their forms, but they awaken our minds and unfold the mysteries we are blinded by. To reach our full potential and to get attuned to higher energies and forces, we must first recognise that being stuck or attached to lower forces doesn't allow us to evolve. The Wisdom Forms of the goddess can be grasped only when we allow her to enter our lives with complete surrender and respect. Each form represents a particular approach to self-realisation, and helps us in areas of life such as health, wealth, fame, spirituality, and even mundane activities of daily life. Her Yoga Shakti does the work and we have to be receptive to this rhythm. Known by many names around the world such as Rajarajeshwari in south India, Tara and Kali in northeast India and Bengal, Nepal and other Buddhist countries, the goddess is ever willing to help us. Also called "The Great World Mother", Kali is the foremost of the Ten Wisdom Goddesses. Since in this book our focus is the Siddha and the Buddhist traditions, we will be deeply focussing on the graces of the goddesses, Kali and Tara.

In the sacred text, *Mahabhagavat Purana*, written in the fourteenth century in eastern India, the original story of the Mahavidyas is connected to King Daksha's famous yagna. In this version of the story, Sati is forbidden by Lord Shiva to attend the ceremony and in her anger she accuses him of neglecting her. Her anger is so great that her eyes turn red and bright in colour, and her limbs tremble. Looking at her fury, Lord Shiva closes his eyes and when he opens them a very fierce female is standing in front of him. As he continues to look at her she turns old and her graceful appearance disappears. She then develops four arms, four hands, her hair is dishevelled, her lips are sweaty, her complexion is dark, her tongue hangs out, and she begins to wave from side-to-side. She is wearing only a garland of severed heads and the half-moon, as a crown. As this form stands before Lord Shiva, blazing like a million rising suns, her earth-shattering laughter fills up the entire world.

Lord Shiva is frightened and tries to run away but this terrible Goddess' dreadful laugh keeps him rooted to the spot to ensure that he does not flee. Sati fills up all directions around him with ten different forms which are called the Mahavidyas. According to the book *Mahabhagvata Purana*, when asked who these goddesses

Lord Shiva

are, Sati calls them her "friends". Soon, Lord Shiva stands still and closes his eyes and when he opens them, a smiling woman looks back at him. When he asks her where Sati is, she replies that she is in front of him. He then asks about the other goddesses surrounding him and she replies with all their names and directions— Kali to the south, Tara above him, Chinnamasta to his right, i.e., the west, Bhuvaneshvari to his left i.e. the east, Bagala to the north, Dhumavati to the southeast, Tripurasundari to the southwest, Matangi to the northwest and Sodasi to the northeast.

In the Hindu book based on the worship of Goddess Tara called *Tantrasara*, there is a fable which describes how the Mahavidyas or the forms of Kali came into being. According to this story, Lord Shiva who was living with Goddess Kali in Satya Yug, grows restless and decides to leave. When he gets up and is on his way out, she asks him where he is going, to which he replies, "Wherever I wish!" She does not reply, and he leaves. As he is wandering, in whichever direction he goes a form of Goddess Kali appears before him. He initially sees the first of the Mahavidyas which is Kali, then he sees her other forms—Tara, Bhuvaneshvari, Bhairavi, Sodasi, Bagalamukhi, Kamla, Dhumavati, Matangi and Chinnamasta. After seeing all these goddesses before him, Lord Shiva realises that he does not want to leave Kali. He also gains *vidya* (the knowledge) that the goddess is everywhere, pervading the entire cosmos and that wherever anyone goes she exists, present in one of her forms.

Kali: The Goddess of Transformation

The mysterious goddess often associated with darker energies, Goddess Kali is called the "Goddess of Transformation". An ally of the forces of death and destruction, she is an enigmatic goddess who is seen as a threat and curse by many; but it is her grace that we

Kali - The Goddess of Transformation

need to worship to end the nights of ignorance and to fight the demons of our life. The word Kali is a feminine form of the word kaal which means time. So Kali also means "time which governs the entire universe". Change is the ultimate reality and also the only constant in this world. This constant immutability is time's secret message to mankind and it is the great force through which each and every organism grows and develops. It takes us many births and deaths to fully understand our soul's purpose and Goddess Kali represents this process through which we evolve and break free from the shackles of birth and death. Like a great womb, time too has a feminine quality to nurture, wait, and love, but our longing for the future makes us believe that time itself is our own, and this can create attachments in our lives. Hence, it is through Goddess Kali that we give up attachments in our lives, and can gain mastery over time itself. To welcome the new, we must let go of the old. This letting go, this destruction of old habits, patterns, attitudes, and way of life, can be brought about through Kali. She helps us release attachments to material things, to go beyond the known, to let go of ignorance and sorrow, sacrifice our ego before the Divine, and it is Goddess Kali who accepts these sincere soul offerings. And gradually, we can become one with time, dissolve into it and like pure consciousness, witness the ongoings of the world more objectively.

Time is prana (the life-force) and since Goddess Kali is Time, she is also the life-force, the Divine Mother of our life, and the source of our vital energy. Our life force or vital energy comes through blood hence Goddess Kali is associated with blood and this is symbolically expressed in many art forms and paintings. She is constantly renewing herself through our physiological processes, and these are like sacrifices that we make towards her. Time also brings about death, hence she is also known as the "Goddess of Death". This death is a spiritual death which paves way for an eternal life that ends all those things that are irrelevant and no longer have any substance. It is said that "Kali is the life that exists in death and the death that exists in life". Thus, every day we must die before her, we must kill all our attitudes, fears, anxieties, and our ego to replenish our life force and to feel the blessings of Kali run through our veins. A meditational approach linked to this goddess is of emptying the mind and absorbing the flame of awareness in our minds. This awareness is of re-igniting the love for the Divine, which is where we have come from, and to where we must eventually return.

Goddess Kali is symbolic of death in all its dark and glorious forms and in many paintings, is depicted as dancing on cremation grounds. Thus, meditating on death is a way we can connect to this powerful goddess. She may appear frightening and destructive but at the core, she is the path to immortality which can lead us to re-experience the immortality of life. She has the power of death, as well as the power over negation, which is the ultimate nirvana, the ultimate liberation every soul seeks. At this stage, there is no mind, no desire, only a peaceful dissolution. When her power connects with our being, this goddess brings about a radical change in our life by helping us break away from all limitations binding our spirit, and takes us beyond our physical form.

Goddess Kali's Shakti is "*Kriya* Shakti" (the power of transformation and action). She blesses us in gaining yogic transformations and takes us to unimaginable realms once we surrender to her will. At a cosmic level, Goddess Kali is linked to *vayu* (the element of air). Just like the air, she is transformative, mobile, and subtle. She is also connected to *Vidyut* Shakti (the power of lightning) or the electrical force that exists in the universe. She is thus quick, unpredictable, and brings about the most radical changes all of a sudden. Her devotees can also experience illumination that appears in a lightening moment. As written earlier, she is a life force that exists in the human body and thus, she is prana, the very breath that we take. When we die, it is this life force that leaves our body and joins the subtle worlds. Thus, in the rhythm of our breath, if we closely observe and concentrate, we can experience the reality of Kali.

It is said that Kali means beauty. Since Kaal means measure or duration or time, this can be taken to mean a measured-out beauty. But this beauty is of terror, destruction, and death. She thus can take the form of or appear in our life as an unrequited love or an unattainable beauty, which represents that divine mystery which can never be grasped in the physical form. Thus, the more we try to find beauty in the external, the more we lose our life. And the more we try to find the inner beauty, the more we go beyond death like Goddess Kali herself. Goddess Kali is the consort of Lord Shiva who is also known as *Mahakaal*, or the "Lord of Time and Eternity". While he has a more passive form, she is the active power, or the flow of grace from his heart. He is the corpse on which she is seen dancing in many paintings. She is thus his life and energy.

In the subtle or auric body, Goddess Kali is said to be located in the Heart Chakra. She is also linked to the heart organ in the physical body, as it is the organ which supplies the blood or the life force to all other organs. Hence, she is also called "Rakta Kali" or "Red Kali", who is the heartbeat of the heart. As Bhadra Kali, she is an auspicious deity and is said to be located in the spiritual heart centre. In this form she gives the devotee the highest transformation, which is self-realisation.

By appearance, this goddess has a very fierce and even terrorising form that leaves devotees awestruck. Dark blue in colour, she wears a garland of skulls and her long tongue sticks out. In many paintings and idols, she is depicted as having two fangs instead of a tongue. She has four arms, four hands and she holds a sword or knife in one hand, and a severed head that is dripping with blood, in the other. Her other two hands are in the form of mudras that grant boons and remove fear. The skirt she wears is made of human arms. She is often depicted as dancing on a cremation ground on top of a corpse which is Lord Shiva himself. Her appearance itself contains multiple spiritual symbols. Blue represents space and eternal time, the chopped head represents cutting off the ego, the garland of skulls represents all the creatures and our own rebirths, which have to die. The skulls represent her ability to help us free our mind from the physical body and identity. Her skirt made of human arms represents her power over all the organs of action.

A powerful mantra related to her is the mantra for Goddess Chamunda who is her fierce reincarnation shown in the story of Devi Mahatmya:

Om Aim Hrim Klim Chamundaye Vicche.

This mantra can be simplified as the supreme word Om, followed by the mantras for wisdom, Saraswati (*Ain*) for purification, Parvati (*Hrim*) for transformation, Kali (*Klim*), and the mantra *Svaha* which consummates the offering to Chamunda. *Vicche* means cut, in the sense of cutting off the head of the demon or cutting off the head of the ego.

A simple repetition of her *Bija* mantra "*Krim*" which is the power of *Kriya* (action) is enough. Devotees can also use "*Klim*" while worshipping her or simply repeat her name Kali. Goddess Kali represents the impermanence of all things and people and this is an important teaching in Hinduism as well as Buddhism, as it is through her that we see the ultimate reality of life, which is death and decay. Thus, knowing Kali is being able to see the child in the old man and the old man in the child. Such a person can grasp time and embrace eternity.

The Kali Yantra is based on the form featured in the Shakta Pramod. The *bhupur* has two lines around it coloured in gold and chrome yellow. These form two layers and a deep blue hue forms the third. The three layers denote the three states of matter, i.e., solid, liquid and gaseous. The layer outside and inside of the *bhupur* has a gold line which helps in maintaining the geometrical structure of the diagram. A partially visible triangle is inside the *bhupur* and outside the circular pattern. This triangle denotes *Tripuramba* or the "Cosmic Mother", and her infinity. The entire world is symbolised by an eight-petalled lotus. This lotus represents the octave of Prakriti, i.e. the elements of air, akasha, earth, fire, water, mind, intellect and ego. The three gold circles inside of the eight petalled lotuses denote the three aspects of time to which the eight petals of the phenomenal existence contribute their karmas. Past, present and future are represented by three golden rings, and the centre is concentric. The triangles overlapping one another are the three gunas— *sattva*, *rajas*, and *tamas*—the modes of Shakti. These three triangles are linked with the rings of time. The *Bindu* in the centre symbolises the goddess herself. In

Kali Yantra

a deep hue of blue, this Yantra forms the complementary colour orange, when meditated on. It cures the devotee of pessimism and depression, makes him ready to accept ideas given by others and also makes him/her more sociable and outgoing. The crimson tone of the central triangle which contains the golden *Bindu* is the shade of love and faith.

Goddess Kali is usually worshipped by warriors and those seeking victory in the battlefield, as even mentioned in the *Agni Purana* and the *Garuda Purana*. The *Bhagavat Purana* represents Goddess Kali as the patron deity of thugs. In the Bengali text, *Mangal Kavyas,* she is represented granting special boons and magical powers to thieves, helping them accomplish criminal deeds. People belonging to the lower castes and tribals are also amongst her followers. In fact, the *Manasara Silpa Sastra* says that Kali's temples should be placed near cremation grounds or near Chandals (very low caste people).

Kalingattupurani, the eleventh century Tamil text, describes a temple located in the midst of a desert, describing it to greatly resemble the goddess's uncivilised persona. The construction of the temple is very fierce—it is made of bones, flesh, blood, body parts of enemies killed in battle, and severed heads. Even the pujas conducted here are horrific and gruesome, and the text describes how warriors and devotees often cut off their heads as offerings to demonstrate their fearlessness. Blood is used to clean the temple instead of fresh water, and flesh is used as offerings instead of flowers. Burning corpses are the lighting lamps. And seated on a *pancha-preta* (bed of five ghosts) is the Goddess Kali herself, using a corpse as a pillow on a bed made of flesh.

Goddess Kali appears in many myths related to Shiva and Sati. In the *Vaman Purana,* it is stated that Shiva called Parvati "Kali" (the black complexioned one) and because of this Parvati once took up austerities to transform her looks. She succeeded, and this avatar was called *Gauri* (The Golden One), owing to her luminous beauty. However, the dark sheath she discarded turned into Queen Kaushiki, who eventually created Goddess Kali in her fury. Kali thus represents a fierce, dark, violent and very aggressive form.

Goddess Kali's stories linked with Lord Shiva are wild and she brings out the destructiveness in him, according to many legends. A tale based in south India tells of a dance contest between the two.

As per the story, Goddess Kali decides to stay in the forest with her fierce companions after she defeats Sumbha and Nisumbha. A devotee of Shiva is distracted by this and asks the lord to help him. When Shiva appears before her, the goddess turns violent and calls the land her own, after which Shiva challenges her to beat him at dance. He performs the energetic Tandav and eventually defeats her. Since it was Kali's bait that provoked him to this violent dance that can signify the end of a cosmic age and can even destroy the universe; it can be seen as a mirror to the goddess' violence. There are many similar illustrations and incidents that describe how Kali enticed or lured Shiva to express his wild and uninhibited side and she is usually shown as the more dominant one.

Goddess Kali thus can be seen as a deity who can change and transform a social order and our personal morals through her fierceness, and as "a slayer of demons", who constantly pushes us out of our comfort zones to face our deepest and darkest fears. It is important to remember to not let this aggression get out of hand, as the goddess who protects can also go beyond the boundary in her frenzy, and destroy.

Her role in Tantrism is a central one. In most Kashmiri texts by Abhinav Gupta, she is described as a very prominent deity in the region's practices of Tantrism. An important symbol found in this region is the Shakti Chakra, which is a wheel of energy that symbolises the evolution and the dynamics of consciousness. This main wheel is often depicted as having additional wheels with the twelve Kalis. Even in eastern India, especially in Bengal, Goddess Kali is the residing figure of Tantric Yoga and is widely worshipped in all her forms. Even though it is Lord Shiva who has all the knowledge of Tantra, it is in Kali's form that Parvati truly expresses her Shakti and prowess, to help human beings transform themselves and the world. The *Yogini Tantra*, *Kamakhya Tantra* and *Niruttara Tantras*, all proclaim Kali to be the greatest of all divinity and even describe her as the *svarupa* (essential form) of the Mahadevi. In a passage of the *Mahanirvana Tantra*, Shiva praises Kali saying, "She who devours time, who alone remains after the dissolution of the Universe, and who is the origin and destroyer of all things."

As an important guide for devotees, Kali's position in Tantra cannot be questioned. This system is based on many rituals which are concerned with the geography of the physical, and transformation of the subtle body. In left-handed Tantrism in particular, sadhana takes a dramatic form and involves the rituals of the *Pancha Tattva* or the five forbidden things viz. meat, wine, fish, parched grain and sexual intercourse. This helps the *sadhak* (seeker) to break away from the barriers of the mind and fragmented reality, and enter the absolute. The seeker also overcomes all dualities that are built up in his perception of sacred-profane, clean-unclean, and eventually, can break the bondage that ties him to the fragmentations and limitations of the society and world at large. In the *Karpuradi-Stotra* (a short work based on the praises to Kali), the *Pancha Tattva* ritual is described in great detail. Performed in the cremation ground (*smashana* sadhana) which is the goddess's favourite place, it is said that when she is confronted boldly by the *sadhak* in meditation, she can grant him great power and salvation. During this meditation, the *sadhak* has to concentrate on the terrible aspects of this black goddess who can help him achieve his desired goals.

As Shiva's consort, she does not fit into the stereotype of a *pativrata,* or the one who is completely devoted to her husband and compliant to his will. In fact, she is the more dominating one, more destructive and takes the upper position or the man's position during sex. Sexually powerful, in the Tantras she is explicitly described as having sex with Lord Shiva. The *Sahasranama Stotra* (the thousand name hymn) stresses on her vigorous appetite and her sexual appeal. She is even described as the one "whose form is the yoni", "who is situated in the yoni", "who is worshipped with semen", "who is always filled with semen", "whose essential form is sexual desire", and many other such names. Thus, the goddess also goes beyond the stereotyped controlled married woman who is sexually satisfied. In contrast, Goddess Kali is voracious and dangerous. She is thus also a symbol of freedom from society's suffocating norms and is usually found in forests, jungles, cremation grounds and similar places which are far away from the civilised crowds. She is raw in her habits, appearance, manners, and values.

Goddess Kali's appearance itself has many Tantric interpretations, particularly her wild and unbound hair, and lolling tongue. In all her dhyan (meditation) mantras, she is always shown with her mouth wide open and her tongue hanging out, as a bloodthirsty goddess. This expression symbolises her great all-consuming appetite for blood. The Daksina Kali, however, is interpreted by Hindus as a sign of embarrassment when she finds out that she is standing on top her husband Shiva's body, and so, literally "bites her tongue". According to Jeffrey Kripal, author of *Kali's Child*, this lolling tongue has deep Tantric connotations viz. sexual gratification and consumption of the polluted or forbidden. This could be true as in many Dakshina-Kali images, in some iconographies and illustrations, Goddess Kali is symbolised as having sex with Lord Shiva, and in some of them he is shown with an erection. Another instance when her tongue is found lolling out is in cremation grounds with a male consort, and in this case, according to Kripal, it shows her enjoyment for different "flavours, for everything that society considers polluted or unclean and is an act of rebellious indiscriminate enjoyment." These habits and appearance of the goddess are often very fierce and untamed for civilised society and could even be repulsive to those with finer sensibilities. However, in Tantra, these are the same narrow-minded, disgusting, repulsive, and selfish conceptions of the world one has to be break away from.

Her loose, unbound hair is a sign of her unconventionality. Most married women tie their hair and braid it neatly with the parting filled with red vermillion which signifies their marital status. The goddess's unkempt hair, along with her nude appearance, her affinity for blood and cremation grounds and her lolling tongue, all add up to a persona that does not fit into any social order, rather it evokes disdain. A cosmic significance of this unbound hair is of dissolution. Her loose hair could also suggest the end of order and chaos. Goddess Kali thus, through her untamed, wild form, provokes ordinary men and women to rise above limitations and taste the world and all that is forbidden, to find that in essence, there is unity and sanctity which is her divinity itself.

Tara: The Saviour Goddess

Goddess Tara is very important for devotees of Hinduism as well as Buddhism. She is counted among the most important of goddesses in the East. As Bodhisattva Tara, she is known as the great consort of Bodhisattva Avalokiteshvara. In the Chinese traditions and legends, this goddess is known as Kwan Yin. Among the Mahavidyas or "The Ten Wisdom Goddesses", she closely resembles Goddess Kali, and is considered to be her first transformation. Time and life are both synonymous with Kali who is closely related to the sound vibrations or the Divine words, which are Tara. Tara is thus, "*Shabda Shakti*" (the power of sound), which is closely connected to the power of time. The word represents consciousness, intelligence, and movement of time. It is said that the vibration of the Divine word is the energy of time.

Tara

The name Tara is derived from the Sanskrit word "*Tri*" which means to take across. Goddess Tara is thus called upon when anyone is in an emergency, crossing a river or oceans, at crossroads when we don't know which way to turn, or in any difficult situation where we need the right guidance. She is thus also called the "Saviour Goddess" as she can save us with her knowledge and wisdom. It is said that her wisdom is as old as the sacred Vedas and in many spiritual traditions her teachings are given great importance. Tara also means star and "*tri*", "to scatter". Thus, just like stars are scattered in the heavens, this goddess guides us and our aspirations along the creative path.

The word Om is closely associated with Goddess Tara. This divine word which begins all sacred chants of the Hindus and Buddhists is called the original vibration of *Pranav*. Interestingly, Tara which also means "the deliverer" is a Vedic name for Lord Shiva and Om. Om is thus also sometimes called Taraka or Tara, for just as a boat leads us to the shore of our destination, this benovelent goddess takes us across (*tarati*) the ocean of ignorance or samsara. As a feminine word, Tara is similar to *nau* (boat in Hindi) and thus she can even save us from shipwrecks and in a metaphorical sense, save us from drowning in our own ignorance or emotional sufferings in life.

Her saving powers also relate to Goddess Durga who takes her devotees through difficulties (*Durgani*). Many a time, she is also referred to as "Durga-Tara", an amalgam of the names of these two goddesses. Goddess Durga empowers us to overcome difficulties, and with Tara's grace we can go beyond them. She transcends all things and can see us through any obstacle, however big or small. She also helps us rise to our complete potential and go beyond the limitations of our minds, and the world at large. Since the bigger obstacle in our path is our own thought patterns and mind, Goddess Tara with her blessings, can help us go beyond these turbulent mentalities which are a fragment of the divine word. The goddess can thus be seen as the personification of the word Om.

Om is the revealer of the worlds and its mysteries. It is the creator and the destroyer of the universe. As the primal sound, it is the ether or the Divine essence of all things. According to Patanjali's Sutras, "Om is the voice of the Ishvara, the Lord, the primal world-guru." For mantras to work and for the lord's secrets to be revealed to us, we need to connect with the power of Om. Om precedes all chants and spiritual mantras as it is the primal unitary sound vibration, and it is only through this sound that we can understand the higher and deeper meanings of every holy scripture. It is said Goddess Tara contains within herself all the mantras and she is the goddess of "Mantra Shakti". She also grants oratory and poetic powers to devotees and those seeking such capabilities must worship her. It is said that the one who is sincerely devoted to Tara can never be defeated in literary talents or in any form of debates.

Goddess Tara is also the purifying force of breath which is the life-force or the prana. Breath is thus described as "The primal sound of life, and the sound of the breath is the original, spontaneous and unuttered mantra (*So'ham*)." Both mind and prana as sound and vibration are rooted in sound. Thus, sounds and mantras possess the power to purify, energise and cleanse the mind.

Different sounds are vehicles of knowledge and Tara is the radiance of this knowledge that we gain from the different meanings of sound. Goddess Tara also represents the nature of inquiry and the drive for knowledge that helps us cross the rivers of ignorance and samsara. This innate aspiration is connected with the goddess and she is hidden in our speech and thoughts, constantly helping us seek the unknown and to go beyond our confined realms. Goddess Tara is particularly connected with the *pashyanti* stage of sound which represents the perceptive or illumined word, and the state of seeing. She represents the sound that is the revealer of truth and to grasp this perfection of true knowledge, we must worship the goddess.

In her manifest form, the goddess is the consort of *Brahaspati* (Jupiter) who is the Vedic God of Wisdom and the ruler of the manifest sound. Goddess Tara relates to the tongue in the abode of speech. Interestingly, *jihva* (tongue) is a feminine word and mystically represents the element of Agni (fire), and the powers of speech of the *Purusha* (cosmic being). Goddess Tara thus rules the power of speech, the discerning ability to taste the flavour of things, and the aesthetic mind at large. Worshipping her and being connected to her can awaken our power to perceive delight or ananda in all that is. She also aids the movement of the soma (immortal nectar) to flow through us. In fact, she is closely connected with the moon. According to a legend in the Puranic mythology, Goddess Tara once had a secret love affair with the moon while being married to Jupiter, and so she is said to have a dual nature which supports knowledge (Jupiter) as well as ecstasy (moon). She also has a son named Mercury (planet of speech and intelligence) from her relationship with the moon.

In an avatar of Goddess Kali, Goddess Tara is Lord Shiva's consort and in her benevolent form she is also called Gauri. Goddess Gauri is the nurturing mother and pure light who increases our spiritual knowledge and helps us go beyond dualities and ignorance. Goddess Tara, thus, takes us back to the Divine Mother who is behind all the worlds. In her wrathful form, the goddess is also known as "Ugra Tara" (the fierce one). Dark blue in colour, she is also called "Nila Sarasvati" (Goddess of Speech). Her wrathful form is also the wrathful avatar of Sarasvati, and Ugra Sarasvati can bless us with the power to win over all knowledge based contests and debates, only if we are devoted to truth.

In the physical realms or the physical body, apart from the tongue, Goddess Tara is also connected with the *Manipura* (navel chakra), which is the centre for *Pashyanti*. As the guru or the Om, she also relates to the *Ajna* (the Third Eye region), as she rises from the navel to the head.

Goddess Tara and Kali are similar in appearance. Deep blue skin, matted hair, eight serpents as ornaments, and a garland of human skulls are the striking feature of Goddess Tara's appearance. She is also illustrated in paintings as dancing on a corpse and is shown as having four arms, four hands in which she carries a sword, head chopper, scissors, lotus and severed head. In accordance with her tamasic nature, her skin is nila (dark blue) and she represents the tamas (the darkness in nature). Goddess Tara is unmanifested sound while Goddess Kali is unmanifested time.

Her appearance is greatly symbolic—the eight serpents represent eight siddhis or a magic power of being able to transform into any shape, lotus is the open heart, scissors show her ability to cut off all attachments, and because of her unitary nature of sound vibrations (*nada*) she has matted hair. In Buddhist traditions, she appears in many coloured forms such as White Tara, Blue Tara, Red Tara and Green Tara, and each of these can be connected to different Hindu goddesses of beauty and wisdom.

The main mantra of this goddess is Om, chanting this single *bija* is enough to worship her. She can also be worshipped by the following mantra:

Om hrim strim hum phat.

This mantra can be understood as follows: *"Om"* is the mantra of deliverance (taraka mantra), *"Hrim"* is a mantra of purification and transformation, *"Strim"* is the feminine nature (*stri*) and provides the power to give birth and sustenance, *"Hum"* is the mantra of divine wrath and protection, as well as knowledge and perceptive power, *"Phat"* too gives protection and destroys obstacles.

Rishi Akshobhya is the seer of her mantra and he represents Lord Shiva's quality that transcends agitation. In the Buddhist tradition, he is amongst the *Dhyani* or Meditating Buddha, and represents the mirror-like undisturbed wisdom that cannot be disturbed and that is free from attachment. When our mind is calm and free from agitation we can fully understand the complete essence and power of this mantra. Om can be freely used without following any particular discipline, and using it can help the seeker gain *Tara Vidya*, i.e., knowledge related to this goddess.

While chanting any of these mantras, the seeker must also call upon her divine grace to inculcate the intention to save the world and its beings and by doing this one can become Tara. Another way is to silence the mind and concentrate on the interval between these sounds, and try to hear Om. Following this sound current to its root in silence can help us return to our Atman or true inner self which is pure silence.

As Tibet's national deity, Goddess Tara also has a prominent place in Buddhist Tantrism. She has both fierce and gentle aspects; however, in Buddhism she is generally manifested in her gentler aspects, and in Hinduism, in her fierce one. Historically, it has been debated that the Hindu Mahavidya Tara is a form of the Buddhist Boddhisattva Tara, and the Hindus give preference to her fierce avatar during worship.

The earliest reference to this goddess can be found in the *Vasavadatta* by Subandhu dating back to the seventh century. In many iconographies, she is shown as belonging to the Dhyani Buddha Amoghasiddhi, and was created out of the tears of Avalokiteshvara. Buddhism was introduced in India around the eleventh century through the works of Atisa who popularised the cult of the goddess in Tibet and through translating several works from Sanskrit to Tibetan. These texts that were circulated came to be known as *Cheating Death*. In all her representations, this goddess is shown as a saviour of the entire mankind, who can even rescue her sincere devotees from the jaws of an untimely death. Her compassion for all beings is true to her nature as the cheater of death. She blesses her devotees with longevity and she even rescues them from troubling situation such as fire, sea-wreck, being trapped, being in prison, or being lost in a forest.

In Tibetan monastic traditions, young monks have to perform several ceremonies in her honour and these are called, "Initiation into life". She protects, preserves, and saves lives, and cannot see her devotees suffering in any way. Apart from these forms, the goddess also has very fierce forms in Buddhism. One such form is Tara Kurukulla. Her power lies in being able to protect the devotee from the evil spirits used by one's enemies. It is said that when she is invoked, she resides in the practitioner himself, and in most cases this is a male adept. Since her force is very potent, this ritual requires a very strong and accomplished male adept. In this ritual, the adept dresses in red clothes and visualises himself in the form of the goddess. He then recites her mantra ten thousand times and makes offerings to her. He then asks her help to subjugate the demon or the person, for which the ritual is being performed.

Her other fierce Buddhist forms include Mahachinnha Tara or Ugra Tara, and Mahamaya Vijayavahini Tara also called "The Blue She-Wolf". Tara worship is deeply rooted in Indian soil as explained in the legend of Vashishtha who, through the left-handed path and ritual of five forbidden things, gained her grace. Her descriptions in Hindu traditions stress on her resemblance to Goddess Kali both in appearance and persona, and also her love for the cremation grounds. These reflect her dark, fierce and terrifying nature which is in contrast to her gentle forms found in Buddhism. There are many similarities between Ugra Tara and Daksina Kali—they are both illustrated as standing on a male figure (resembling Shiva), both are dark blue in colour, both wear a tiger skin or very little clothing, both wear skulls around their necks, both have a lolling tongue, and blood oozing from their mouths. They are often mistaken for one another and share epithets in their names in hymns dedicated to them. For instance, Tara is called "Kalika", "Bhadrakali" and "Mahakali".

Just like Goddess Kali, Goddess Tara loves blood and in a hymn called "Mundamala Tantra" she is called "She Who Enjoys Blood Sacrifice" and "She Who is Smeared with Blood". The Tara-Tantra describes the goddess' love for human blood in particular and it is said that this blood is taken from specific parts of the devotee's body such as forehead, hands, breasts, and the area between the eyebrows, which are connected with the energy centres or chakras in the spiritual body. Goddess Tara is also connected to Lord Shiva and her name is often associated with him, viz., "Hara-vallabha" or "Sankara-vallabha" (beloved of Shiva), "Hara-patni" (wife of Shiva, wife of Mahabhairava), among others. She is thus connected to ascetics and yogis in myriad ways. There are many myths and legends which also describe the connection between these two deities.

Left-handed Tantric rites are often used to worship this goddess, just like Goddess Kali. Even her rituals revolve around the power of the forbidden and attempts to transmute forbidden objects into spiritually transformative instruments. Just like Goddess Kali, Tara's favourite haunt is the cremation ground. In many of her depictions, funeral fires are seen burning in the background, jackals are shown and it is said that she should be worshipped in the dead of the night. In her thousand name hymn, she is called "Smashana Bhairavi" which literally translates to "Terrible one of the cremation ground". Even her temples and shrines are found in and around cremation sites. Tarapith, which is her most famous temple, is located near a cremation ground in Calcutta. She is also said to symbolise the powerful fire of the funeral pyre.

Symbolically also, both these goddesses have great similarities. Tara, too, is depicted as being naked, wearing severed heads as ornaments and standing above a male corpse. Unrestrained, fierce, wild and dominating, she rebels against civilised society and its narrow mentality. She is also associated with destruction and dissolutions of all things. In contrast though, she also has a gentle maternal aspect and is also identified with the fires of cremation which are like a purifying aspect that mark the transition from death to another existence. She is thus also very purifying, creative, and transformative. Interestingly, she is also identified with the sun's excessive heat.

Her necklace of skulls has the same symbolism as that of Goddess Kali. The skulls also represent the sounds of alphabets and associate her with *Shabda Brahman*, i.e., the primordial creative force linked with the power of sound. The girdle of severed arms that she wears represents destruction of accumulated karma that can free a person from the cycle of rebirth. Her sword and scissors symbolise her power to cut through ignorance and limited consciousness that bind a person. Her weapons thus destroy as well as transform, positively. She thus enables her devotees to be free from all bondage and to succeed by eliminating all the unwanted nonsense related to the mind.

The Hindu Tara has a maternal and gentler side and is slightly different in appearance. Potbellied, with large and full breasts, she represents creation and individuation. She is said to be "filled with the universe, which is about to emerge from the void". In the hymn of a thousand names she is called, "*Jalesvari*" (Mistress of Rain), "*Vrksamadhyani-vasini*" (One Who Dwells in Trees), "*Jagaddhatri*" (Mother of the World or World Nurse), among others. Also called a saviour, many people describe her as "She who takes one across samsara, she is Tara". Her blessings are readily available and do not lay emphasis on puja (worship), japa (chanting) or dhyan (meditation) by the devotees. She is also called "The One Who Liberates" and she helps her devotees cross over bodily problems, matters of fate, and matters of materialism. She is also illustrated in many paintings with an oar in one hand ferrying her followers across the ocean of samsara which indicates her spiritual role in our destiny in crossing the ocean of ignorance towards enlightenment.

Her most dramatic and striking avatar as the maternal goddess is evident in Tarapith in Bengal, where she is shown breastfeeding Lord Shiva, in the manifested form she took before Vashishtha. This idol mirrors her nourishing and gentler aspect that nurtures and protects her devotees. The fierce aspects associated with her take place in the adjacent cremation ground where blood sacrifices are made to quench the goddess' thirst in return for boons. Purification rituals are also carried out and goat sacrifices are common. The shrine of Bamakhepa (Rampurhat, Birbhum district, West Bengal) is also important in this respect. (These shrines are discussed in detail in a later chapter.)

Although the aspects of the goddess in Hindu and Buddhist traditions are contrasting—the Hindu Tara (like Goddess Kali) shocks her devotees with her fierceness and the Buddhist Tara showers them with compassion—both the Buddhist Tara and Hindu Tara have one goal, which is to lead devotees to liberation.

Shakti and Tara—Identical Identities

There are many researches since ancient times to identify the true connection between the goddesses Shakti and Tara. A recent research by V.H. Sonawane has discussed and illustrated a number of images of the Indian goddess, Lajja Gauri, displaying her pudendum by squatting with her legs wide apart. Lajja Gauri literally means "modest" Gauri. Gauri is a name often given to Parvati in many religious texts. This is explained in the fable where Parvati is caught in a dalliance with Shiva, and they are interrupted during lovemaking by a devotee. But according to author Hasmukh D. Sankalia, glossing Lajja Gauri as "a shy woman is euphemistic" and it really means "a shameless woman". This is again substantiated by the etymology of the word "lajja" proposed by R.C. Dhere as coming from the old Kannada words *"lanji"* or *"lanjika"*

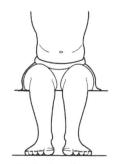

Pralambapadasana

Padmasana

which means an adulteress or harlot.

Sonawane also observes that the goddess appears in many Shaivite iconographies and concludes: "Thus, she can very well be considered as a manifestation of the Shakti aspect of Shiva." However, he also adds that it's important to consider a similar female figure in a Buddhist panel in Aurangabad who "appears to be naked, except for jewellery, and squats to display her pudendum. Yet, she is placed in a panel with a Buddha image. How should we identify such a figure?"

The haphazard arrangement of the cave suggests that perhaps the construction was commissioned by a variety of donors and is not part of the planned iconographic organisation of the cave. However, the iconography of Buddha appears as either in *pralambadasana* or in *padmasana*, and usually performing the Dharmachakra mudra. However, in this particular panel, the squatting, front-facing female takes the place of the proper right-hand donor figure. Thus, it is difficult to relate to why the Hindu Lajja Gauri is part of the Buddhist iconography, and whether she is really a Lajja Gauri.

Numerous publications and scholars of the subject have confirmed that the sure way to identify this goddess (whatever name she takes), is her act of exposing herself by raising her knees. However, it is unclear as to whether this posture is a sexual one, or whether it indicates parturition. She is worshipped today by women in order to promote fertility, particularly in barren women.

This was probably the purpose of the goddess earlier as well, although the third century inscription on a Lajja Gauri from Nagarjunakonda specifically states that the donor is a *jwaputa* (one who has her child or children alive). The donor was an Ikshvaku queen, Kharhduvula, and this was a dedication or a token of gratitude for success in worshipping the goddess. However, fertility, and either a sexual or birth-giving posture can be seen as something facilitating it. The most likely explanation, in fact, appears to be that the posture was used with both meanings; and it is probable that the "two" postures, representing (potential) sexual intercourse and resultant birth are linked in the worshipper's mind, as they are in reality. That the position is a sexual one, however, is somewhat difficult to support from artistic and textual evidence.

The Lajja Gauri figures appear explicit with full frontal exposure, and almost always without male partners, with the artist's intention being the exposure of the yoni and not the presentation of a sexual act. In a relief, on the eighth century Huchchimalli Temple at Aihole, the squatting female actually reaches out and grasps the enormous phalluses of two flanking males. While the exposure of the yoni can be seen as a sexual posture, the evidence suggests that it could mostly be a birth-giving posture. This position, called *uttanapad* and glossed by Monier-Williams as "one whose legs are extended (in parturition)" finds graphic depiction in a late twelfth century Chalukyan sculpture showing women giving birth. Its association with birth and fruition, however, is seen in much earlier art as well as in this small, first century BC terra-cotta, in which a goddess removes (gives birth to) a sheaf of grain from her vagina.

The Aurangabad figure compares to both the Matrikas and the Lajja Gauris, in having the right arm raised with the elbow resting on the knee. This figure can also be seen in association with the Buddhist goddess Vasudhara, whose most characteristic attribute is the *Dhanyamanjari* (sheaf of grain). Is the Aurangabad figure therefore a Tara, and specifically Vasudhara? This is again speculation, as Tara's mannerism and postures appear differently in texts.

The Aurangabad illustration, thus, has characteristics of several goddesses such as a goddess giving birth to vegetation, the Lajja Gauri and Vasudhara, and each of them relate to one another in a general way as goddesses of fertility and fruition, and this is clearly the meaning of the Aurangabad figure as well. Nevertheless, that she displays her genitals, however discretely, as compared to the usual Lajja Gauri images, must put her most fully into the Lajja Gauri category and into a unique category for a goddess in a Buddhist context.

Many Buddhist caves in India which can be dated back to the sixth century have images of Goddess Tara which continued until the beginning of the Muslim rule in India. These also indicate the Shakti cult encroaching the Mahayanic tradition of Buddhism. According to Hirananda Shastri, Goddess Tara always appears in a Buddhist guise in Hindu Texts, and even in the Puranas her lineage is evident as she bears the image of Akshobhya on her head and is worshipped through "*Chinachara*", i.e., the Chinese methods. Even in the Puranas, she is called "Maha Shakti" and "Tara Amba"— the patron deity of those crossing the seas, and it is said that she

Vajra - tara in Ratnasambhava, Svayambhu Stupa area, China

also controls floods. Since ancient times, she is called "Dhruva Tara"—the one who guides fishermen and sailors crossing the oceans, and like a shining star, guides them ashore. She's a favourite goddess in western India and her depictions are found in Buddhist caves in north Deccan, Kanheri, Ellora and Ajanta, and in caves in Aurangabad, Nasik and Panhale Kazi. These regions again prove her connection with seafarers.

The similarities found between Tara and Parvati are also quite prominent. Another name of Parvati is Durga, who is given the status of "Mother" in Hinduism. Tara occupies a similar place in Buddhism. The prayer verses related to her images which are found in Ellora caves are also found in the *Markandeya Purana*. In his book *The Indian Buddhist Iconography,* Dr. B. Bhattacharya has described several important names and avatars of the goddess. In the *Sadhanamala*, the names Janguli, Parnashabari, Maha-china Tara, and Khandiravani are mentioned. Mahashri Tara, Vashya Tara, Shadbhuja Sita Tara, Dhanada Tara, and Sita Tara are her other names. Maha China Krama Tantra, which is a left-handed tradition, deals with the goddess and is completely absorbed into the Hindu Tantric pantheon.

An important form of this enchanting goddess is "Vajra Tara" who emanated from Ratnasambhava. This image has also been noticed in the Svayambhunath Stupa area, and is also found in parts of China. Ugra Tara, also locally known as "Vajra Yogini", is renowned in Nepal and she is also said to emanate from Dhyani Buddha Ratnasambhava. According to Dr. B. Bhattacharya, she was brought into India by Bengali Buddhist priests around AD 1350 from Dacca, owing to the Muslim invasion in Bengal. Since the seventeenth century, Hindus have been worshipping Goddess

Bhavani who is essentially Vajra Yogini.

Pratima Kamat, Head of the History Department at Goa University, in an article, has published her observations on this fascinating goddess. Goa is a coastal region surrounded by many water channels and a striking feature of the cultural legacy of Goa is the maritime *"Mahishasuramardini"* of the Mhadei. She is the "Boat Deity" or the goddess worshipped by the seafarers of the Mhadei river valley. The lineage of this deity can be traced through earliest references to the Kadamba dynasty that ruled over the region during the early medieval period.

The author has documented and closely observed: "Fifteen sculptures in which a female deity, locally known as Santeri/ Shantadurga, Jogeshwari, Navadurga, or as an anonymous *parivar devata*, is depicted either seated atop or standing in a boat (one of them even sits on a boat shaped like a fish); two images of Gajalakshmi with howdahs in the shape of a boat; three sculptures of Brahmani Maya with a boat carved on the pedestal, and six of male deities who are shown either standing fully armed, with a boat etched on the pedestal, or riding a horse positioned above the boat-like pedestal."

Further she writes that most of these Devi (goddess) structures have a votive origin, i.e., these are dedicated or given in fulfilment of a vow. She has found similarities between boat-goddess Tarini and the boat-god, Tar-Vir, which bear an obvious resemblance in culture and iconography to the Goddess Tara-Tarini of the Orissa coast.

The worship of Tara and Tarini is found in Orissa's Ganjam district (which has the famous Taratarini temple), Ghatgaon and Ratnagiri (where the Ashtamahabhaya Tara is worshipped). All these are the patron deities for men of the sea, merchants and fishermen, for safety and success along the coastal areas. The Ratnagiri Tara is believed to save her devotees from eight great fears, of which one is shipwreck and *jalarnavabhaya* (fear of drowning in a sinking vessel).

Goa's boat deities or coastal deities watching over the coasts are found away from the coast, in the sub-Ghat talukas of Sattari and Sanguem, against the backdrop of the Sahyadri Mountains. They are also found in the villages of Keri, Bhuipal, Nagvem, Dhamshe, Guleli, Shayll-Melauli, Zarme, Sonal, Sanvarde, Bhironda, Malpann in Sattari; Ganjem in the Ponda; and Barabhumi, Surla and Talldem of Sanguem.

The sculptures are found along the banks of Mhadei River and its tributaries. Those planning a visit can see them inside a temple, in the open lush greenery, near a stream, in the periphery of the *Devarai* (sacred grove), and even outside the Bondla wildlife sanctuary. Carved out of schist stone, locally known as Pashaan, all sculptures came alive by the works of local temple architects and sculptors. A distinct local influence in their iconography is thus seen, such as a Sattari flavour and even an amalgam of various artistic forms and iconographies from different belief systems such as folk, Brahmanical, as well as Jain and Buddhist influences.

She further adds that, "In the Devi Mahamatya, the Devi is hailed as Durga, the boat that takes men across the difficult ocean of worldly existence, devoid of attachments". She is also the saviour of one who is tossed about in his boat by a tempest in the vast sea.

Durga is also known by the names "Tarini" and "Tarita"; Tarini means boat and is also a Sanskrit word for saviour. The goddess is hailed as Tarini in Arjuna's hymn to Durga in the *Mahabharat*. Gayatri, the primal form of Tara or Bhavatarini, is called "*Bhayahaarini Bhavataarini*", i.e., the one who removes fears and ferries across the river of life. The only maritime reference for *Mahishasuramardini* is the epithet, "Daughter of the ocean", in the *Mahishasuramardini Stotram*.

Thus, it is clear that Tarini is spiritually similar to Tara as they both are deities assisting and protecting souls to "cross to the other shore". In her many avatars, Tarini, as Santeri or Shantadurga, is also considered to be a symbol of fertility. Like Goddess Ganga, she is the river goddess representing the Mhadei and as the Buddhist Tara, she rescues and ships her devotees to safety; and above all, as *Mahishasuramardini* (the boat-goddess), she is the protector and slayer of the enemies of the local sailors and merchants. This is also a great historical aspect mirrored in the Goan culture, roots, and history, as the talukas of Sattari and Bicholim are important trade routes and are also home to sacred spots that have Buddhist and Jain connections. According to Goa's history, Buddhism and Jainism flourished in this region during the ancient and early medieval periods, and places like Kothambi, Kudnem, the caves of Lamgaon, and Colvale are crucial to both religions. This thus helps us trace how

Tara Statue at Padma Samye Ling Retreat Centre & Monastery in New York

elements of the Jain Yakshi and Ambika, found their way into the conceptualisation, and even the artistic execution of the maritime Mahishasuramardini. The author also found a Buddhist or Jain monk close to the Sanvarde Tarini, and the sculpture in Shayll-Melauli has an image of a Buddhist monk on its base. Along with the boat, most of these sculptures have very distinctive nautical and marine motifs, such as oars, anchors, mast, sail, pennant, fish and crocodile.

Tarini is thus a syncretic vision of the Shakti of the Mhadei river valley who is a reflection of the "shared faith" that defined the cosmopolitan Sattari in the early medieval period. This region only reflects the wide and deep range of local, Sanskritic, Buddhist and Jain traditions that remind us how inclusive, democratic and colourful the Indian civilisation once was.

1.5 The Tantric Guardian Ganesh

Ganesh is a deeply loved god of the Hindu pantheon. Known as the "Remover of Obstacles", he grants many boons to his devotees and is also said to grant firmness to all his worshippers meditating on him. His name is especially chanted before the commencement of all undertakings for good luck, glad tidings and an abundance of positivity. He is also said to be the "Lord of Brahmacharis and Celibates".

There are many legends in the *Puranas* that trace the birth of this god. According to one story, Ganesh was formed from the *ubtan* or the cleansing unguent that Goddess Parvati removed from her body. Once, when the guards of her quarters were absent, she took this *ubtan*, formed a childlike form from it and breathed prana (life) into him. She appointed this child as her guardian and gave him a sceptre and strict instructions not to allow anybody in her private room. After some time, Lord Shiva came there and was stopped from entering the palace. Displeased and angry at this, he cut off the child's head with his *trishul* (trident).

When the goddess heard of this she was very upset and asked Lord Shiva to bring the child back to life. While Lord Brahma comforted her, Lord Shiva went to search for a child's head that he could fix on him. As it was night, all children were asleep with

Lord Ganesh

their mothers. However, he came across a baby elephant, and Lord Shiva cut off his head and fixed it on top of the child's body and brought him back to life. He was thus named Ganesh where "*gana*" means existing beings and forms of his followers, and "*isha*" means Lord. There are many different stories surrounding his birth. However, at their core one thing is clear—Ganesh is the creation of the Divine Force. He is the guardian of the place where the Divine Mother resides. It is only after he grants permission, that the devotee can enter the gates of the Divine. In Tantric worship particularly, his name is invoked right at the beginning. He is also worshipped at the beginning of all undertakings—however big or small—whether it's a journey, writing a letter, building a house, or starting a business. A short, potbellied figure, his small eyes shine like jewels, he holds an *ankush* (hatchet), *pash* (lasso) and a conch in his three hands. His fourth hand, at times, is depicted as holding a *laddu* (an Indian sweet). He is shown accompanied by a rat who is also his *vahana* (vehicle). His elephant-like head and plump body attracts all children. There are also people who find his appearance laughable. Those who see the divinity in Ganesh and his form are

Ganesh Yantra

able to still their rational mind and are free from doubts which can cloud their decisions and thinking as they do not gauge situations or people by outward appearance alone. Those who find faults in his appearance are influenced by their rational mind, and their spiritual path thus becomes obstructed. By surrendering to Ganesh, we subdue our rational minds and control it through our faith which is the most powerful force in the universe.

Ganesh attained this merit in the Hindu pantheon because of his pure heart and virtues of prudence and wisdom. An interesting story explains why he is considered to be the guardian or lord of all creation. According to sacred texts, Shiva was considered the sole guardian of all gods and goddesses and the one who protected all beings, spirits and demons. However, because he immersed himself deeply in the blissful state of samadhi, the gods found it very difficult to communicate with him. In fact, it is said the Ganas spent a lot of time chanting hymns and praying to him, to gain his attention. They all needed a patron who would always be available for guidance and provide them with the security they often needed.

Lord Brahma and Lord Vishnu were then approached by the Ganas and they persuaded them to appoint a new "Ganpati" or "Ganesh" (leader of the Ganas). Through a counsel, Lord Vishnu suggested that they may choose between Kartikeya and Lambodar (pot-bellied). And thus a contest was held to gauge which of them was suitable for the role. Lord Vishnu was the judge and Lord Shiva and Goddess Parvati were also present. The challenge for both sons was to go around the entire universe and come back, and the one who would come back first would be declared Ganesh. Kartikeya set off on his peacock but Lambodar did not move. However, on Vishnu's insistence to join the contest, he got up and first bowed to his parents. He then paid homage to all the gods and goddesses present, and finally took off on his rat. However, instead of going around the entire universe, he circled Parvati and Shiva. After doing so, he declared, "I have completed my task. I have gone all around the universe." The entire audience of gods and sub-gods were impressed that instead of going around the entire universe, he had chosen to encircle Parvati (Primordial Prakriti) and Shiva (Divine Father).

Ganesh then explained his action to all the gods present before him, saying that the world was a phenomenon of relative existence, i.e, maya (illusion), which is far removed from absolute reality and truth. The Divine Father and Mother are the source of all creation, and the source of all that truly exists. This wisdom and virtue was appreciated by the entire audience present there who named him Ganesh, "Leader of the Ganas" or "Lord of all Creation".

The mantra connected to Ganesh is:

Aum Gan Ganapataye Namaha.

This mantra is from the *Ganapati Upanishad* and it is called the "Mool Mantra". Chanting this divine incantation is said to remove all evil, negativity, blocked energies, and obstacles from one's path. Each Ganesh mantra has a particular specific power of the god associated with it, and when chanted properly with Pranayam, yields very good results. This mantra mainly means bowing down to the lord of the world. Reciting this mantra daily with complete concentration and an open heart ensures protection from all evil, and it is said that negative forces can never enter the mind or home of his devotee. Chanting this mantra 108 times is fruitful, and if done continuously for forty-eight days, it becomes an Upasana. The devotee may even gain siddhis (spiritual powers) as a divine gift. This mantra can also be used for the benefit of mankind and for healing. However, its misuse could lead to a curse or punishment from the Asuras.

Meditating on Ganesh's Yantra is said to help the sadhak gain balance. The *bhupur* is a radiant green or viridian, similar to the Shri Yantra or the Tara Yantra. Green shade represents balance and meditating on this hue is said to produce red which is its complementary colour. Red represents life, freedom and inspiration.

The eight-petalled lotus of this Yantra in the shade of vermilion denotes "the octave of Prakriti", or the primordial nature. This includes the elements of akasha, air, water, fire, earth, sattva, rajas and tamas. The six-pointed star of this Yantra symbolises balance, created by one upward pointing male triangle, and one downward pointing female triangle. The upward facing six-pointed yellow coloured star in the middle symbolises the male sap, i.e, the elixir of immortality. This triangle's colour is the same as Lord Ganesh's skin colour. The *Bindu* (dot) right in the middle of this triangle is Ganesh himself, and meditating on it is the main aim of Yantra worship. The golden hue of the *Bindu* is very attractive and soothing to the eyes.

II

Gorakhnath: The Thread that Binds Shaivism and Vajrayana Buddhism

Let us now pay homage to a great seeker who devoted himself to this prolific knowledge of yoga and emerged as the greatest yogi ever born. It was he who laid the core foundation and paved the way for a school of thought that is rooted in the Indian tradition for centuries. That founder's teachings, vows, and philosophies form the backbone of yoga and the attainment of immortality. That great teacher was Gorakhnath.

An important fable traces the birth, the rise and the gradual awakening of this great founder.

The story of his birth is as engaging as that of Matsyendranath, who is his master, guru, spiritual guide and guardian deity. It is said that Matsyendranath travelled far and wide disguised as a Brahmin saint, seeking alms, and in return granting boons to people who merited his grace, blessing them by fulfilling their wishes. On one such journey, he came across a hut where a woman lived with her husband. She gave him a hearty meal and treated him with respect but did not ask for anything. Lord Matsyendranath sensed her sadness and asked her the reason for it. The woman spoke of her longing to have a child. Giving her some holy ash, Matsyendranath asked her to eat some of it and apply some on her forehead, saying that with Lord Shiva's grace she would get her heart's desire. The woman narrated this incident to her neighbour who told her that taking ash from a perfect stranger was foolhardy as it could be a jinx or curse that could ruin her. In her naivety and fear, the woman threw away the holy ash on a dunghill and let the incident pass.

Twelve years later, Lord Matsyendranath passed by the woman's hut and told her that he wanted to meet her son. The woman was shocked and told him what she had done in her foolishness. Lord Matsyendranath told her that her lack of belief did not make his prediction untrue. She then took him to the dunghill and with his faith in Lord Shiva, he invoked the boy. And behold! From the dunghill arose a little boy smeared with dung. He was thus named "Gorakhnath" (Lord of the Cattle) or "He who was Protected by the Earth". He became Lord Matsyendranath's devoted disciple and successor to his legacy. Through his teachings, he gained the wisdom and power to lay the foundations of *Goraksha Paddhati* or the *Goraksha Samhita*, which defines the deeper nuances of Hatha Yoga.

According to Shankaracharya, the personality of Gorakhnath was surely that of a *Paramahansa* (one who has total control over his breath). The ashram tradition in those days was in a depleted state. The traditions of Jainism and Buddhism allowed any person, in any state, to renounce the world. The result was that India became overrun with renunciants having immature bodies and minds. Thus, the Nath Panthis, the Siddhas and the yogis of real stature pronounced themselves as beyond any ashram culture. The same tradition progressed as neither Hindu nor Muslim, beyond religion, caste or class.

Like Shankaracharya, Gorakhnath renounced the world at a very early age. He and his followers gave birth to the above-mentioned group. Gorakhnath added his influence and execution to the highest ideal professed by Shri Shankaracharya in his comments on the *Shwetashwatar Upanishad*. It is almost impossible to find the origins of a renunciant such as Gorakhnath as his renunciation is not just a change in name, but is as good as a new birth.

In ancient and modern scriptures the name of Gorakhnath does not differ much. In the scriptures like *Hatha Yoga Pradipika*, *Vibhinna Tantra* and *Shyama Rahasya* he is known as Goraksha while in the scriptures like *Maha Arnav Tantra, Yoga Sampradaya Vishkruti, Siddha Siddhanta Paddhati, Amaruk Prabodh* and *Yoga Martanda,* he is known as Gorakhnath. In *Sashya Viharsuchi*, he is known as Goraksha Appa. In the *Puranas* there are many stories related to the birth of Gorakhnath in Nepal. In some *Puranas,* we find that he was born to a Brahmin on the banks of the river Godavari. There are many stories which prove his relation to Lord Shiva and Matsyendranath. Some *Puranas* say that he was the "son of god". The birthplace of Gorakhnath is considered to be north India, in Gorakhpur, Nepal and Punjab, among others. There is also a school of thought that says he was born on the banks of the Godavari, in Chandragiri, or in the village of Badav in south India. There is a lot of discussion about the period of his birth. It is said that he took an avatar in the four Yugs: In Peshawar, Punjab, in the Satya Yug; in Gorakhpur in the Treta Yug; in Dwarka in the Dwapara Yug; and in Kathiawad Gorakhpuri in the Kali Yug. Some experts have interpreted this information in a different way to mean that he was born in Peshwar and then did the pilgrimage to Gorakhpur, Kathiawad and Dwarka.

There are many definitions of the name Goraksha in the *Gorakhshanath Stotra.* "*Ga*" means "full of virtues", "*Ra*" means "of beautiful form", and "*ksha*" means "never ending, ever blissful spirit, *Akshaya Brahman*".

There are so many references to Gorakhnath in the *Puranas*, that it is very difficult to find the truth behind these stories. According to the *Shiv Purana*, Gorakhnath is an avatar of Shiva. It is written in the *Goraksha Geeta* that he helped Brahaspati (Jupiter) to protect the chastity of Indrani. He is regarded as one of the Navnaths in the *Skanda Purana*. Though there are many stories, the fact that Gorakhnath is referred to with great respect in almost all the *Puranas* proves that he was a man of great stature and extraordinary valour and wisdom.

Dr. Hazaari Prasad Dwivedi declares Gorakhnath a "*mahapurush*", a superhuman by stature. He invites our attention to many important virtues and facets of Gorakhnath's personality. With the above discussion it is clear that Shankaracharya was a Shaiva and he unified the Vedic Shaiva renunciants. All other Shaiva renunciants were brought together by Gorakhnath. The impact of Shankaracharya in the fields of philosophy and spirituality was so great that whenever a discussion is held on the subject, the name of Shankaracharya is bound to come up. Gorakhnath's personality was religious and he was so expansive and serious in the field of religion and spirituality, that history cannot be discussed without his name and lifework. He had a direct connection with society and the life of people. In these terms, he was a leader of the people. He had immense fame and recognition among the masses. His disciplined dealings in life, his mind control and his patience in spreading the yogic knowledge make him an inspirational personality even after so many centuries. The scope and the magnamity of his work make him extraordinary even today.

The book written by Gorakhnath in Sanskrit, *Siddha Siddhanta Paddhati*, proves that he had great command over the language. There are many stories in the *Puranas* where the virtues of Gorakhnath are described in detail. It can be concluded that Gorakhnath had great presence of mind, was very handsome, and could achieve different forms through yogic power and travel, in his astral form. He was proficient in playing the *mridangam* (south Indian drum). He had indepth knowledge of dance. There is enough proof of these virtues in many folktales.

Generally, even a virtuous man finds it difficult to keep a high moral standard in view of the temptations of life, but there was a great confluence of virtues with very high standards of morality and courage in the personality of Gorakhnath. He always used his knowledge and skill for the benefit and betterment of the people. He didn't have any desire for materialistic possessions or the company of women. He believed every woman to be his mother. When Matsyendranath hid a gold coin in his bag to test him, Gorakhnath created a huge mountain of gold through his yogic power. Finally, Matsyendranath threw the bag itself in the river. Gorakhnath even distributed food to the poor through his yogic power. He did not believe in any differences of caste, class, race, or creed. According to him, all men were equal. He stayed away from meat eating and all intoxicants. He did not have any home to call his own and was forever on the go. He has described the various places from his pilgrimages in his books. He always considered a young woman his sister, and an elderly woman, his mother. He had intense anger and irritation about the attitude of men towards a lady if it was filled with lust.

There can be no doubts about his vision and intelligence. His books *Amaroughshasanam* and *Maharthmanjari* show that he had excellent knowledge about Indian spirituality and philosophy. He had a lot of struggle with his contemporary scholars as he was always a humanitarian who helped his followers through thick and thin. He did not agree to any theory which did not lead to the progress and betterment of the people. He had to face many battles and prove himself. He always advised his followers to stay strong-willed and keep the faith. He also had to confront some violent Muslims and he advised them to stay away from violence by creating the *pir* tradition within the Nath cult. The *Hatha Yoga Pradipika* written before the fourteenth century also has the name of Shri Gorakhnath as one of the great Siddhas.

Another legend that describes Gorakhnath and Matsyendranath's beautifully complex relationship is the tale of "Matsyendra's Fall" described in Bengali dramas such as *Minchetan* (The Awakening of Mina) and *Vijaya* (Gorakh's victory).

The yogic verses of these texts describe the tension between yogic mastery and the female force when faced with female sexuality. It also talks about human weakness in general. As related earlier, Matsyendranath gained the esoteric knowledge through Lord Shiva. The Goddess, who slept through the teaching discourse, then cursed the yogi that one day he would fall asleep and forget everything he had ever learnt about yoga. This prediction did come true when Matsyendranath entered Kadali Rajya (the plantain forest or kingdom) located in Kamarupa, in Assam. In his desire to experience the luxurious life of kings, Matsyendranath forgot his yogic duties and ideals and became enamoured of Queen Kamala. He entered her husband King Trivikrama's body through Parakaya Pravesha and enjoyed a life of sensual pleasures, wealth and debauchery. Decades later, Gorakhnath, his greatest disciple, found out from another Nath, Siddha Kaneri, that his guru was close to death in Kadali Rajya where he was entrapped by sixteen hundred women. The kingdom of Kadali did not allow males, except for Matsyendranath, who was already residing there. To save his teacher, Gorakhnath disguised himself as a woman and entered the kingdom with a musical troupe. Finding his teacher so close to death in a hapless state, he fiercely beat the *mridangam* and sang, "*Jaag Macchendra, Gorakh Aaya*" (Awaken Matsyendra, Gorakh has come). Listening to the beats of the *Nada Brahma* (sound of the Universe) and the voice of his disciple, Matsyendranath came out of his trance temporarily.

To restore his master's yogic powers and to get him attuned to his Shaktis once more, Gorakhnath took him to the forest, and once again sang, "*Kaya Sadha, Kaya Sadha, Guru Mochandar*" (Perfect your yogic body anew, Guru Matsyendra).But to get his teacher completely conscious he needed to shock him, and so he killed Binduknath (he who is formed froma drop of yogically transformed semen), Matsyendranath's son whom he (Matsyendranath) had fathered with Kamala. He skinned the boy's dead body, washed off all the impurities and hung the skin on the roof like that of any beast. Both Matsyendranath and Kamala were appalled by this act. Gorakhnath then created 108 Binduknaths in front of them. This is when Matsyendranath realised the "*Moh-maya*" he was drunk on, the attachments he had formed with the worldly pleasures, and the temptations he had given in to. His spiritual self was once again awakened, and he and Gorakhnath left the kingdom of Kadali. (It is also said that the women of Kadali tried to lure Gorakhnath through their charms but the determined and pious yogi turned them all into bats!)

2.1 Gorakhnath's Descent and Timeline in Historical Texts

Often called a "superhuman" by his followers, Gorakhnath was said to be unbound by time and place, which were just relative for him.

His followers call him a "*Paramhansa*" (one whose mind chants "*so*" with inhalation, and "*hum*" with exhalation [*Sohum*], constantly and automatically) which is the highest regard given to an ascetic, and given only to one who has controlled his senses through meditation. His disciples describe him thus:

"He is beloved of God and his worship has been accepted by the Almighty. You can ask what you please of him."

His appearance has been described to Puran Bhagat by his disciples thus:

"Very great is his beauty, say all men and women; no maid in India's court has greater beauty. He is like the swan of Sarowar."

Though the exact time and days of his appearances are unknown, many instances of his visits have been recorded.

*Jain Temples from Amba Mata temple,
Girnar, Gujarat*

Gorakhnath temple, Girnar

Gorakhnath is said to have stayed near Pashupatinath Temple in Kathmandu. It is also safe to assume that Gorakhnath was essentially a Vajrayana Buddhist and deeply connected to Shaivism because of his teacher Matsyendranath. Some say he was a native of Punjab and from there travelled to many parts of India, and his chief seat is at Tilla Jogian Temple, in Jhelum district. Baba Farid, who visited Girnar in 1244 and died in 1266, is connected to Gorakhnath. There is also an old shrine dedicated to Gorakhnath on Girnar Hills. According to legend, Goddess Parvati sang songs and hymns praising Lord Shiva, on these hills. It was at this exact spot that he finally appeared before her. In many legends of Sind, it is mentioned that this was also a favourite place of Gorakhnath where he often meditated, and that his *dhuni* still exists there.

His spiritual descent has been recorded by many historians and by various people. However, the most authentic source is considered to be Kabir's *Gorakhnath ki Goshti* (story), where Gorakhnath calls himself the grandson of Adinath, and son of Matsyendranath.

Jnaneshvar, in one of his most well-known quotes in the *Jnaneshvari*, affirms that he was a practitioner of yoga. *Goraksha Amar Samvad* is all about Gorakh and many lines from this work link their literary descent. They also confirm the fact that the Nath sect had very close relations with Jnaneshvar's ancestors.

The *Jnaneshvari* gives a definite timeline to Gorakhnath's emergence. The book goes back to AD 1290, so we can assume that his presence was prominent around the tenth or eleventh centuries AD. Other important citations that confirm this are mentions of Rani Pingla, Gopichand, Bhartruhari and Bhoja which can all be traced back to the early eleventh century AD.

The greatest contribution of Gorakhnath to mankind is making the knowledge of yoga accessible and understandable to all. There are many yogic works which describe in detail, the life of the Nath-gurus with special reference to Gorakhnath who laid its foundations and roots. But words are insufficient to describe the greatness and the role of this reverent being. To understand his work, it is important to trace the cult of the Nath Siddhas or Kanphata yogis (as they are also colloquially called owing to their split ears and the distinctive large earrings they wear in the hollows of their ears) and to understand their way of life, principles, and the legends surrounding their unexplained, and at times, eccentric rituals.

2.2 Gorakhnathis: Their Vows, Principles and Way of Life

The devoted followers of Gorakhnath are called Naths (masters) and Kanphatas (split-eared) and are also popularly known as "Gorakhnathis", as a reference to their famous founder. Pitamber Datta Barthwal, in his work *Siddha Sahitya,* states that "Nath" was a title that meant guru or lama in Bengali Vajrayana or Vajranathi Buddhist traditions, where such references were made to Saraha-pa and Kanha-pa and they were seen as "One whose mind is unwavering". Gorakhnathis represent a distinct class of yogis and are far different from other ascetics because of their beliefs, teachings, and way of life. They are found in many parts of India, in what was earlier Central Provinces, Punjab, Gujarat, and Maharashtra, and especially near the Northern Deccan, near the Ganga and Nepal.

Kanphata yogis have some very unique characteristics. Of great importance and interest are their split ears and the huge earrings by which they can be easily identified. During the last stage of their initiation, their chosen guru takes a two-edged knife to split the central hollows of both ears. These slit openings are then covered with neem sticks and once the wounds are healed, the sticks are replaced with large ear ornaments or mudras.

Interestingly, this ritual is symbolic of the devotee's faith in Lord Shiva and Gorakhnath, and it is also believed that splitting this *nadi* enhances yogic power that can make him immortal in the course of time. David Gordon White explains this phenomenon as: "Ear boring, besides opening a hole in the disciple's ear, also opens, as if by synecdoche, a subtle channel inside the head of the initiate.

Once open, this channel too becomes a conduit to yogic powers and bodily immortality. In certain sources, it is further maintained that the guru actually penetrates, puts his mouth in the mouth of his disciple, somewhere inside the latter's left ear, at the opening of the channel called the "Conch" (*Sankhini Nadi*)."

After the piercing, either flat (*darsan*), or cylindrical (*kundal*) earrings can be used. *Darsan* earrings are considered very sacred and this word itself inspires great reverence. It is often used when someone has had a divine experience or vision of the Brahman. Many different earrings of different metals and materials are used. Earthen or clay earrings are the least expensive and most popular, but they break easily. Earrings made of horn or rhinoceros leather are more durable and thus are a favourite among many Kanphatas. Earrings of crystal, metals like gold, and others studded with precious stones, are also popular.

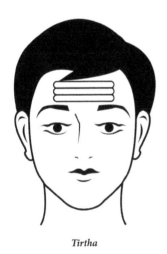

Tirtha

Wearing earrings is absolutely essential and if one breaks accidentally, the yogi cannot converse with another, eat food, or perform any religious rites till a pair is substituted. Kanphatas must also guard against their earrings being torn out or being damaged, as without them, they are considered cast-offs who have to leave the place where they live, never perform sacred ceremonies again, and in some extreme cases, they die or are buried alive.

Another important accessory with phallic significance that Kanphatas carry is a "*singnad*", which is a whistle made of either a rhinoceros horn, or black buck horn. It is blown before morning and evening worship, before meals and before performing duties. Some yogis fasten a *janeo* (scared thread) to the whistle along with a silver toothpick which is used as a protective talisman to keep evil energies away and this is called a "*singnad janeo*".

Some yogis wear around their loins, an *arband-langot-nag*, which is a rope made of black sheep wool. As the word explains, besides this rope, these yogis wear nothing else, though some use a thin strip of cloth instead of wool. Another important thread worn by many Kanphata yogis is the "*halmatanga*" which has many important regulations associated with it. For instance, after wearing this thread the yogi has to immediately go out to beg alms.

Wearing rosaries made of Rudraksha berries is common among Kanphatas, and these consist of 32, 64, 84 or 108 berries or even more. These are for spiritual reasons, as well as for keeping a check on the number of chants recited. The number of faces the Rudraksha has is very significant. Three represents the trident, four stands for the Vedas, six represents the six systems of philosophy, eight represents the eight-armed Durga, while nine stands for the nine Naths. Ten is for the ten avatars of Vishnu, and eleven is very auspicious as it is worn only by celibates and is very dear to the Mahadev Shiva. A rare Rudraksha is the double faced or double Rudraksha (called Shiv-Shakti or Gaurishankar) naturally joined, which is sacred for both Shiva and Parvati and only kings possess it. It blesses the owner with an abundance of wealth and everything his heart may desire.

Kanphatas also use ash for markings on their body and for protection against evil forces. The most common markings for yogis include the *Tripund* (three horizontal lines) on the forehead made of sandalwood paste, ash or clay. Some also draw similar lines across the body to show their connection to Shaivism. Some yogis wear a black horizontal line with a single black dot, as symbolic of Bhairav and a red circle below this, to represent Mahabir or Hanuman. There are many varieties of *tika* and each yogi has a different deity and significance associated with it.

With regard to hair, the practices differ. Some yogis shave off the entire head while others keep long, unkempt and matted hair. Most yogis are seen in dhotis or ochre coloured robes, and also in plain white. There are also many who go unclothed with just a loin cloth. During cold weather, some add a scarf, jacket or *arband* (a girdle of wool). Ochre coloured turbans are often worn and a cone-like cap of nine sections is also common. Skull caps in white in the usual Hindu pattern are worn and on special festivities, heads of monasteries wear turbans made of black sheep wool in flat or cylindrical shapes.

A Kanphata yogi will never leave home without the *khappar*

(begging bowl) made from coconut shell (*dariya narial*) or a brass *tomri* for receiving alms. Some may carry a trident while begging but it is essential to carry a wallet or bag with their belongings, which is sometimes used for begging, as well. Other important things for a Kanphata yogi are: fire-tongs for daily use as well as to use for defence purposes, and the *dhuni*—fire with a burning log of wood which is mandatory for every Kanphata to own in his household. A staff made of bamboo or metal is also used. A crutch is also very important for yogis especially as good support while meditating, and also during burial.

Certain common practices found among the Gorakhnathis are often misunderstood. It is said that some are jugglers or palmists, some make and sell charms, practise witchcraft, some are involved in exorcism, and some in medicine and yoga. Some pretend to cure diseases by chanting texts, rid children of the evil eye, while others claim to have supernatural powers and even alchemical powers to convert base metals into precious metals like gold and silver. Interestingly, Gorakhnath was also known for his art of advanced alchemy.

There are some yogis who engage in elite professions like working in the army of kings, and selling silk threads, expensive clothing and wares. Some are even involved in rich commercial ventures, in agriculture and farming.

Each yogi has to follow a certain set of rules and each yogi vows to follow a certain path to stay focussed in his spiritual journey. Among the important vows undertaken by yogis, some include not taking up any kind of employment and not engaging in trade, but instead only begging door-to-door for alms and food, chanting "Alakh! Alakh!" or "Gorakh! Gorakh". While their meals are usually vegetarian, comprising rice, millets, vegetables and fruits, some also eat fish and mutton, but most don't eat pork as it is considered unclean, and also beef as the cow is considered sacred by Hindus. Meals also differ from region to region and depend on the castes existing there.

Some Kanphatas practise controlling their breathing patterns through the *nadi*s, while some even take a *maun vrat* (eternal vow of silence). They do not enter homes of people and most of them sleep in tents or huts which are temporary. Most of them are penniless and do not work for their livelihood. The life of a yogi is full of

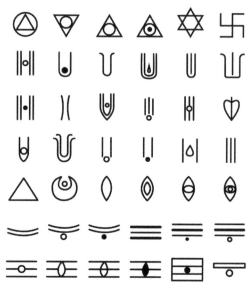

Different Types of Tilaka
Top Row (left to right): 1-5 The Lord Brahma and / or the Trimurti,
(far right) Shakti Rows 2-4 : The Lord Vishnu and or the vaishnavas
Rows 5-7 : The Lord Shiva and / or the Shaivas

difficulties. When Ranjha (the legendary youngest son of an affluent Chaudhary from Punjab who joined the Nath cult to win back his love, Heer) wanted to become one he was told: "The taste of a *jogi* (yogi) is bitter and sour. You will have to dress like a *jogi* in dirty clothes, have long hair, cropped ears and to beg your way through life. You will have to meditate on your guru and hold your breath in your midmost throat. You will have to give up the pleasures of birth, to cease to rejoice when friends come or grieve when they die. You will have to abstain from casting eyes on women. You will have to become divinely intoxicated by taking *kand, mul, post,* opium, and other narcotic drugs. You will have to think the world a mere vision. You will have to go on long pilgrimages to Jagannath, the Godavari, the Ganges and the Jumna. Jog (yoga) is no easy task. You Jats, luxury loving princes, cannot attain *jog.*"

Even Puran Bhagat (one of his best followers), was told by Gorakhnath: "*Jog* (yoga) you must not think of. The performance of *jog* (yoga) is beyond you. You will have to suffer hunger and thirst, to bear trials with patience and to renounce the world. You will have to leave behind all the pleasures of sense and to enter upon a life most difficult to pursue."

Gorakhnathis take a vow of celibacy and this rule is strictly practised at most monasteries, especially at Dhinodhar, Devi Patan, and Gorakhpur. However, in many areas it is found that the Kanphatas marry, and Brahmins preside over their marriage ceremonies. In fact, in Gorakhmandi, both *mathadaris* and celibates are found, along with *gharbaris* (householders). *Grahasta, bindi-bagi, samyogi* are other names by which householders are known. Many gharbaris are found in the Himalayan region and many families follow the lineage system in preserving the temple rights, passing them for generations, from father to son.

Married yogis are often held in contempt and some are even fined for just smoking with celibates. These yogis choose a wife from their own caste and avoid a union in the same *Gotra* (sub-sect). However, they continue to practise yoga and wear the distinct earrings and *Janeo* (sacred thread), along with the other articles of clothing. Rules for *gharbaris* differ in every region but most of them are not allowed to eat or live in the monastery.

Interestingly, the Shiva Samhita allows householders to be employed or to run businesses. It is believed that "success for the masterful householders, who are attached to the practices of yoga, must arise by the means of *japa*. Therefore, let the householder exert himself. Established in the house, with ample household, householders also engage in self employment having renounced attachment and engage in yoga practice secretly. The householder sees (increasingly) the wonderful marks of success, and, having carried out my instructions, should enjoy (bliss)." Becoming milkmen, farmers, tailors, weavers, soldiers or money-lenders is also common. The occupation of married yogis also depends and differs across the country in different regions and castes.

2.3 The Order of the Kanphata Yogis

Most yogis are casteless and there are no restrictions on eating, drinking or smoking habits. However, it is seen that Hindu and Muslim yogis do not eat together and women are not allowed to eat with the male yogis. Mostly, a young age is preferred for those wanting to become Kanphatas. Each guru tests the candidate's willpower and ability for a period between forty days and three to six months.

Two stages define the initiation process of yogis: the first stage of becoming an *Aughar* and the second stage of splitting the ears to become a complete yogi. The former involves many rituals and rules leading to discipleship, and the latter commits the yogi to the clan. Initiations are usually conducted at important pilgrimage centres or at a monastery, and can also take place at any Bhairav, Shakti, or Shiva temple.

Many Kanphatas add a "Nath" to their name to show their association with the other Gorakhnathis. Important monasteries of these yogis include the monastery at Tilla in Punjab, and the one at Gorakhpur, which is dominant in Uttarakhand. It belongs to the Dharamnathi sect and apparently overlooks the workings of 360 other, lesser known institutions. The monastery at Tulsipur belongs to the Ratannath branch of the Gorakhnathis. All these establishments are of great spiritual importance and exercise wide influence over the people. Their *pir* or *mahant* (spiritual head) is chosen differently by each tribe in every region.

Life in monasteries follows a simple routine. Each yogi has a separate room for privacy but they are accessible at all times to the public. Begging is part of the yogi's routine, and so are conversations with other fellow yogis, listening to religious discourses and interacting with the public who seek help or guidance. The dead yogis are buried by fellow-yogis and there is a large number of rituals and ceremonies that follow. The grave is known as a samadhi, and depending upon the class of the yogi, that is, whether he was rich or poor, he is buried in different parts of India. A year later a *Shraaddh* or *Barsi* is celebrated with a specific set of rules and ceremonies involving chants, material gifts, and food.

Though Gorakhnath's followers and devotees are spread far and wide across the world, there are twelve main sub-sects which were formed after his death. There are other divisions and schools led by individual gurus who belong to this same comprehensive group, but not all of them get that respect or following.

Traditionally, there are eighteen *panths* of Lord Shiva and twelve of Gorakhnath, but a clash between these two groups destroyed twelve groups of the former, and six groups of the latter. The remainder of the two groups i.e. twelve groups, form the main order of the Kanphatas.

The six Shaivite sects that have survived are: (i) Pagalnath of Peshawar and Rohtak (ii) Kantharnath of Bhuj in Kacch (iii) Pankh (iv) Kantharnath of Bhuj in Kacch (v) Ban of Marwar, and (vi) Rawal of Afghanistan.

The six surviving sects of Gorakhnath are: (i) Paonath of Jaipur (Jalandharpa, Kanipa, Gopichand) (ii) Hethnath (iii) Cholinath of the Aipanth of Devi Bimla (Bombay) (iv) Chandnath, Kaplani, (v) Bairag, Ratadhonda Marwar, Ratannath and (vi) Dhajjanath (Mahabir).

Each of the panths has different principles, with a different history and location.

The Kapalika School was introduced by the Naths, and only twelve important Naths possessed the knowledge of the doctrine of this school. These are: (1) Adinath (2) Anadinath (3) Kalanath (4) Atikalanatha(5) Karalanath (6) Vikaralanatha (7) Mahakalanath (8) Kala Bhairavanath (9) Batukanath (10) Bhutanath (11) Viranath and (12) Srikanthanath. The names of their twelve pupils are: (1) Nagarjun, (2) Jada Bharata (3) Harischandra (4) Satyanath (5) Bhimanath (6) Gorakshanath (7) Charpatanath (8) Avadyanath (9) Vairagyanath (10) Kanthadhari (11) Jalandhara and (12) Malayarjun.

In another list we find the following names of the nine Naths: Gorakshanath, Matsyendranath, Carpatanath, Mangalanath and Ghugonath. These Naths are believed to be immortal demigods and preachers of the sect for all ages, and it is also believed that they are still living in the Himalayan region. Sometimes, they are regarded as "guardian spirits" of the Himalayan peaks.

PARAMPARA (TRADITION) : as given by Pangarkar, based on Namdev references

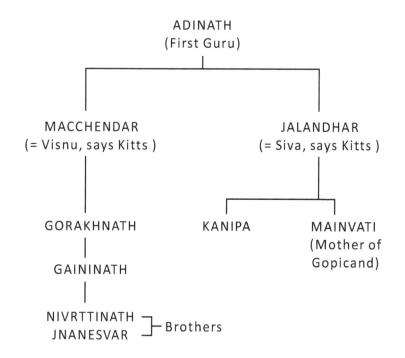

(Source : *Gorakhnath and the Kanphata Yogis*, George Weston Briggs.)

PARAMPARA (TRADITIONS) OF BAHINA BAI
ADINATH (Siva)
(taught he Yoga to)
PARVATI
|
MATSYENDRA
(who heard it as Siva taught it to Parvati)
|
GORAKHNATH
|
GAHINI
|
NIVRTTINATH
(While N. was a child but yet a Yogi)
|
DNYANESHVARA
|
SATCHIDANANDA
further on
VISHVAMBHARA
|
RAGHAVA (Chaitanya)
|
KESHAVA CHAITANYA
|
BABAJI CHAITANYA
|
TUKOBA (Tukaram)
|
BAHINA BAI
(B. 1628; D. 1700)

PARAMPARA (TRADITIONS)

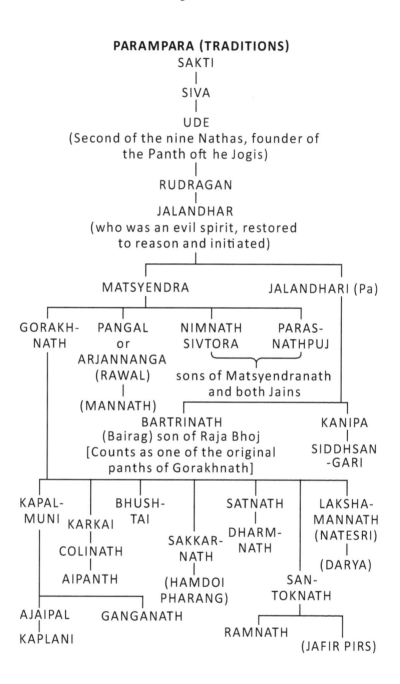

SAKTI
|
SIVA
|
UDE
(Second of the nine Nathas, founder of
the Panth oft he Jogis)
|
RUDRAGAN
|
JALANDHAR
(who was an evil spirit, restored
to reason and initiated)

MATSYENDRA   JALANDHARI (Pa)

GORAKH-   PANGAL   NIMNATH   PARAS-
NATH   or   SIVTORA   NATHPUJ
          ARJANNANGA
          (RAWAL)   sons of Matsyendranath
          | and both Jains
          (MANNATH)

BARTRINATH   KANIPA
(Bairag) son of Raja Bhoj |
[Counts as one of the original SIDDHSAN
panths of Gorakhnath]   -GARI

KAPAL-   BHUSH-   SATNATH   LAKSHA-
MUNI   KARKAI   TAI | MANNATH
        | SAKKAR- DHARM-   (NATESRI)
        COLINATH   NATH   NATH |
        | | (DARYA)
        AIPANTH   (HAMDOI   SAN-
                          PHARANG) TOKNATH
AJAIPAL   GANGANATH   RAMNATH
KAPLANI   (JAFIR PIRS)

(Source : *Gorakhnath and the Kanphata Yogis*, George Weston Briggs.)

2.4 Sacred Texts by Gorakhnath

As with every creative genius, Gorakhnath's teachings are still alive through oral tradition in the form of folktales, songs, and poems. Most of his teachings are also easily accessible through some of his epic works which are awe-inspiring and deeply philosophical.

Various books written in Sanskrit include *Amanaska Yoga, Amaraugh Shaasanam, Avadhoot Geeta, Goraksha Kalpa, Goraksha Kaumudi, Goraksha Geeta, Gorakshchikitsa, Gorakshpanchak, Gorakshpaddhati, Goraksha Shatakam, Goraksha Shastra, Gorksha Samhita, Chaturashityaasana, Jnyanaprakash Shatak, Jnyanamrit Yoga, Nadi Jnyan Pradipika, Maharthamanjiri, Yoga Chintamani, Yoga Martand, Shri Nath Sutra, Siddha Siddhaant Paddhati, Hatha Yoga* and *Hathayoga Samhita.* The similarity in their names suggests that perhaps these could have been written by one of his students at a later period. Nevertheless, they are considered to be reliable sources of his yogic knowledge. It is important to note that Gorakhnath's verses were written in an unorganised manner, and hence it is difficult to trace the exact source of his works.

It is agreed worldwide that *Goraksha Shatak* is the most authentic work on this great yogi, and it is available in many forms such as *Jnyan Shatak, Jnyan Prakash*, names which have a close resemblance to the books written by Gorakhnath himself, especially *Goraksha Paddhati* and *Hatha Yoga Pradipika,* written in the fourteenth century. However, there is a lapse of a century between the book by Briggs and the one by Kuvalyananda, and they are very different in the verses described.

The *Siddha Siddhanta Paddhati*, the *Goraksha Shataka*, the *Mahartha Manjari* and the *Amaraugh Prabodh* seem to be most honest and genuine sources of his knowledge and works. The *Goraksha Paddhati* is divided into two parts, the first being *Goraksha Shataka, Goraksha Jnyan* and *Jnyan Prakash Shatak* or *Jnyan Shatak*, and the second one being *Yoga Shastra.*

Works like *Goraksha Shatak Tika, Goraksha Shatak, Tippanna, Goraksha Kalpa* and *Goraksha Paddhati* are very similar in content, and are only known by different names. In *Goraksha Paddhati, Goraksha Shatak* is called *Goraksha Samhita.* Recently, the Varanasi Sanskrit University published a book called *Goraksha Samhita* which acknowledges the *Goraksha Shatak* as the most important book, but this again is a very debatable subject. Many experts argue on this matter as *Goraksha Samhita* seems to be older than *Goraksha Shatak,* as the former is even mentioned in the *Goraksha Paddhati.*

Gorakhnath seems to be the author of *Amaraugh Shaasanam* and *Maharthmanjari* and what makes these books so special is that they are written in colloquial Kashmiri. He has also penned a critical appreciation in the same discourse using the pseudonym "Parimal" in Sanskrit. Pundit Mukundram Shastri has called this book Gorakshaaparparyaay shri manmaheshwaraanandaachaarya virchita. This book defines thirty-six principles of the great guru but according to Pundit Vrajavallabh Dwivedi, this work was authored by Maheshwaraanand in the thirteenth and fourteenth centuries.

The book *Amaraugh Prabodh* deeply explains the Shaiva connection to the Nath cult. Hence, it is safe to assume that *Siddha Siddhant Paddhati, Amaraugh Prabodh* and *Goraksha Samhita* are significantly important.

The epic *Siddha Siddhanta Paddhati* describes Gorakhnath's emphasis on *adhikar* (power/rights), and is very valuable from a yogic perspective for two reasons. First, it explains the path, principles and perspectives of penance related to the Nath tradition and thus, without the knowledge of *Pindbramhand* philosophy, a yogi's path is incomplete. Six major concepts explained in this book are *Pindotpatti* (origin of the bodies, cosmic as well as individual), *Pind-Vichaar* (deeper contemplation on the constitution of the bodies), *Pindsanvitti (true insight into spiritual nature of the bodies), Pinda-dhara (container and sustainer of the bodies), Pind Samarasa-karana* (supreme ideal of a yogi's life) and character of an Avadhoot yogi respectively. The other reason for the book's importance is that it explains the different facets of yoga practice, and encourages internalisation and inner penance. The sacred values of *aadesh, kundal* and *bhajan,* are defined and explained in great detail.

Amaraugh Shaasanam is published in Kashmir Sanskrit Granthavali. It is vital for understanding the relationship between Shaivaagam and Shaiva Nath, and it also has a general summary of the principles of Vivruta. This book is divided into two sections: the first describes "*Sharana*" and the other describes "Siddha Siddhant Paddhati". Terms like *nadi, granthi, kundali chakra* and *amrut saadhan* among others, are explained in great detail and readers will feel deeply drawn to the supreme yogi Maheshwar.

The main objective of the *sharana* (surrender) is to achieve the siddhakadhayadha. There is a discussion on Shakti Prabodh and Shabda Sadhana. The book describes *Sahaj* Sadhana as the ultimate liberation, that is, a state of mind that can be totally grasped by another mind. Reading both parts in depth can help a person gain innate knowledge about Kaya Siddhi and Amrit Sadhana through the Yoga Sadhana prescribed by the Nath tradition. Hence, *Amraugh Shaasanam* is essential to understand the principles and path of penance of the Gorakhnathis.

The name *Goraksha Samhita* appears in many books and many of its verses are mentioned in the *Akulkeer Tantra* written by Matsyendranath. Both these works are similar in their content.

All the verses after the third verse, in the first part of *Goraksha Paddhati* are from the book *Goraksha Samhita* published from Prabhas Paatan, Kathiawad. The name Goraksha Samhita appears in the fourth verse. Gorakhnath bows to Minanath in *Goraksha Samhita*, and this book has two parts. Various facets of Shadang Yoga are described such as asan, *pransanrodh, pratyahaar, dharana,* dhyaan and samadhi. The knowledge of *shatchakra, shodsh adhar, trilakshya, vyom panchak, nav dwaar,* and *panchadhidaivat* situated in the body are intrincic to the knowledge of yoga. There is a discussion of *nadi* shastra, as well as the chakras. There are elaborate rules given for the awakening of the power for the yogi doing penance. There is also an elaborate explanation of the mudras and different bandhas, in addition to Pranavabhyaas, the ritual and types of Pranayam and the naadishodhan. To summarise, though the subject matter of this book is not different from others, it includes a thoughtful discussion on the act of penance.

From an overview of all these books, one can conclude that the main focus of Gorakhnath had always been on yoga and the knowledge gained from the penance of yoga. Pind-bramhand-dnyaan, Hatha Yoga as well as Raj Yoga command great importance in his books. The ingenuity and honesty of these books are well proven. There is definitely a dearth of ancient handwritten scripts but these books are accepted all over as written by Gorakhnath himself.

Gorakhnath's writings in the Hindi language command no less importance. These writings are in the regional language forms of the thirteenth and fourteenth centuries, written in the different contemporary styles of popular writing of that period. They necessarily portray the thoughts of Gorakhnath himself, as the tone, thoughts and *bhaav* (emotion) do not have any deviation from those in the Sanskrit books. Signs and symbols of their ancient link are sprinkled all over. Some words (like *bum or tofh*) suggest that these writings may be of the later period. These works of Gorakhnath have been edited by Dr. Pitamber Dutt Barthwal.

Thirteen compositions which are accepted as the most genuine ones are compiled in the original book. There are two annexures in the book which include Gorakhnath's major poetic works such as *Sabadi, Pad, (Raag Saamugri) Shishya Darsan Pransankali, Narvaiibodh, Atma Bodh, Abhaiyatra Jog, Pandrahatithi, Saptavaar, Macchindra Goraksha Bodh, Romavali, Gyaan Tilak* and *Panchmatra*. Writing compilations in the first annexure are *Goraksha Ganesh Gushti, Dnyaandeepbodh (Gorashdatt Gushti), Mahadev Gorash Gushti, Sishta Puraan, Dayabodh*, and some other compositions. *Saptabaar-navgrah, Brat, Panch Agni, Ashtamudra, Chaubees Siddhi, Battis Lacchan, Ashtachakra*, and *Raharasi* are published in the second annexure. The handwritten scripts of these books are from the seventeenth century. Among all of these, the *Sabadi* is the most authentic book. Though the language used in *Raag Saamugri* is ancient, it is quite disorganised.

In short, after analysing most of the Hindi literature available on the subject, one can conclude that though the language of the Hindi compositions on Gorakhnath is very simple and direct, the style in which they are written is similar to that of Sanskrit texts. There is technicality involved and the original tone is that of control and effortless living. These two virtues are essential for yoga and the yogi.

At the root of this is the principle of the guru and Pindbramhand philosophy, along with the penance of yoga. Gorakhnath has professed that to attain Parampad, its secretive nature is necessary, and for its attainment, experience and knowledge, Hatha Yoga and Raj Yoga are necessary, in the same order. Hatha Yoga helps to attain Siddha Kaya and Raj Yoga helps to attain Param Jnyan.

In simple words, his goal was to merge the human consciousness into super-consciousness. There are numerous symbolic references to Gorakhnath's advice on how to achieve this goal included in yoga penances such as *Bindu sadhana, Agni sadhana, Nadanu sandhan,*

Shabda sadhana, Amrutpan, Maanasniyaman, Navadwaarrodh, Pranayam, Unmaniyoga, Viparitkarani, Nadi Sadhan, Dashamdwar Sadhana, Vajroli, Amroli, etc. The utility of *bramhacharya, Bindu-raksha, yam-niyam,* the importance of speech and behaviour, not going to extremity in anything, moderate behaviour, the uselessness of shallow scholarly knowledge, joyous life, renouncing bad behaviour and renouncing the outer behaviour, has been professed with perspective to control diksha. The eligibility and rights of both, the guru and the disciple, their behavioural readings, the principles of human consciousness and supreme knowledge and their equanimity, is accepted as essential to the yogi and his knowledge, from the point of view of the *siddhanta* (principle). Having said all this, the main tone of the *Gorakhbaani* is that of control, which is helpful to both, the yogi and the householder. In fact, in many places, Gorakhnath has given more importance to the controlled householder.

If Gorakhnath's Hindi and Sanskrit compositions are to be evaluated in relation to his personality, it would be revealed that his advice was not just for the yogis but was also very useful, apt, and important for the common man. These virtues are very much essential for a leader. He had the exceptional qualities of penance, religion, social life, generosity, compassion, and had no enemies. It is because of these qualities that even today he is remembered by educated, as well as, uneducated devotees.

2.5 Sant Jnaneshvar and the Nath Cult

At the end of the *Jnaneshvari* (XVIII.1750-61), Sant Jnaneshvar has described his association with the Nath Sampradaya. This mystic poet's lineage can be traced directly to Gorakhnath. The first student, Matsyendranath attained the secret knowledge from Lord Shiva, who in turn, imparted it to Gorakhnath years later. Gorakhnath bestowed the secrets of this vast and mysterious doctrine to Gahininath who was Nivruttinath's guru. Nivruttinath was Jnaneshvar's elder brother who taught him extensively and thoroughly about yoga. All the different branches of *Shakta, Kapalika,* and Buddhist Tantra arose out of the *Agamas* (Shaiva scriptures) and claimed their origin in Lord Shiva. Matsyendranath was the first human guru of the Nath tradition and the prophet of the Kaula sect. This mystic and powerful cult left unforgettable impressions on the brilliant mind of Jnaneshvar.

According to the Tantric text *Shaivagama*, the ultimate truth is Adinath Shiva. Self-illuminated and known to only himself, he has Goddess Shakti as his consort, and he is infinite and imperishable. Like Sankhya's Prakriti, Shakti is the primordial energy contained within all beings, or we can say that she is the cause of the origination, continuance and dissolution of the world. Continuously active, she becomes manifest or remains in an un-manifest form. But unlike Sankhya's Prakriti, she is not independent of God and is not unconscious, but has a conscious form and hence, the Shaiva doctrine appears to be based on dualism.

The Nath Sampradaya has inherited its philosophical tenets from the Kaula sect and Matsyendranath is part of its foundations. In his norms for a yogi's discipline, Gorakhnath has laid importance on purity of mind and body, dedication to knowledge, aversion to ostentatious rituals, and non-consumption of meat and wine. Gorakhnath places great emphasis on yoga and dispassion, and it is because of this that Jnaneshvar has called him "The lake of lotus-creeper in the form of yoga and the conquering hero of sense-objects". (*Jnaneshvari*, Chapter XVIII, 1755.)

According to Sant Jnaneshvar, even if the world is real, its appearance is not. Just as one wrongly perceives a serpent in a necklace, or silver in a shell, so is perceived the world's appearance. And it is this false perception that comes in the way of true knowledge (15.46). However, these notions cannot last before knowledge. In the sixteenth chapter of his extraordinary work *Jnaneshvari*, Saint Jnaneshvar praises his preceptor as one who dispels this world appearance. He also did not accept the belief that the world is the play of the Supreme (*Chidvilasa*) like Ramanuja, according to whom the visible world is too real and is the cosmic play of the Supreme.

Even the sacred doctrine of *Shankara Bhashya* differs from the *Jnaneshvari* in its view of which yoga is considered more important in the *Geeta*. The philosopher Shankara regards the Yoga of Knowledge as primary along with the Yoga of Action, and the Yoga of Devotion as secondary and merely supportive to it. According to him, the seeker attains liberation in the following order: purification of the mind through a combination of the paths of Karma Yoga, renunciation, the way of knowledge, and self-realisation.

In Sant Jnaneshvar's opinion, all forms of yoga are equally valid and one has to adopt the path that is most suitable to his/ her aptitude and spiritual goal. In the sixth chapter of his book, while commenting on the Yoga of Meditation, he has spoken at length about the Yoga of Kundalini and called it "*pantharaja*" (the best way to self-actualisation). This view is not fully in conformity with Shankara's view. Additionally, Sant Jnaneshvar has stated that fulfilling one's duty is integral to Nitya Yajna, and that if it is performed in a selfless spirit and with dedication to God, it leads to liberation, independently. He further adds that to reach the peak of liberation, one has to walk on the path of devotion and that can only be attained step-by-step by performing one's duty (Karma Yoga), through complete, non-dual devotion to God and attainment of knowledge. It is only through this way that that the seeker becomes a "*jnani-bhakta*" (the knowledgeable one), who is most precious to God and becomes one with Him.

On the other hand, the other commentators hold that liberation is achieved through devotion to a personal God, and that even after attainment of liberation the devotee retains his individuality and lives in the presence of God. It is thus obvious that Sant Jnaneshvar consulted the *Shankara Bhashya* and not the other commentators. However, he did not follow it blindly, but formed his own views about the message of the *Geeta*.

Roots of Jnaneshvar in the Nath Panth

Being a disciple of Nivruttinath, who was himself a disciple of Gahininath, Jnaneshvar undoubtedly was a Nath Panthi himself. Though Jnaneshvar was very well-versed in the yogic and the Tantric ways of the Nath Panth, it is of utmost importance that he brought devotion in this path, as an ultimate way to conquer duality.

The Nath Panth had always given utmost importance to devotion towards the guru. But Jnaneshvar established the *Bhakti Marg* (the path of devotion) on an independent and firm pedestal.

Patanjali's yogic sutras (principles) and meditation techniques enjoy the highest status in the quest of spirituality. But they are filled with hardships and atrocities for the body of the *sadhak* (disciple). Jnaneshvar brings in the essence of these sutras and blends them most beautifully with this kingly path of devotion. This path of devotion professed by Jnaneshvar is his greatest contribution to the Nath Panth.

The devotion Jnaneshvar professes is beyond the attainment of knowledge. He considers devotion as the ultimate loyalty, objective, and goal of life. He explains that to love God like one's own, maintaining non-duality with Him and at the same time enjoying the celebration of duality in the world as its expression, means devotion.

Jnaneshvar explained this boon of ultimate devotion to the Warkaris and the Bhagavat Dharma which emerged in the simple minded, uneducated and devout masses of society. And the society happily relaxed in its love towards God. The concept of one being his own disciple was also one of the important facets of this great non-dualistic devotion. This path of devotion has more ease of execution, more surety and has the ultimate loyalty amongst its *sadhaks* compared to Hatha Yoga.

Jnaneshvar states that this ultimate devotion and the non-dual state of mind surpass all other yogic methods and even the final liberation. Jnaneshvar can thus be called a yogi who is a king of saints and a god of love.

The path of devotion he professes is connected to Karma Yoga. As he blends action, renunciation, knowledge and devotion in Karma Yoga, he creates a new word, "*Krama Yoga*" which is elaborated in the verses 50 to 66 in the XVIII chapter of the *Jnaneshvari.*

He says that in the path of *Krama Yoga*, action, knowledge and devotion together help in the attainment of final liberation. In this path there is neither renunciation, nor is there giving up of action. He further says that a living being is incapable of non-action.

Jnaneshvar was saddened by Tantric misbehaviour and the dark ways that Tantra developed during the particular period. He wanted the *sadhaks* to focus on an ideal mental frame and ideal behaviour all throughout.

He describes the devotion towards the guru professed in the Nath Panth very lovingly, delicately, and emphatically. He says in the thirteenth chapter that there is no beloved closer to you than your guru. A sadguru is an exposed spirit and service to the guru is the mother of all good fortune. He places the guru on the highest pedestal and loyalty and love towards him flourishes independently on the paths of devotion, as well as on the yogic paths in the Nath Panth. Devotion towards the guru as a principle has been emphasised in his book *Anubhavaamrit* more elaborately. The concept of the guru having a dialogue as a disciple himself, and Shiva himself coming to the state of Shakti or Uma is not new to the Nath Panthis.

Thus, Jnaneshvar expounds the principles of the Nath Panthis and says that this multifaceted world is, in fact, the expression of "The One Principle", and is inspired by it. He explains that the "One" became "many" to counter loneliness, and the rest of the maya or this world was created to enjoy the beauty of the one spirit in various forms. One comes across beautiful and expressive explanations of this inspirational and ever blissful state in the literature written by Jnaneshvar.

Jnaneshvar and the Geeta

It is interesting to trace Jnaneshvar's initiation into the Nath cult, and then his writings of the *Bhagavad Geeta*. In chapter X (ovi 19) of his work *Jnaneshvari*, he has written that his guru commanded him to explain the knowledge of Brahman in the form of the *Geeta*, in the ovi form. Additionally, he wrote his commentary to destroy the poverty of thought and reveal the knowledge of Brahman to all. Shaivites were drawn to the *Bhagavad Geeta*, as it dealt with devotion. Thus, in turning to the *Geeta*, Jnaneshvar was following this tradition and using it as a reference point to offer and extend his spiritual understanding of the pious stanzas. Even after he imbibed the "*Brahmavidya*" (scriptural knowledge of the *Geeta*), he continued his interest in Kundalini Yoga and his devotion to his gurus. All these instances find detailed mention and space in the *Jnaneshvari*.

Kundalini Yoga was not taught in the *Geeta*, and Jnaneshvar states that "Lord Krishna had made a casual reference to this secret of the Nath sect and that he has elaborated this before the audience." (ovis 291, 292) By including Kundalini Yoga in the *Jnaneshvari* and extolling it as the "*pantharaja*" (the great path) he has accorded to it the same status as that of Dhyan Yoga in the *Geeta*.

Devotion to the guru is integral to understanding the deeper nuances of the *Jnaneshvari*. An entire chapter in the "Kularnava Tantra" explains how a disciple should worship his guru. It is said that "*The sacred sandals (paduka) of the guru form his ornaments;*

the remembrance of his name is his japa; to carry out his commands is his duty; and service to the guru is his worship." The *Geeta* calls service to the guru (*acharyopasana*) as one of the characteristics of a *jnani*. However, Sant Jnaneshvar has explained this devotion to the teacher in ninety ovis and at the beginning of every chapter he sings praises and pays obeisance to the guru.

The Nath Sampraday lays special stress on diksha (initiation) and on *shaktipat* (transference of power) from guru to disciple. It is said that no mantra becomes fruitful unless the disciple hears it from the mouth of the guru. Thus, transference of power is especially important in the awakening of the Kundalini, and the Shakti lying dormant in the muladhara chakra is awakened instantly by the guru's touch. This transference of power is mentioned in the *Jnaneshvari*. Its eighteenth chapter states: "He who was experiencing the universe as a dream during the sleep state of ignorance, woke up to experience the bliss of the Brahman when the guru patted his head and awakened him."(ovi 403). He further adds, "In order to grant what the Lord could not give through words, the Lord hugged Arjuna, and then 'the two hearts mingled and what has in the heart of the guru was transferred to the heart of the disciple'. Thus Krishna made Arjuna like himself without removing the duality between the guru and the disciple."

Yoga and Knowledge

Just like Shankaracharya, Sant Jnaneshvar must have also realised that yoga does not become complete without knowledge. While commenting on the *Brahmasutra* II 1.3, Shankaracharya states: "One does not enjoy the bliss of Brahman through Sankhya knowledge and the practice of yoga." In the *Amritanubhava* (727), Jnaneshvar calls the yogi "the moon in the daytime", i.e., the yogi becomes as lustreless as the moon before the sun of knowledge.

The legend of Changdev explains this theory well. Changdev was a great yogi, who had taken initiation from the yogini Muktabai, Sant Jnaneshvar's sister. Changdev had practised yoga for many years and had attained many miraculous powers which had built up his ego. When Sant Jnaneshvar and his other siblings received a blank note from him, his sister Muktabai aptly remarked that Changdev had no respect for knowledge. Jnaneshvar then wrote sixty-five verses on the blank paper and sent it back to him. Changdev had great difficulty in interpreting his words. So, to demonstrate his powers, he rode on a tiger with a poisonous cobra as a whip and visited them accompanied by thousands of devotees. Looking at this scene, Muktabai and her brothers decided to teach him a lesson. They patted the wall and it rose up in the air. They then used it as a vehicle to approach him. Using a non-living object as a vehicle left everyone awestruck. Changdev overcame his pride and became their devoted disciple. The verses Sant Jnaneshvar wrote on that blank note came to be known as the "Changdev Pasashti".

In the books *Jnaneshvari, Amritanubhava* and *Changdev Pasashti*, Jnaneshvar has disclosed the knowledge of the Self. Nicknamed, "The Prince among *Jnanis*", he is a "*Sthitaprajna*" after practising the path of knowledge. The *Geeta* states that tranquillity abides in a *Sthitaprajna* (ch. 2.70) and that "Even if all the currents of the rivers become swollen and join the sea, the latter does not become disturbed and remains serene." Jnaneshvar had attained this rare serenity. Although Brahmins had persecuted the three brothers and sister as being offspring of a monk, he praised them as "gods on earth, the fountainhead of all sacred lores and austerities incarnate." Among the characteristics of a man of wisdom as stated in the thirteenth chapter, the first and the chief is *amanitva* (non-arrogance). As for the attribute of humility, Jnaneshvar says, "If a person casts off all vanity of being great, forgets his learning and becomes humble, then know that he has attained knowledge of Brahman."

All the qualities of a *jnani* found in the *Geeta* apply to Jnaneshvar. "He who has attained knowledge sees no distinction in all beings, as he has discarded egoism, nor does he discriminate between a mosquito, an elephant, a cow and a dog."(Geeta V.18)

Devotional Love

The *Geeta* describes devotion as based on meditation, but there is also a reference to devotional love in it. In the tenth chapter it is said that God grants *Buddhiyoga* to those who worship him with love (verse 10). Further, in the eleventh and the twelfth chapters, Krishna tells Arjuna to work for him (*matkarmakrit*, V.55) or be devoted to work for him (*matkarmaparama*, V.10). Shankara's interpretation states: "One should perform his works with dedication to God." But Abhinavagupta takes *matkarma* as Bhagavat Dharma which consists of worship, austerities, scriptural study, sacrificial rites and more. But the word Bhagavat does not occur in the *Critical Edition of Mahabharata*. So the Bhagavat Dharma seems to have germinated from these sayings in the *Geeta* and spread in north India before the second century BC. Sant Jnaneshvar however, knew the *Bhagavat Purana,* to which he refers in Chapter XVIII (ovi 1132).

Some scholars have even said that Jnaneshvar has taken more than half his illustrations from the *Bhagavat*. Many references to Puranic stories in the *Jnaneshvari* can be linked with those mentioned in the *Bhagavat Purana*. Jnaneshvar mentions nine-fold devotion in "Adhyay VI" (ovi 127), where he says that "Arjuna was the chief deity of the eighth kind of devotion named friendship." He has given a marvellous description of the kirtan bhakti in the ninth chapter (ovi 97-112). Such devotees, he says, sing songs of God's praise and dance with the joy of devotion. They have made all talk of atonement redundant, as there is not a trace of sin left in them. They take his name as Krishna, Vishnu, Hari, and Govinda, and spend their time in discussion over the nature of the Self.

When devotees sing praises to God, they give and receive a healing touch to the miseries of the world and fill it with the bliss of self. Through their devotion, these devotees turn the world into Vaikunth (the Divine abode of Vishnu). In fact, the *Geeta* also states that God may not be found in Vaikunth or the region of the sun, and he may even pass by the minds of yogis, but he will surely be found where his devotees sing his praises aloud. "To utter the name of God even once by mouth is the reward earned by rendering service to him in thousands of years; yet the same name ever dances on their tongue. One cannot compare them with the sun, the moon or the cloud, as the sun sets, the moon is full only at times and the cloud becomes empty after a while. But the knowledge of these devotees never sets, they are always full of devotion, and they flood this world with the knowledge of the Self."

Jnaneshvar and Namdev

The friendship of these two saints is divinely remarkable. Sant Namdev was dazzled by the deep knowledge and devotion of Sant Jnaneshvar based on non-dualism. Jnaneshvar was awed by the intense devotional love and the depth of feeling Namdev held for

Vitthal. In chapter X, he has given a beautiful description of what two devotees do when they meet. "They must have conversed with each other and danced with joy in the fullness of knowledge and devotion. They must have exchanged their experiences and shared their knowledge and devotion with each other. Just as when the water in two lakes shoots up, the waves of one mingle with the waves of the other, so the ripples of their mirth must have mingled together. They must have spent days and nights in singing the praise of God and in discussions on the Self." Theirs was a spiritual friendship. Namdev realised that devotion remains incomplete without self-knowledge and he went to Visoba Khechar to take initiation. Jnaneshvar on his part became a devotee of Vitthal and turned to *madhura* bhakti (devotional love).

Non-Dual Devotion

Most people experience devotion in one of two ways. The devotee ascribes the human attributes to God and worships God with form. Or, he projects these divine qualities to an extraordinary and remarkable person and worships him as an avatar (incarnation of God). According to the *Geeta*, most devotees worship God to gain wealth, to attain relief from misery, or for knowledge. But very few devotees worship God without entertaining any desire in their minds.

Most scholars believe in the spiritual premise that devotion is only possible through duality between God and the devotee. The schools of Ramanuja (*Vishishta Advaita*) or Vallabha (*Shuddha Advaita*) are non-dualistic but their devotion is based on a distinction between God and the devotee (unlike Advaita philosophy of Shankara which says that the Self and Brahman are the same). According to their beliefs, "a liberated soul does not become one with God, but retains his individuality and enjoys independent life in the proximity of God." In contrast, Jnaneshvar regards such devotion based on distinction as unchaste and narrow-minded. In the fourteenth chapter of the *Jnaneshvari* he has written: "It is not that one should attain God realisation after the dissolution of the world but that one should try to apprehend God along with the world. If God is worshipped with the knowledge that he has pervaded this whole universe, it becomes chaste, non-dual devotion. Even if there are waves in the sea, they are all water. So the *jnani bhakta* sees God in the universe and worships him with the intensity of devotion." He says, "Whatever creature one meets, one should regard it as God; such is the nature of non-dual devotion." (ovis 379, 380) At the end of the twelfth chapter, the *Geeta* mentions the characteristics of a *jnani bhakta*, beginning with "without hatred towards any being." This attribute can be clearly seen in Sant Jnaneshvar as he had no hatred even for wicked or bad people. In his "Pasaayadan" (last prayer) he has asked God not to destroy wicked people but to destroy their wickedness.

Another attribute of a *jnani bhakta* is that he does not trouble the world, nor is he troubled by it. In the thirteenth chapter, Jnaneshvar writes on non-violence saying that "a *jnani* takes great care that he does not trample any creature and cause harm to it as God is imminent in it." It is also interesting to note that through devotion based on non-dualism, he also devoted himself to devotion of God with form. In chapter XII of the *Jnaneshvari*, he says, "Even though a person has become a yogi by practising the means of Karma Yoga externally and of Dhyana Yoga internally, he attains intense love for my form with attributes. O Arjuna, he alone is a devotee, a yogi and a liberated soul. I am so fond of him as though he is my beloved and I the husband. He is dearer to me than my own Self. This simile too is inadequate to express the relation between us. The account of my true devotee is a magical formula (mantra) which infatuates the mind. One should not say such things, but I had to say them because of my love for you. When the subject of my devotee is broached, my affection for him doubly increases." (ovis 155-160) "Just as the devotee feels an attraction for Me, I too have a 'passion' for him." (Ch. XVIII, ovi 1349)

The personal connection of a true devotee becomes so intense with God that, at times, he may feel that God has left him and he experiences an agony of separation. In Western books of devotion, this is described as the "Night of Darkness". Jnaneshvar has described the pangs of separation in his *gaulani* (cowherdesses) and *virahini* (a wife suffering the pangs of separation from her husband) *abhangs*. The devotional love (*prema-bhakti*) of Jnaneshvar is touching. Ramanuja believed that "no one can attain liberation without *Prapatti* (complete self-surrender to god), without which one cannot gain the grace of god. It is not necessary for him to perform actions or yoga!"

Gurudev Ranade explains this beautifully in the following lines: "The Gita is not a book of ethics but of spiritual life. It teaches not human but divine action; not the disinterested performance of duties but the following of the Divine will; not a performance of social duties but the abandonment of all standards of duty (*sarvadharma*), to take refuge in the Supreme alone; not social service but the action of the God-possessed, the Master-men and as a sacrifice to Him, who stands [14. R.N. Dandekar Vedic Mythological Tracts Delhi 1979, pp.55, 341] behind man and Nature (*Essays on the Bhagavad-Gita*, p. 43)."

In the eighteenth chapter of the *Jnaneshvari,* Jnaneshvar has said that one should also worship God through performance of his duty. According to him, "one should place his actions like flowers at the feet of God." In his last prayer, he prays to God to let the sense of duty dawn upon the world.

Jnaneshvar and the Warkari Order
After meeting Namdev, Jnaneshvar was introduced to other Warkari saints like Sena Nhavi, Savata Mali, Narahari Sonar, Gora Kumbhar, and Chokhamela among others. These Warkari saints fulfilled all their duties with dedication and worshipped Lord Vitthala with devotional love according to the Bhagavat Dharma. The spiritual meaning they found in everyday life with ordinary people is especially commendable.

"Onions, radish and vegetables, these are my Vithabai (Vitthal)" said Savata Mali.

"O Lord, I am your goldsmith and carry on the business of your name; I blow the bellows of *jeeva* and Shiva and beat the gold (taking the name of God) day and night," said Narhari Sonar.

Jnaneshvar left a lasting impression on the minds and hearts of all these saints and they took refuge under his wings. Jnaneshvar, who was a Siddha and part of the Nath sect, also became the "*Mauli*" (mother) of the Warkaris and all devotees. Even after seven centuries, it is a very heartening fact that his devotees flock in thousands to Alandi at the time of Ashadhi Ekadashi, when the palanquin containing the *paduka*s of Jnaneshvar is taken to Pandharpur, and they walk this distance in rain and sun, singing the "Haripath". On Kartiki Ekadashi, a fair is held at Alandi where lakhs of devotees visit the place and sing his praises.

Jnaneshvar and Patanjali

The *Vedas* and the *Agamas* are perhaps the greatest philosophical and spiritual books ever written. The ultimate aim of these works is to help the individual attain moksha (liberation) and experience Brahman (the ultimate truth). However, these books largely differ in their teachings, ideologies and philosophies.

Like the *Mahabharata,* the *Vedas* and the *Upanishads* consider the origin of the science of yoga to be the *Hiranyagarbha* (golden womb), from which the creator of the universe, Lord Brahma, emerged. The *Agamas* believe that the author of this science of yoga is Adinath or Shiva, and all of these are written in the form of conversations between Shiva and his consort. Patanjali is a follower of the Upanishad traditions. The philosophy of the sacred text, *Patanjali Darshana,* is that Sankhya, the Ashtanga Yoga which Patanjali propagated, was in vogue several centuries before Patanjali (300 BC).

A number of *Upanishads* such as the *Chandogya Upanishad* and the *Shandilya Upanishad* have references to Ashtanga Yoga. The yoga philosophy explained by Yajnavalkya to Gargi and other disciples is exactly on the same lines and very similar to Patanjali's. According to Yajnavalkya, the philosophy of Ashtanga Yoga was learnt by him from his masters, and this is testimony to the fact that Ashtanga Yoga as a spiritual system is indeed very ancient, and was already in practice before Patanjali. Thus, all theories and principles mentioned by him can be referred to the Upanishads and the Sankhya philosophy. However, he has contributed to the *Yoga Sutras* and has defined the concept of *Ishvara* (PYS 1.240) but this is his own standpoint and does not in any way relate to the established tradition. According to his concept, "*Ishvara* is not a creator but a person whose sins are destroyed." This theory is closely linked with the Jain Darshana.

In contrast, Jnaneshvar was initiated into the traditions of the Nath Sampradaya, and his philosophies differ greatly from that of Patanjali's *Yoga Darshana.* Sanskrit books such as *Goraksha Gita, Goraksha Paddhati, Siddha Siddhanta Paddhati, Amaraugh Shaasana,* and *Amaraugh Prabodha,* among many others define the essence of the path of the Nath Panth and are like a mirror reflection of the teachings of Sant Jnaneshvar.

Thus, there are many differences between the paths of these two philosophers and spiritual masters. And each of them is relevant to understanding and shaping the path of yoga in myriad ways. Some of the anomalies are listed below:

1. Patanjali's system of Ashtanga Yoga is based on his *Yoga Sutras* whereas Jnaneshvar's yoga system is based on the principles of Hatha Yoga, founded by the Siddhas. There are many followers of Ashtanga Yoga around the world. Many great yogis such as Gorakhnath recommend the system of Sadanga Yoga described in the *Goraksha Paddhati,* and this path avoids *Yama* and *Niyama* which is considered vital by Patanjali. The justification given by yogis is that if an individual can obtain mastery in meditation, their entire lifestyle is metamorphosed in such a way that they start following the *Yama* and *Niyama* which are important rules and individual rules of conduct, respectively. These six aspects of yoga are physical postures, pranayam, pratyahara, dharana, dhyan and samadhi.

2. The Nath cult lays great emphasis on purification of the entire body of the seeker in accordance with the rules mentioned in the *Gheranda Samhita.* This process includes complete purification of all vital organs of the body such as stomach, small intestines, large intestines, nasal passage, food pipe, eyes, ears, throat and nervous system. Only after this *"shuddhi"* is carried out, is the seeker considered eligible for yoga. However, in contrast, Patanjali's *Yoga Sutras* do not mention these preparatory steps or rules.

3. Learning the various physical postures for mind-body healing is included as part of the yoga systems. However, each seeker has to learn all the important postures and among these he has to practise the Siddhasana or the Vajrasana. This is considered to be the most important posture for all future sadhanas. This posture is explained in great detail by Jnaneshvar in the sixth chapter of the *Jnaneshvari* and it is considered a must by the Nath cult in many of their sacred texts. However, Patanjali differs on this. According to him the seeker can sit in any convenient posture of his/her choice and thus, he calls this sutra the *"Sthira-sukham asanam"* (the steady and seated comfortable posture) that is performed with willingness and acceptance by the seeker.

4. For the Nath cult, a guru is of utmost importance and each

and every work of their sacred teachings in the Shastras begins with gratitude and a deep reverence to the masters— Adinath or Shiva. Even the *Jnaneshvari* starts with the saying "*Om Namoji Adya.*" This acknowledgement to the gurus is not given in Patanjali's *Yoga Darshana.*

5. According to the Nath Siddhas, the human body consists of essential centres or vital points and voids (*Akasha*) and each seeker must have complete knowledge of these to become a perfect yogi viz, the six chakras, sixteen vital points, two *lakshyas* (concentration points) and five voids, all situated within the human body. This physiological discussion is not part of Patanjali's *Yoga Darshana.*

6. The Nath cult compares the human body to a beautiful house with nine doors. It is believed to be formed out of five essential elements and each element has its own deity. These nine openings are two eyes, two nostrils, two ear holes, mouth, anus, and sex organs. The deity of earth is Brahma, of water is Vishnu, of fire is Rudra, of air is Ishvara, and of space is Sadashiva, and each and every seeker aiming to become a yogi must know this. Such explanations and theories are missing from Patanjali's *Sutras.*

7. In many of the theory books of the Nath cult, the location and functions of the seven chakras (energy centres) which are connected with spiritual growth and transformation is explained in vivid detail. These are the Muladhara chakra (located at the base of the spine), Svadhisthana chakra (where the reproductive organs are located), Manipura chakra (located near the navel/stomach), Anahata chakra (located near the heart), Visuddha chakra (located near the throat), Ajna chakra (located in the forehead, between the eyes where the Third Eye is activated), and the Sahasrara chakra (located in the crown). Interestingly, these subtle auric energy centres were founded by the great rishis. Through their sadhana, they discovered these and taught the seekers the powers available by activating these chakras through the path of yoga and meditation. These explanations and theories of immense knowledge are missing from Patanjali's *Yoga Sutras.*

8. Further describing the human body's anatomy, the Nath cult states that there are seventy-two thousand nerves in

the body of human beings and out of these, ten *nadis* are of utmost importance. Of these, the *Ida, Pingala* and *Sushumna* are vital. *Ida* is the *Chandra Nadi, Pingala* is the *Surya Nadi* and *Sushumna Nadi* is also known as *Agni Nadi.* Patanjali's *Yoga Sutras* do not make any mention of these. However they mention a few *nadis* like *Kurma Nadi,* only in few words, devoid of detailed explanations.

9. The Nath cult has deeply studied and analysed the concept of prana and according to them, the human body has ten different types of air or *Vayus* which are: *Prana, Apana, Samana, Udana, Vyana, Naga, Kurma, Krikala, Devadatta* and *Dhananjaya.* Each of these is located in a specific part of the body and is responsible for specific purposes and functions in the body. When we breathe, the air we take in gets divided into ten branches like a stream of water which starts from the Himalayan Mountains and gets divided into several branches. Each branch becomes a river and is given a separate name. Medical practitioners and science cannot explain this as, miraculously, it is only the great yogic sages and teachers who have "seen" these different streams of air inside our body through their sadhana. These descriptions are missing from Patanjali's *Yoga Sutras.*

10. When we inhale, the sound of "So" is produced, and when we exhale, the sound of "Hum" is heard. Each practitioner can experience this sound of "Sohum" with continuous practice. In a single day, we breathe twenty-one thousand six hundred times, and this sound known as "mantra" is continuously heard in the body twenty-one thousand six hundred times. If this is reflected upon and deeply observed by the practitioner, it can turn into a sadhana which is important to every yogi of the Nath cult. This explanation or theory is not found in Patanjali's *Yoga Sutras.*

11. Jnaneshvar's *Yoga Sadhana* lays emphasis on the Kundalini Shakti which forms a part of the Tantric sadhana of the Nath cult. This process is described in great detail in the sixth chapter of the *Jnaneshvari*. A practical approach, it is based on the premise that the whole universe is created out of the cosmic play of energy between Shiva and Shakti which is Maha Kundalini, and a small part of this energy is contained in every

human being in the form of the dormant Kundalini (*Supta Shakti*) at the base of the spine. Yogis describe this as energy coiled three-and-a-half times like a serpent at the end of the *Sushumna Nadi*, and is termed by them as "Bramhandi te Pindi". This phrase means that "whatever exists in the universe also exists in the human being in the subtle form." This energy can be activated and the Nath yogis, especially Gorakhnath, have devised many ways for this. Jnaneshvar's path is explained in the sixth chapter of the *Jnaneshvari* and also mentioned in almost all the books of Hatha Yoga and the Nath Panth, and in some *Upanishads*. This energy can also be activated by Mantra Yoga, Laya Yoga and Bhakti yoga. The practitioner who succeeds in activating this Shakti experiences divine bliss and is blessed with many siddhis (spiritual powers). Patanjali's *Yoga Sutras* make no mention of Kundalini Shakti.

12. The Nath cult also describes a very mystic method called *Shaktipat* through which a master can transfer spiritual energy to the initiated aspirant, and can even activate the Kundalini energy of the disciple. This transfer can be done by simply touching a specific part of his body or simply by looking at him, and can also take place if the disciple is at a great distance. This is a profound mystical act which is shrouded in mystery among the yogis and only a few of them are adept at this. After the transfer of energy, the devotee experiences a number of supernatural happenings and a tremendous flow of (liquid) light, among other out-of-body experiences and divine visualisations. This mystical and profound concept of *Shaktipat* is not found in Patanjali's *Yoga Sutras*.

13. The Nath cult lays great emphasis on the practice of certain physical postures known as mudras. These are very useful in meditation and also in the activation of Kundalini energy and the six chakras. It is therefore necessary for every seeker to learn these. According to ancient texts, there are twenty-five mudras and out of these, ten are most important. Regular practice of mudras with concentration can help the devotee get rid of each and every disease, and gain healthy immunity and longevity. Mudras are nowhere mentioned in Patanjali's *Yoga Sutras*.

14. There is a big difference between the dhyan meditation of

Patanjali and that of Jnaneshvar. Patanjali gives the definition of dhyan in Sutra No. III.1 and III.2, which are as follows: "The aspirant has to concentrate on a specific or vital part of the body or on some external point. This process is known as *Dharana*. When the aspirant gets success in the concentration on that particular point, for a sufficiently long time, it becomes 'dhyan'. For the concentration on that particular point, the aspirant has to use his mind." In contrast, in Kundalini Yoga, the devotee does not have to use his mind but instead has to practise "Kumbhaka" wherein the function of mind totally stops. Instead of concentrating on any particular point, the devotee has to activate the Kundalini energy which is a superior way and is mentioned even in the esteemed publication *The Serpent Power* by Sir John Woodroffe, which many learned scholars and philosophers refer to.

15. Patanjali has broadly divided samadhi into *Samprajnata* samadhi and *Asamprajnata* samadhi. However, the state of samadhi has been studied in detail by the Nath cult and is followed by Jnaneshvar too. The Siddhas have classified samadhi into six types: 1) Dhyan Yoga samadhi 2) Nada Yoga samadhi 3) Rasananda Yoga samadhi 4) Laya Yoga samadhi 5) Bhakti Yoga samadhi and 6) Raja Yoga samadhi. How each samadhi can be experienced is also discussed in detail. Scholars and philosophers can refer to chapter seven of the *Gheranda Samhita* which gives the entire description.

2.6 Fables, Legends and Superstitions

Just like ordinary people, the Kanphata yogis have their set of beliefs, superstitions, and practices. They worship all the gods of the Hindu pantheon, observe fasts on certain days, and some even carry on the traditional medicinal system involving witchcraft, magic, and exorcism. Some yogis abstain from eating fish because Matsyendranath, whom they worship as a god, was born from one. Red dal or grains of masoor are considered taboo as they resemble drops of blood. Observing breathing patterns is the most popular way to cure and detect diseases, and so is the use of exorcism. Along with this, Kanphatas are also reputed for using charms, evil eye protection, drugs, magic spells and even ash from the *dhuni* for healing purposes. They also use many amulets made of a combination of metals like silver and copper, to be worn around the neck or on the fingers.

In many stories Gorakhnath is described as "a great magician and healer" whose powers know no limits. He can change his form at will, appear anywhere across time, disappear at his wish, and grant life-changing boons to his devotees. There are many instances of his great deeds. Once he scattered ashes over a dry garden where flowers began to bloom. His magic bag contained many gifts and boons in the form of apples, flowers, ashes, and barley-grains. These transformed or carried the magic of blessing people with sons, gems, wealth, clothing, and innumerable desires that their hearts desired. The ashes especially, which were from Gorakhnath's sacred fire in Patiala, were believed to be so powerful that they could transform men into animals and vice versa. Apparently, it was from a similar bag that Puran Bhagat took the magical grapes and rice that blessed his step-mother, the queen Lunan, with a son (Rasalu).

He also owned a magic carpet (mat) which was so telepathic and sensitive to his disciples' needs that whenever someone far away needed help the carpet would tremble, alerting the yogi to the plea for help. It is said that it is on the same carpet that Gorakhnath went to heaven. It is also said that even Lord Vishnu created the world by taking these ashes and scattering them on the waters.

Siddhas are greatly respected as semi-divine beings who become exceptionally pure with the practice of yoga. The *Nanak Sakhi* describes an instance where a great saint had visited the yogis. There, in the Himalayas, it is said that he met Gorakhnath, Bhartruhari, and others. On another occasion, he met eighty-four Siddhas who performed unusual miracles in front of him through their powers. They could make a stone move, cause a wall to move, make a deer skin fly,and even light a fire out of nothing.

Gorakhnath's many miraculous deeds are described in many folktales and towns and villages across Punjab, Bengal, Sindh, Deccan, Nepal, and Rajputana, and even in parts of Tibet and Pakistan. He is also the patron saint of the royal house that rules Nepal. According to some legends, it is said that his followers, the Kanphata yogis, were originally Buddhists but became Shaivites at the end of the twelfth century for political power and social acknowledgement, after the fall of Nepal's Sena dynasty. However, there is another mythological tale connected to his teacher Matsyendranath (described earlier), in which he was called when there was no rainfall in the country for a span of twelve years.

It is said that Goraksha country and the Gorkha city in Nepal get their name from Gorakhnath, who lived in the city in a small cave, where an old shrine dedicated to him is found even today. In the Sindh province, Gorakhnath is called Datar Jamil Shah, and according to one historical record he was the teacher of the north Indian *pir*, Gugga. In many texts, he is seen as a manifestation of Shiva himself. In the Rasalu legend, he is described as a god.

Gorakhnath and the Legends of the Kingdom of Nepal

The Kingdom of Nepal has a long association and is deeply connected in many religious ways with the blessings and teachings of Matsyendranath and his disciple Gorakhnath. Even today, after centuries, both these great yogis are respected by followers who sing praises of their powers and deeds. The Nath cult is influential in many parts of this kingdom. Symbols related to Matsyendranath are praised by titles such as "Shri Karunamaya", "Shri Loknath", and even their precious coins have "Shri Gorakshanath" inscribed on them.

There is an interesting story about King Narendradev, who ill-treated Gorakhnath. It is said that once when he visited the kingdom with his guru Matsyendra, there was only one boy, Vasant, who treated him with respect. Pleased and impressed by his selflessness and love for his widowed mother, Gorakhnath said that he wanted Vasant to take over the entire kingdom of Nepal and would like her permission. Vasant's mother was shocked but respected the yogi's words and told him that her son would now be his servant. Gorakhnath took the little boy near the secluded banks of the river Sarovar and asked him to make human figures out of mud. Vasant followed his orders and built thousands of human figures. With his mystic yogic power, Gorakhnath instilled life into all these non-living figures and blessed them, saying that they would now have to follow Vasant's orders and help him take over the kingdom of Nepal. Feeling blessed and motivated, Vasant took his army and led them to battle with the king. A big war ensued and with Gorakhnath's *Iccha Shakti* (will power), the king's army was defeated, and fled the battlefield. Vasant emerged victorious, and the king fell at Gorakhnath's feet asking for forgiveness for his sins. Gorakhnath then told him that he missed out on a great opportunity in his life and so would have to repent for the same. The only way out of his misery would be to adopt Vasant and bring him up as his own son. The king found a new lease of life and in front of the entire court, with the blessings of the great yogi, he declared Vasant as king. Gorakhnath told Vasant, "The first duty of the king is to look after all the needs of his people and he should never forget this." Eventually, King Vasant named his kingdom "Gorkha", after him. Even after ten generations, the Gorkha kingdom is ruled by the Shah clan. Nara Bhupal Shah, Naresh Dravya Shah, Ram Shah, Prithvi Narayan Shah and Yashovarma are some of the famous kings who carried on the legacy of praying to Gorakhnath.

Another legend relates to King Meghraj, who was born in Dang (Ratanpuri) in Nepal. As a youth, he went to the forest for hunting and shot a deer. As he chased the bleeding deer, he came across a mahayogi wearing long shiny earrings. He had hypnotic eyes and blood marks on his ribs. Realising his mistake, the king begged for forgiveness. The mahayogi blessed him saying that non-violence is the greatest religion, and every living being should be treated as one's equal. Animals and birds are created by God and only He has the right to take away their life. If you want to hunt and kill then you must first kill your indecisive heart because once you do that, you will truly gain power and strength. God and his creations are inseparable, as divine essence resides in every being. Hence, killing someone of the same flesh and blood is a sin. The path of yoga is to liberate you from worldly desires and sins. And for this, you even have to kill your own heart. In a yogi's life, there is no body, heart, flesh, blood or desire. There is only place for the Divine and the guru's teachings. The great yogi who spoke these words was Ratannath, descendant of Gorakhnath. The young man became his student and after blessing him, Ratannath asked him to chant "*Pranav-rupini hans gayatri mantra*". The king built a grand temple in the kingdom of Dang and worshipped the *Amrut Patra*. Even today, there is a place called Shri Nath Tirthavalli, dedicated to Gorakhnath and opposite it is an idol of Ratannath. The Shakti Peeth Devi Patan has a shrine of Baba Ratannath, where it is believed that he meditated and gained many yogic powers and knowledge.

In the regions of west Nepal, Tibet and many parts of Asia,

Ratannath influenced many people and showed them the path of the Gorakhnathis. It is said that Ratannath walked barefoot on the earth and talked about the greatness of yoga, and how fulfilling it can be in a person's life. According to him, the path of a yogi is without fear, attachments and sins, and is always free. People who do not attain any knowledge of the path of yoga will never be able to understand the path of the *Parmatma*. In Patiala, Punjab, in Govindgad Mandal is his samadhi and every year there is a fair held in his honour. Ratannath was also a special *Kripa Patra* (blessed devotee), who was blessed by the Divine grace of Gorakhnath.

Another interesting story is that of Bappa Rawal, who belonged to the Rajputana lineage. This story describes how Bappa became connected with the Gorakhnathis. It is said that he used to tend to a small herd of cows in jungles surrounding Eklingaji, north of Udaipur. Every day, he was accused by his master of stealing all the cow's milk, as his best cow had no milk after the day's grazing. Disturbed by this, he started to keep a watch on this cow during the grazing hours and decided to follow her. He soon found that she emptied all the milk on a phallic symbol (five-faced Shiva linga) of Mahadeva Shiva, and it was on this spot that Bappa Rawal built the famous temple of Eklingaji. Here he met a sage who eventually became his teacher and who told him about the many stories and mysteries related to Lord Shiva. Eventually, Bappa Rawal was blessed with the power of divine weapons. The sage gave him a blessing that he would be invulnerable to weapons. The sage was Gorakhnath. He gave Bappa Rawal a double-edged sword. [In *The Alchemical Body: Siddha Traditions in Medieval India*, p. 120, David Gordon White posits that this is chronologically impossible.] It was with this sword that Bappa defeated his enemies and won his way to the throne of Mewar. Eventually, he won many battles with his bravery, and became one of the greatest rulers of the entire Mewar dynasty. Interestingly, it is said that Bappa Rawal moved further to the east to found the house of Gorkha, which became the kingdom of Nepal. The Gorkhas in Nepal take their name from Guru Gorakhnath, and the first one was Bappa Rawal himself.

Gorakhnath and the Tale of Gugga Pir

In *Gorakhnath and the Kanphata Yogis*, George Weston Briggs writes: "Many of the legends, some of which have been recorded by Temple,

Legends of the Punjab; by Synnerton, *Romantic Tales of the Punjab*; by Grierson, *The Story of Manikchandra* and in *The Adi Granth*, are sung even today by Gorakhnathis, and by other wandering singers as well, through the villages of the land. Amongst the most famous of them are those of Zahra, or Guga Pir, Puran Bhagat and his brother Raja Rasalu, Gopichand, Hir and Ranjha and Rani Pingla."

One such tale is of Gugga Pir. It is believed that Gugga was born thanks to the blessings of Gorakhnath. According to this ancient story, his father Raja Jewar married Rani Bachal, whose twin sister was also married in the same kingdom. Rani Bachal was childless and started praying to Gorakhnath after he set up his *dhuni* in their garden. However, her twin sister Rani Kachal surreptitiously took the yogi's blessing by disguising herself as her sister, received the holy ash from him, and soon gave birth to two sons, Arjan and Sarjan. When the queen found out about this she told Gorakhnath what had happened and after many requests he gave her the same guggul candies (guggul is an Ayurvedic herb used to treat people suffering from infertility) and she soon conceived. He even predicted that her son would grow up to be a very powerful man who would defeat his cousins Arjan and Sarjan. When the king heard the news of his wife's unexpected pregnancy he thought this could taint the family's name in society and so decided to kill her by sending her away. While Rani Bachal was on her way in a bullock cart, a snake bit the bullock but because of her blessed baby's mysterious powers, they were both saved. The baby was eventually named Gugga after the holy fruit. Gorakhnath then appeared in King Jewar's dream and ordered him to bring back his queen, and the king agreed to do as directed in the divine message. After he grew up, Gugga became famous as one who had power over snakes.

Gugga became engaged to Siriyal, daughter of Raja Singha of the Singhgad kingdom from the region of Kamrup in Assam. This union was blessed by Gorakhnath himself. When Siriyal's father refused to give him his daughter in marriage, Gugga went to Basak Nag (Naga king), the king of the snakes, and threatened him and his house with extermination if his betrothed was not brought to him. Basak's nephew thereupon contrived to bite Siriyal while she was bathing in a tank. When Gugga heard of this, he played the flute in Gorakhnath's name and the snake began to dance to his tune. Gugga then took Siriyal's body to Singhgad and with Gorakhnath's Yoga-

Shakti, she came back to life. Soon after, the couple was married in a grand ceremony and the bride received expensive ornaments, sarees, and many other luxurious items, along with a chariot, soldiers and attendants. However, Gugga did not feel content after marriage. He was seeking spiritual fulfilment and chose to make Gorakhnath his teacher. After his father's death, his cousins Arjan and Sarjan took over a kingdom in Delhi. Gugga defeated them to emerge victorious but he was still dissatisfied. He decided to leave the world to meditate in a faraway forest. It is said, his guru Gorakhnath used his *chimta* (holy tongs) from Gorakh Tilla, caused the land to slide, and eventually both the horse and Gugga disappeared in the deep recesses of the earth and took samadhi. Gugga was buried after dying, and was also given the Muslim name of Gugga Pir. Today, he is worshipped by many people from the low castes such as sweepers and leather workers. It is believed he has power over snakes and can save the lives of people who have been poisoned by one. Barren women seeking children pray to him as it is said he can give children to the childless. There are many shrines which are dedicated to him in Rajasthan, and in Punjab many shrines related to Gugga are found even today built next to the sacred places of his master, Gorakhnath.

Smaller temples are found in other Indian regions of Himachal Pradesh, Maharashtra, Gujarat and Uttar Pradesh. An annual month-long fair is held in Rajasthan's Ganganagar, and there is also a temple of Gorakhnath located here. There is lots of music and dancing by people who come here in thousands every year to pay homage to the gods. There is also a temple in Guwahati dedicated to Princess Siriyal where yoginis seek blessings. Gugga has been immortalised in many religious stories as Gorakhnath's *Kripa Patra* who received his divine grace.

Gorakhnath and Heer Ranjha

In the immortal love story of Heer and Ranjha it is said that Gorakhnath played a very important role. This story has inspired many artists worldwide and also set an example of pure love in the hearts of many romantics.

It is said that in the sixteenth century, in the Takht Hazara village in Punjab, there lived Muijuddin Chaudhary, a very wealthy Jat, with his family. The youngest of his four sons was Dheedo (Ranjha) who lead a very sheltered and relaxed life, and enjoyed playing the *bansuri* (flute) all day. After his father tragically passed away, he could not take the taunts and harsh attitude of his brothers and left home. While wandering one day near the Chenab River he saw Heer, a very beautiful girl who was the daughter of Chaudhary Meher Chuchak who belonged to a Jat family of the Sial community. They soon fell in love. She offered him a job as a cattle rearer in her estate, after her father permitted it. Gradually, their love blossomed but Heer's family did not approve of him and told her that he wasn't the right man for her. But Heer couldn't leave Ranjha. However, she was soon forced to marry Saida Khera from the nearby village of Rangpur.

Over time, Heer was heart-broken and depressed, and Ranjha decided to become a yogi to get his love back. He learnt that the great Gorakhnath and his Gorakhnathi yogis were at Yogi Tilla (also called Baalnath ka Tilla). Ranjha played such a melodious tune from his flute that Gorakhnath came out of his meditative trance state. Ranjha then pleaded before him, confessed his deep love for Heer and his desire to get her back. He called him a "param karuna maya yogi", and asked for his guidance to become a yogi and to help him in his mission. Gorakhnath, however, told him of the hard life the yogis led and how being such a sensitive and sheltered person, he would not be able to walk on this difficult path. Ranjha was very adamant and wanted his "prem sadhana" to be fulfilled. Gorakhnath again told him how after becoming a yogi, he would have to stay away from being tempted by a woman and see every woman as his sister or mother. Ranjha was determined and after many pleas and requests, Gorakhnath's compassionate heart melted, and Ranjha was given his blessings, five paisa and *supari*. His ears were then cut like the other Kanphata yogis by Gorakhnath himself, who gave him *kundal* earrings to wear. He also gave Ranjha ash from his *dhuni*, and told him to walk on the path of Alakh Niranjan i.e, Mahadev Shiva and leave behind the past, not worry about the future, and not have preconceived notions of the world in the present. Ranjha requested him to direct him to a path that would help him attain his love Heer, as loving someone is not a sin. He said he had taken "*yog diksha*" (initiation into yoga) only for her. Gorakhnath then went into a meditative state and after a while blessed him that he would be successful and get his heart's desire.

Ranjha then wore the ochre robes of a yogi, took his *jhola*, and, playing his flute, set off to see Heer at her husband's home in Rangpur. Heer ran away with Ranjha and came back to her father's house. Her father agreed to get them married. But out of embarrassment and societal pressure, her family gave her poison and she died. She had once even told her friends to call her by her beloved's name "Ranjha", as in his love she had lost herself and become one with him. When Ranjha heard the news of her death, he committed suicide. Though this story had a tragic end, Gorakhnath's blessings made their love immortal and it is believed that in death these lovers were finally together and happy.

Gorakhnath and Puran Bhagat (Choranginath)

Other famous people in Punjab who became followers of Gorakhnath include Puran Bhagat and his half-brother Rasalu. According to legend, Puran's father's younger queen, Luna, ordered that Puran be amputated and killed. Her soldiers cut off his hands and legs and threw him in a well in the forest. However, after twelve years Gorakhnath and his yogi followers came to Sialkot and transformed the dry lakes into overflowing ones, and spread lush greenery everywhere. He also found Puran in the well when the *pari*s (fairies) sent to him by Puran told the great yogi that he was asking for help. At first Gorakhnath couldn't discern that Puran was innocent and he even threatened him saying that if he was a monster or an evil spirit he would throw his magic sandals at him and sink the whole well into hell. However, once he saw him, with a single look he knew that Puran was innocent even after the false stories Queen Lunan had told him. Another version of this story however says that Gorakhnath had tested Puran Bhagat's innocence by using his teacher Matsyendranath's name and throwing a thread that was spun by an unmarried virgin into the well.

Both stories describe how Gorakhnath restored his limbs by sprinkling amrit (holy water) on him along with a prayer. Puran then remained inside the well for twenty-four years and when Gorakhnath passed by that spot again, he requested the great yogi to initiate him. To test his mettle and dedication, Gorakhnath sent him to Sundran, the queen of Simhala, who had fallen in love with him. Later, however, Gorakhnath found that Puran had remained celibate. He then gave Puran Bhagat earrings for his initiation from his magic bag, and while piercing them with his own hands whispered in his ears, *"kanon mei phunk lagai"* (blew into his ears). Later, Puran through his powers, granted Queen Luna a blessing which was her son and his step-brother Rasulu. This young prince led a very adventurous life, full of joy and many mysteries. Both Puran and Rasulu eventually became devoted Gorakhnathis, and even Rasulu's parrot considered him as a guru. Even today, the well called "Puran's Well" is full of water. Punjabi women visit it every new moon and take its cool healing waters to drink as it is said that it can bless the childless devotee with children.

Gorakhnath and the Legend of King Bhartruhari

As mentioned earlier, the black buck is a very sacred animal for yogis. Its horn and skin is used by them for making important items such as clothing and earrings. There is a very significant story connected with this. Once, King Bhartruhari was out hunting when he killed a stag. While taking back its dead body, many deer followed him. Gorakhnath descended from the Toranmal Hill and came to the site where the black buck was killed. He told the king, "If you do not have the power to give someone life, you do not have the right to take one. Look at the pitiful glances of the deer who have followed you and are silently mourning and asking you for the black buck's life." King Bhartruhari realised his folly and told the yogi that he was sorry and wished to repent for his sin.

It is believed that this black buck was actually Gorakhnath's student in disguise who had used this animal's body to meditate and gain yogic knowledge peacefully. While dying, the stag said to the king, "Give my feet to the thief, that he may escape with his life; my horns to the yogi, that he may use them as his whistle (*nad*); my skin to the ascetic, that he may worship upon it; my eyes to a fair woman, that she may be called *Mriga Naini* (having eyes like a deer); and eat my flesh thyself."

Gorakhnath then took some holy ash from his bag and threw it on the lifeless body of the stag who miraculously came alive and ran away with the other deer deep into the forest. Looking at this unusual sight, King Bhartruhari was dumbfounded. He fell at Gorakhnath's feet and requested him to make him his student. But Gorakhnath told him that before walking on this path, he must first take permission from his wife Pingala. The king came back to his kingdom and narrated the entire incident to the queen and spoke about the magical and life-giving powers of the yogi. He told her that becoming his student and gaining this knowledge could give real purpose to his life and liberate his soul, but for this he wanted her consent. This shocking request became the talk of the entire kingdom. The queen was very upset and heart-broken as this yogic path would mean that she would no longer have her husband and would have to become a Sati as per her wifely duties. Looking at the sad state of his queen and the unrest of the people, the king changed his mind and spent some years in the kingdom itself.

Over time, he lost interest in all his royal duties and realised that Queen Pingala's wifely love was a barrier in his path of becoming a yogi. He decided to test her loyalty. He went hunting in the forest with his men and killed a wild animal. He dipped and stained his royal clothes and told his soldiers to take them back to the kingdom and give the queen false news of his death. The queen, however, believed it as the truth and so did the people in the kingdom. Everyone was sorrowful and eventually the queen became a Sati and died. After sometime, the king secretly came back to the kingdom and realised what had happened. He wept over her ashes. Many days passed and he continued to stay close to the site of her death and kept crying "O Pingala! O Pingala!" When Gorakhnath heard of this in the Girnar Mountain, he came to meet the king and offer condolences. He bought a *patra* (earthen bowl), broke it in front of him and wept over it crying "O *patra*! O *patra*!" The king then asked him why he was crying over an earthen pot. He replied saying that now that this was broken, he was wondering how his tears could bring it back to him. The king told him that he could replace this bowl with a golden one for him, but his Pingala could not be brought back to life.

To prove his point, he told the king that he could bring Pingala back to life but she would not be the same as before, just like the original bowl which can never be replaced. He then asked the king to close his eyes for a moment. Once he did so, he took out some ash from his bag and with his life-restoring yogic powers, sprinkled it fiercely on the earth. He then asked Bhartruhari to open his eyes and when he did, he was shocked to see thousands of Pingalas in front of his eyes. When he moved forward to touch one of them, Gorakhnath stopped him and said that till such time that he did not recognise his queen from the others, he could not touch any of them.

The king was bewildered as it was difficult for him to decide and recognise which one of these figures was his lovely wife. Looking at his confusion, all the Pingala figures told him in one tone: "Every person who has been born on this earth has to eventually die and this is the ultimate truth of life. You must leave behind these illusions and attachments and try to gain closeness with the *Parmatma*. It is your good fortune that Maha Yogi Gorakhnath is with you." Saying this, they disappeared.

Bhartruhari came out of this state of attachment to worldly desires and fell at the yogi's feet. Gorakhnath gave him yoga-diksha and took him back to the kingdom. The soldiers and his people greeted him with joy, but after realising that he had given up his title as king to become a Nath yogi, they were sad. Bhartruhari then wore the ochre coloured robes of a yogi, took a begging bowl and went to every house begging for alms, crying out "Alakh! O mother, give me some food." All the female attendants of the court and the women folk of the kingdom told him that they were his servants and were embarrassed that he was seeking food in such a way from them. He then told them, "I am not King Bhartruhari, but just Yogi Bhartruharinath. See me as your son and give me whatever you like. I cannot stay here much longer as I have to go back to my guru." The women gave all their ornaments and food to him because they did not want to send him back empty-handed. Without a second glance Bhartruharinath went to offer his services to Gorakhnath. Soon Gorakhnath took Bhartruhari to Girnar, and there explained the principles of the Nath Panth, yogic philosophies and the ways of yogic life. Bhartruhari soon became a great and knowledgeable student. Gorakhnath also explained to him about the *Nad-Bindu* (holy sound–dot) and told him to concentrate on this path as it would lead him to the Alakh Niranjan Mahadev Shiva himself. Chanting *Shiv Shiv* Bhartruharinath crossed the borders of his kingdom and dedicated his entire life to yoga and the Nath cult.

Gorakhnath and the Fable of Gopichandra
Gopichand faced many difficulties when he wanted to become a yogi. Mainly because he had to give up his throne, title, wealth and lifestyle if he chose to become a yogi. In the Punjab legend of Shantinath, it is described how Gopichandra was afraid of Jalandarnath.

This story is related to King Manik Chandra of Bengal who was married to Maynavati, sister of the affluent King Bhartruhari. They had a son named Gopichandra. King Manik Chandra was afraid that due to his pious queen Maynavati's faith in yogi Jalandarnath, his son might get influenced into becoming an ascetic himself, so he restricted Jalandarnath's entry into the kingdom. After his death, Queen Maynavati insisted the yogi initiate her son into the yogic practice and share the knowledge with him. However, Gopichandra's wives built up wrong impressions in his head and he ended up naively believing that his guru was a magician who was cheating him to take away his kingdom. He then ordered that his teacher be taken away and thrown into a well in Patan and there Jalandarnath was covered with dung and other dirt to ensure that he wouldn't be able to come back out. When the queen heard of this incident, she was very upset and she also learnt that to free Jalandarnath, his student Kanpanath (Kanipa) was on his way to destroy their kingdom. The queen who was torn between her belief in the yogi and her loyalty to her people and son decided to seek Gorakhnath who appeared before her after listening to her heartfelt prayers. She requested him to protect her son and people. Even Gopichandra came before him and requested his help as he was afraid of being killed and cursed by Kanipa. The soft-hearted and generous Nath told Gopichandra to take a cart full of the best food and drinks and set off to meet and treat Kanipa with love, respect and affection, and then come back to the kingdom. Gopichandra did exactly that and a few miles outside the borders of his state, he found Kanipa and his disciples. He offered them his hospitality and respect, and in return the yogis blessed Gopichandra. He then came to the kingdom and related the good news to Gorakhnath.

Soon after, Kanipa and his disciples left the forest, came to Gopichandra's kingdom and began cursing and chanting evil words to destroy its existence. However, they soon realised that none of their powers were working as the kingdom and the people were untouched. Through his yogic instinct, Kanipa soon sensed that Gorakhnath was in the kingdom. The students however, in their loyalty to Kanipa and Jalandarnath, did not acknowledge the great yogi, and disapproved of the bond he shared with Gopichandra. They soon left from there and reached the site where their guru Jalandarnath was trapped in the well. They began to remove the dirt and dung from the well and tried to clean it, but to no avail. Soon, all of them were tired, and slept. But the next day, the well appeared to be the same as before with all the dirt and dung. They all once again started to clean it fiercely and this went on for three days, but still they did not succeed. The students then decided to pay due respect to Gorakhnath and seek his help. They reached Gopichandra's kingdom and expressed their faith in him. Gorakhnath then told them to walk together to the well where Jalandarnath was trapped. He also asked them to prepare for a feast the following afternoon and invite everyone as he would be helping Jalandarnath come out of the well. The disciples went back to the well and narrated the entire incident to Kanipa and they began to prepare for the feast the next day. Gorakhnath also asked Gopichandra to make two artificial figures resembling him at the earliest.

The next day, people gathered in thousands near the well to watch Gorakhnath help Jalandarnath out of the well. Soon, he arrived at the site and people took the *prasad* (sacred food offerings) of the feast. Gorakhnath, with his yogic powers, scattered some holy ash on the well. Soon, all the dirt and dung started to come out on its own and in a few minutes the well was completely empty. They could all see Jalandarnath in a samadhi state and Gorakhnath signalled to Gopichandra to come there. He then told him to stand behind one figure and call out to Jalandarnath. Gopichandra stood behind the fake figure and called out to Jalandarnath: "Guruji! Please come out of the well". In return, his teacher asked, "Whose reflection and words are these?" To this Gorakhnath replied, "This reflection and voice belongs to your student Gopichandra." On hearing this, Jalandarnath immediately cursed him to die and the fake figure was destroyed. Again when Gopichandra called out to him, he cursed him back and the second figure was destroyed. The third time, Gopichandra himself stood before him and repeated in a pleading voice, "Guruji! Please come out of the well". This time Jalandarnath answered saying, "Who are you who has survived even after two death curses? Are you really Gopichandra?" On Gorakhnath's instructions, Gopichandra replied, "Yes, Guruji. It is I, your student and servant Gopichandra."

To this Jalandarnath said, "Dear Son! I will come out of the well. But you who are still standing alive, should now become immortal," and he came out of the well. The crowd of people who witnessed this epic scene rejoiced and Kanipa and his disciples were ecstatic. The great yogis, Jalandarnath and Gorakhnath, blessed the crowds and Gopichandra sought his master's forgiveness by touching his feet. Just like Matsyendranath was rescued by his student, Kanipa rescued his teacher, and Gorakhnath once again fulfilled his moral duty.

2.7 Blessed Places of Vibrancy and Worship

Kanphata yogis treasure many things as sacred including earthen earrings, *dhunis* at Pai Dhuni (Mumbai), Gorakhpur, Dhinodhar, and four ancient cauldrons at Dhinodhar. The rivers Ganga and Godavari are considered pure while the temple of Sivaramandap with the bronze statue of Nakaland and the Mount of Rawa Pir at Dhinodhar, are piously worshipped. Many Naths also pray to the *padukas* of Matsyendranath and Gorakhnath on Shivratri.

Trees are also worshipped as spiritual symbols. Interestingly, villagers in Punjab worship the anola tree on the fifteenth and eleventh day of Phalgun, and its fruit is used for the finial of Buddhist temples. Animals like cow, rhinoceros, black buck, dogs and snakes are held in high reverence. The rhinoceros, especially, is worshipped by rulers of Nepal and the earrings made from their horns are prized. Even the rare black buck is held in high esteem and its horn and skin are used by the Kanphatas for holy purposes. Many fables link Gorakhnath and serpents especially the water-controlling or rain serpents found in Nepal. Lord Shiva is also worshipped as Nageshwar, "Lord of the Serpents" in Benares and Uttarakhand, and as Rikheshvar in the Himalayas. Snakes are also divinely associated with water and rain, and images of Bhairav and Nagas are found alongside the Devi and Shiva-linga. Black dogs are greatly valued as legends link them to Bhairav.

Gorakhnathis also worship nine Naths (spiritual guides) who get their names from Shiva or Adinath. Gorakhnath is considered the chief of the Naths and the other eight are Matsyendranath, Mangalnath, Ghugonath, Prannath, Suratnath, Cambanath, Charpatnath, and Gopinath. The Naths are revered as guardian sprits protecting the Himalayan peaks. The nine Naths are also said to correspond to bodily orifices of the Tantraraja Tantra that features names of nine *abhishekas* (initiations), in which the core nine gemstones (used widely in astrology) are placed in medicated water. These nine gemstones are also said to correspond to eight bodily *dhatu* and identified with nine heavenly planets.

Gorakhnathis also worship eighty-four Siddhas (famous saints - see Appendix) who have attained the stature of being semi-divine beings through their purity and sincere practice of yoga. These are again residents of the Himalayas, and Mahadev, Bhartruhari and Gorakhnath keep these perfect yogis company.

Both Naths and Siddhas follow Gorakhnath in his spiritual wanderings and it is believed that small trees with sugar candy spring up wherever they go. It is also said that there are many siddhis (spiritual powers) that are connected to him through many folktales and legends, and they help him in his spiritual tasks.

Among the festivals, Shivratri is the biggest festival for Gorakhnathis. The Kanphatas fast, stay awake all night, and sing songs in honour of Matsyendranath and Gorakhnath. Goddess Shakti is also worshipped during this time and both these observances are said to bring devotees closer to God, to help them attain all their desires, and to ease their final release after death towards immortality.

Kal Bhairav, who is considered an avatar of Shiva, is worshipped during Kartik, on the dark eighth day of the lunar month at Bhudargad (Kolhapur), Devgad (Sindhudurg), and Bhairavnath, all of which are places with important temples. During this time, a procession takes place in Kathmandu. The Hindu festival of Nag Panchami in the month of Shravan is also significant for Kanphatas and the festival of Guga known as Chari Mela is also celebrated five days later with song and food.

Each Kanphata has a particular shrine or place of worship that is located in a different part of India. But there are some places of historical and spiritual significance that they all visit for pilgrimage. These sacred places include Kashi (Benares), Prayag (Triveni), Pushkar, Brindaban, Kedarnath, Badrinath, Haridwar, Dwarka, Darjeeling (in the northeast), Nepal, Assam, Amarnath in Kashmir, Rameshwar in the south, and Hinglaj (Baluchistan) in the west.

The cave temple at Gorkha in Nepal is very sacred and is nicknamed "The Sacred Hearth of the Gorkha Race". The town and the shrine at the cave get their name from Gorakhnath who is believed to have lived there. Kathmandu is very sacred considering the large number of shrines scattered across its length and breadth, which worship Matsyendranath and Gorakhnath. Interestingly, the word Kathmandu means "Kath Mandir" or "Temple of Wood" built in honour of Gorakhnath by Goddess Lakshmi in AD 1600. Bagmati, which is a few miles from Patan, is home to a temple dedicated to Matsyendranath. Pilgrims who visit the Pashupatinath Temple dedicated to Lord Shiva are blessed that they would never visit as a lower life form again.

Kistipur has a temple of Bhairav, and Kathmandu is home to a temple of Kal Bhairav. At the monastery of Ratannath located in Sawari Kot, it is believed that an image, the Cangra Tang Pahar contains the holy spirit of Gorakhnath. Kanphatas are also found in various shrines of Bhairav situated at Kumaon and Garhwal Hills. At Srinagar, Gorakhnath is revered as an incarnation of Lord Shiva and Kanphata yogis have an establishment built there. These yogis are also seen at the Nandi Devi temple at Nainital. There are many other religious establishments with historical importance built by yogis of different divisions, where devotees can seek blessings and a few moments of peace.

The twelve important members of the division have many buildings and sacred spots in Haridwar. Benares is renowned for three places of worship—the temple of Kal Bhairav, Gorakhnath ka Tilla and Lath Bhairav. Gorakh Tilla or Gorakhnath ka Tilla was once known as Tilla Balnath and is the most revered spot of the three. According to legend, Gorakhnath settled here after Shri Ramchandra became a teacher to his adopted student Balnath in the Treta Yuga (the third Yuga in which lord Vishnu reincarnated as Vamana, Parshurama and Rama). Special religious festivals or melas are held at this Tilla every year in March.

The Devi Patan temple and its adjoining monastery are both under the control of Kanphata yogis and are located on a hill near Tulsipur in Balrampur district, which is close to the Himalayan and Nepal borders. This temple is among the fifty-one Shakti Peeths where the dismembered organs of Goddess Durga (Sati) fell. According to the famous legend, when Lord Shiva carried her burnt body, her right hand fell at this spot and sank into the ground. The word "*Patan*" is derived from the Sanskrit word "*Pat*" which means to sink or fall, and also implies a hole in the earth. The Devi Patan is also referred to as Pataleswari, and Patala is said to be home to dragons and nagas. A story in the epic Ramayana connects Sita to this holy spot.

According to legend, after Rama rescued her from Ravana, she was accused of being an unfaithful wife. To prove her loyalty, she gave an *Agni-pariksha* (ordeal by fire) and returned to Ayodhya with Rama. Later however, Rama sent her back into exile, accusing her once more. In Valmiki's hermitage, she gave birth to Luv and Kush, who grew up in the forest, listening to Valmiki's compositions of the *Ramayana*, which described in detail their father's heroic deeds. After many years, Rama performed the great horse sacrifice and in one of the ceremonies, he heard a poem describing his deeds from two youths, whom he recognised as his own sons. After listening to this, he asked for Sita and she was once again asked to prove her innocence to be able to return to the palace. Crying, Sita called to Madhavi or "The Earth Goddess", and requested a hiding place. Her earnest request made the goddess appear on her throne and she placed Sita by her side. It was at this place, Devi Patan or Pataleshwari, where she disappeared into the earth.

The annual mela or religious fair at this temple is of great interest around the world. Every year in early April, the fest commences when the *pir* (abbot) from the monastery of the Kanphata yogis arrives at Sawarikot or Dang Kangra in Nepal. Many sacred rituals follow with elaborate ceremonies of food, garlands and processions full of song and dance.

Apart from the holy legends surrounding it, the Devi Patan temple is renowned for being home to many experts in Hatha Yoga. In its possession are nine tax-free villages, and much of its income comes from monetary offerings made by devotees.

Kanphata yogis worship the female energies or the yoni symbol as much as the Shiv-Linga for attaining samadhi and the rituals of "left-handed attainment" or *Vamachara* rites of the Undivided Supreme are given a lot of importance. It is said that these rituals are carried out in secrecy as they are considered licentious. However, many yogis follow this path and indulge completely in eating flesh, drinking wine, and performing orgies. These incidents are believed to be found in the hills of Garhwal and many yogis in the plains and mountains admit to possessing this knowledge. In this path, women receive freedom to indulge their carnal passions and disregard the rules and regulations laid down by society and by pleasing this aspect of Goddess Shakti they ultimately gain union with the Supreme Divine.

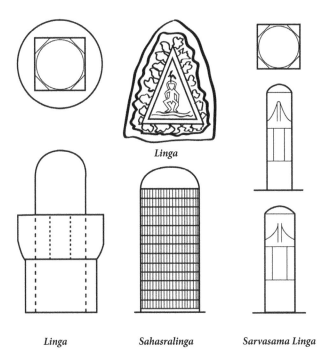

Linga

Linga   Sahasralinga   Sarvasama Linga

An important place of worship is the Adi Shakti Tarapith of the Buddhist goddess Tara who is worshipped deeply by Tantric practitioners. Located near the banks of the Dwarka River in West Bengal, it is surrounded by rural environs of thatched roofs and huts. However, these only add to the rustic charm and air of antiquity of this sacred site. According to the self-immolation story of Sati, when Lord Shiva carried her dead burnt corpse, this is the spot where her eyeball fell. Since the eyeball is called "tara", this place was named Tarapith. Earlier this place was also known as Chandipur.

The goddess is worshipped in both her fierce aspects (of Kali) and the peaceful motherly visionary form of Tara in accordance with the Buddha's vision and that of his disciple Vashistha who belonged to the Tantric tradition. There are many legends and stories associated with this holy place and it is said the goddess can bless devotees with enlightenment, fulfilment and many siddhis (supernatural powers).

It is believed that in the legend of *Samudra Manthan* (churning of the ocean), after Lord Shiva drank the poison to save the entire universe and mankind and became *Neelkanth,* "The Blue Throated One", he experienced an intense burning in his throat. To give him respite from this pain, Sati took the motherly form of Goddess Tara and breast-fed him. Another story narrates that Vashistha was a devout follower of the goddess but failed to please her. After a divine voice guided him to seek the guidance of Lord Buddha in Tibet, he approached the enlightened one, who told him to practise *Vamamarga* (left-handed Tantric worship) using *"Panchakarma"*, the five forbidden things viz. *madya* (wine), *mansa* (meat), *matsya* (fish), *mudra* (yogic pose) and *maithuna* (sexual intercourse). During the time of his practise, Lord Buddha had a divine vision in which he envisioned Tarapith and told Vashishtha that it was the perfect place to enshrine the image of the goddess. Vashishtha reached Tarapith and began to chant the "Tara mantra" three hundred thousand times. This penance pleased the goddess who appeared before him. Vashishtha requested the goddess to appear before him in the form of a mother breastfeeding Lord Shiva, in the same way that Lord Buddha had envisioned her. The goddess fulfilled his wish and Vashishtha immortalised that primordial image in a stone idol that is worshipped till today.

Apart from this idol, another image of the deity seen at this temple is of Tara in her fiery form (like Kali) with four arms, wearing a garland of human skulls and with a protruding tongue. The goddess' forehead is smeared with vermillion or red kumkum, and priests take a speck of this as a mark of divine blessings and apply it on the foreheads of devotees. Among the offerings, coconuts, bananas, silk saris, and bottles of whisky are generally the norm.

Taking a holy bath in the sacred tank adjacent to the temple before and after worship is also common. Interestingly, the waters of this tank are assumed to possess healing properties that can even restore life to the dead. Making blood and animal sacrifices of goats is also common. A small quantity of the blood of the goat is collected after killing and offered to the deity, and some is taken by the devotees and applied to their foreheads as a gesture of respect to the goddess. Another intriguing site close to this temple is of a cremation ground where it is believed that Goddess Tara can be seen camouflaged by the shadows, drinking blood of the goats that have been sacrificed at the altar to appease her anger and seek her favour.

This place is also believed to be her favoured place as skeletons and bones are found here and hence this is the chosen place for many Tantric practitioners to perform their Tantric sadhana. Among the many mysterious aspects of the rituals of this place, it is said that skulls of virgins and people who have committed suicide (which are considered powerful), and other good skulls, after curing, are used for drinking and worship.

Another shrine important for yogis is the Bamakhepa temple (Rampurhat, Birbhum district, West Bengal), named after the "mad saint" who practised the *Vamamarga* (left-handed Tantric worship). It is believed he was a devoted disciple of the goddess who lived near the temple and meditated in the cremation grounds. As a young teen, he left the house and sought guidance of a saint named Kailashpati Baba, who lived in Tarapith. He perfected yoga and Tantric sadhana, and soon became the head of the Peeth. People came from far and wide to seek blessings and cures for their suffering. However, he was disliked by the temple priest as he often ate the offerings made to the goddess. Legend also relates how one night, Tara appeared in the dream of the queen of Natore and told her that Bamakhepa was her son and that he must be fed first by one and all. Soon, people followed the goddess' words and Bamakhepa was treated with greater reverence. It is also said that once, the goddess appeared in Bamakhepa's dream in the cremation grounds in her ferocious avatar and she then took him to her breast and fed him.

Another temple which embodies the feminine power is the Guhyeshwari Temple located in Kathmandu, Nepal. Built in the seventeenth century by King Pratap Malla, this temple has beautiful architecture adorned with floral motifs and snakes, and it only allows Hindus to worship. Non-Hindus can gain blessings and admire the temple's simple beauty from outside. According to legend, Sati's vagina had fallen at this site making it an Adi Shakti Peeth where her yoni (vagina) is worshipped. Its name is derived from the Nepali word "*guhya*" which means vagina, and "*ishvari*" which means goddess. A similar shrine is found at Kamakhya Temple in Guwahati, Assam, where according to legend, the goddess's organs of regeneration fell.

Close to the Guhyeshwari shrine is the revered Pashupatinath Temple dedicated to Lord Shiva. The Linga is said to be *Svayambhu* (self-created) and an interesting story explains how it was discovered. It is believed that Kamadhenu, the wish-fulfilling cow, used to offer her milk to a single spot every day and after noticing this curious habit for many days, the farmers dug the land of that particular place. To their astonishment, they found the phallic Shiva-Linga, which is worshipped till today. Another legend says that once Lord Shiva took the form of an antelope and was roaming around the banks of the Bagmati. The gods found him and dragged him by his horns to force him to once again transform into his divine form. The broken horn was worshipped as a Linga but over the decades, got buried and lost. Many centuries later, farmers found it through the Kamadhenu cow. Since all animals are sacred and precious for Mahadeva, this temple was named Pashupatinath (The Lord of Animals). Today, this temple is a UNESCO World Heritage Site and an important place of pilgrimage for all Hindus around the world. On special occasions like Ekadasi, Sankranti, Mahashivratri, Teej Akshaya, Purnima (full moon day), the temple is a splendid sight. Devotees take ritual baths in the Bagmati River on all important festivals. A shrine dedicated to Gorakhnath is also found here.

Interestingly, it is also believed that the Linga of the Pashupatinath Temple is said to have the same origin as that of the Gokarneshvara Temple situated in the coastal region of Karnataka. During the Malla period, south Indian Shaivite Brahmins and Tantrics controlled the Pashupatinath Temple and according to Carlo Levi, it was the yogis from this region who "transformed Pashupatinath from an indigenous deity into a form of Shiva."

Most yogis are Shiva devotees or Shaivites but they do acknowledge other gods of the Hindu triad in their prayers and chants. The pictures on the face of the dharamshala on top of the Dhinodhar hills, the picture of his mighty bird (Garuda) chariot at Puri, and the Rudraksh with ten faces are all related to Lord Vishnu. In western India, many Vaishnavite devotees revere the religious teachings of Gorakhnath and many architectural elements of

Garuda

Gorakhpur contain symbols and images related to Lord Vishnu. Even the Shiva Samhita makes it essential for devotees to chant the name of Lord Vishnu when paying attention to the balancing or healing of the chakras.

In the Shiva Yoga cult, the practices of meditation along with physical discipline are equally important. Hatha Yoga features the practice of shreechakra and vamachakra rites, use of psychadelic drugs and the use of *dhauti* (internal cleansing). All of these help to reach samadhi and to merge with all the creative forces, and superhuman and divine forces of the universe.

Shiva is known by many names in the Indian subcontinent— some of these names include Pashupatinath and Shambhunath in Nepal, where devotees even offer sacrifices of blood. Worshipping his consort Shakti, and Bhairav or Kal Bhairav, is equally essential for yogis and Shaktas. He is also known as Bhut Bhairav (Lord of malignant ghosts) and his symbol is a black dog. It is said that Bhairav guards all the temples of Lord Shiva and Shakti like a door-keeper and guardian spirit. In Benares he is also nicknamed Kotwal (police officer). In Garhwal and Kumaon Hills, the principal place to worship him is Kedar. His pictures are also found in many sacred spots of Lahore Gate, Amritsar and Takhsila Gate. In fact, every shrine in Punjab is in some way dedicated or related to Bhairav.

The core essence of the *Rig Veda*, and even the Dyaus–Prithvi parenthood discusses the male and female principle as responsible for the creation of the universe. In the Samkhya system, the male and female forms are represented as *Purusha* and *Prakriti*. Shiva is also referred to as "*Ardhanari*" with both male and female principles united, and by the yoni-linga symbol.

The Tantras explain in great detail the functions and importance of the masculine and feminine forces. All chakras work because of the duality and harmony between these two principles. According to this, Shakti is the feminine principle and holds the *Bindu* (drop of Shiva) which then forms into a *Nada* (female element) which encompasses names of all things that are created. *Kaam-Kaal* is the heart of creation which is formed by the union of Shiva-Shakti and their unique energies.

As mentioned earlier, Shaktism is a branch of Shaivism and is crucial to the understanding of the Tantras. The Goddess or Devi is Shiva's consort, and is also an independent deity known by many names including Bhavani, Gauri, Uma, Parvati and Jaganmata. In violent and angry avatars she is known as Kali, Durga, Bhairavi, Chandi, and Shyama. As Goddess Durga and Kali, she is symbolic of the destructive forces of the universe. In Bhishma Parva of the *Mahabharata*, Shakti is known as Kapali, and her followers appease her by human and animal sacrifices. Her shrine at Kamarupa in Assam is considered the centre of Tantric worship as it is from here that her teachings spread to Tibet and Nepal, and she is also linked with Vajrayana Buddhism (in the incarnation of Tara).

The vital place of worship is the Kamakhya temple situated on a hill close to the banks of the Brahmaputra River. This site is even mentioned in the *Padma Purana*. This hill is also called Kamagiri and Nilachal. According to legend, this is where Sati's dissevered organs of generation (reproductive organs) fell, and hence this place is among the fifty-two Shakti Peeth. This is also the region according to epics where Kama was reduced to ashes by the glance of Shiva and returned to his natural form (Kamarupa). Architecturally stunning, the most striking and biggest building is of the Goddess Kamakhya (Goddess of Sexual Desire). In the depths of the shrine is a cleft in the rock through which an underground spring flows from a phallic yoni-shaped cleft, into the bedrock. A temple of Bhairavi is located below and many devotees from Bengal visit it when on a pligrimage. In ancient times, blood and human sacrifices were common as the goddess is appeased by love and sacrifice; however, in 1832 the government banned this. The most privileged and central scriptures of the sect are the *Mahanirvana Tantra, Kalika Purana,* and *Yoni Tantra.*

The legends associated with this place are especially interesting.

The name originates from two stories. One relates that Kamadeva, "The God of Love" lost his virility because of a curse. He sought the Godddess Shakti's womb and genitals and was freed from the curse. This is where "love" gained his potency and thus the deity "Kamakhya" Devi is worshipped here, and Kamadeva is known as the "God of Love and Sexual Desire". Ancient stories also believe this place to be the place where Shiva and Sati had their amorous encounters and romantic interludes. Since the Sanskrit word for lovemaking is "kama", the place was named Kamakhya.

Another legend says that Narakasura was a demon-god who fell in love with Goddess Kamakhya Devi and wished to marry her.

Since a goddess cannot marry an asura (demon), she decided to test him with a trick. She challenged him saying that she would marry him only if he built a temple for her within one night. In order to please the goddess, Narakasura agreed and finished building most of the temple overnight. However, before the final steps of the temple could be completed, the goddess got scared and sent a cock to crow at the temple. The asura was tricked into believing that morning had dawned and he killed the cock on the spot. He also realised that he had not been able to fulfil the challenge, and left. It is said that this architecturally stunning temple which is visited by many even today, was the creation of Narakasura.

Another ancient legend connects this place with Lord Brahma. Once, his supreme power was challenged by Goddess Shakti, who told him that that Brahma could thereafter create only with the blessings of the yoni, as it is the sole creative principle that regenerates and brings new life. After a long period of penance, Brahma brought down a luminous body of light from heaven and placed it within the yoni circle which was created by the goddess, and placed it at Kamarupa Kamakhya.

Kamakhya Devi is also called "The Bleeding Goddess". As mentioned earlier, the mythical womb and vagina of Goddess Shakti fell in the *Garbhagriha* (sanctum of the temple). In the month of June, the Brahmaputra River near Kamakhya turns red, and it is said that the goddess bleeds or menstruates during this time. Every year, the temple is closed for three days and holy water is distributed among the devotees. Scientifically, this natural phenomenon cannot be explained. Some people assume that priests pour kumkum (red vermilion) into the waters which lends it the colour. Others consider this a symbol of menstruation as this process represents a woman's creativity and power to give birth. The temple of Kamakhya and its Devi are thus praised and worshipped as they celebrate this life-giving Shakti (power) within every woman.

In his book, *The Alchemical Body*, David Gordon White writes: "In a more abstract schemata of yonipuja, the Tantric worship of the female sexual organ, the yoni is represented as a downturned triangle, at the heart of which is, once again Kamarupa, the abode of the Goddess Kamakhya, who is identified with the Kundalini and with feminine materiality (Prakriti) in the form of menstrual flux (pusparupini). At the pitha of Kamakhya itself, Assamese tantrics identify their "lineage nectar" (kulamruta) with the Goddess' menstrual fluid (or the commingled sexual fluids of Shiva and the Goddess); it is at the time of the Goddess' menses, in August and September, when the water that oozes from this stone becomes reddish in colour, that their annual gathering takes place."

Yoni Lingam

The powers of the goddess' menstrual blood are directly linked to its redness. Persons suffering from leucoderma come to Kamakhya to smear their bodies with the goddess' menstrual blood, thus

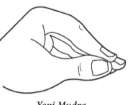

Yoni Mudra

"colouring" themselves with the ooze of her red mineral hierophany. The *gerua* (ochre dye) with which the Nath Siddhas colour their *kantha* (traditional garb) is said to originate from the blood of the Goddess Parvati, who resorted to self-mutilation to dye the robe of Gorakhnath. Cloth dyed in this colour is considered by the Nath Siddhas to aid in *virya-stambhan shakti* (yogic semen retention). This red mineral manifestation of the goddess is also capable, according to the *Kalika Purana*, of transmuting base metals into gold. According to medieval legend, a sealed cave containing a pot of *rasakumbha* (mercury), the drink of which confers immortality, is located in its vicinity.

Suprisingly, the word Kamakhya means "old mother" in Assamese.

Gorakhsetra or Gorkhatri in Peshawar is an important place for Gorakhnathis. Other important yogic shrines include those located at Jalalabad, Kabul and Kohat. Sialkot is renowned for being the abode of Puran Bhagat, who is among Gorakhnath's disciples. Other legendary shrines include Guga's temples at Sultanpur, Batra and at Birag Lok, near Palampur.

Lahore's Ai-panth monastery at Taksala Gate, Bhairav Temple at Durgiana, Amritsar, temples in Ladwa, Ambala, a monastery at Kirana, and buildings in Bohar in Rohtak, are among the pious spots for Kanphatas.

Many places in the region of Sindh possess sanctity and are

considered to be crucial to every Kanphata's religious journey. Koteshwar, Nagar Thatha, Pir Arr and Hinglaj are the main shrines, each with engaging legends and stories related to them.

Located seventy miles from Karachi is Nagar Thatha or Nangar Tatta, which attracts Gorakhnathis for its limestone pebbles and lumps (scientifically called nummelite), strewn on its grounds. These stones are considered very powerful for yogis and are used to make *thumra* (rosaries) which pilgrims wear on their way to Hinglaj. There are many descriptions related to these stones. They are called "Seed of the Creator" or a combination of cereal grains which is believed to be loved by Lord Shiva. Hence the combination of semen and blood is present in the *thumra* made from these stones, and it is said that Gorakhnathis use the large *thumra* stone for pregnant women to have an easy delivery. The *thumra* is washed in water and the liquid is given to the expectant mother to drink.

The rosary with the smaller beads is called Hinglaj ka Thumra and the one with bigger beads is called Asapuri. Yogis and all devotees visiting this shrine first buy the rosaries at Nagar Thatha, offer the *thumra* to the goddess at Hinglaj, and then wear it as a blessing. On reaching Asapuri Devi's shrine on the return journey, the other rosary is offered to the goddess and worn as a blessing. All these places have many Shiva-Shakti legends associated with them, hence pilgrims have to stop by and pay their respects. According to legend, the sacredness of Asapuri is said to be because Ramchandra on his way to Hinglaj, left his staff at the shrine.

Hinglaj is considered the most crucial shrine for Gorakhnathis who believe that to become a perfect and expert yogi and for completing their spiritual journey they must pay homage to this blessed place. About eighty miles from the Indus, located on the Makran coast is Hinglaj, which is among the fifty-one Peeths and it is believed that it is here that Sati's crown of the head or the *brahmarandhra* (crown area) fell. This area of her worship is also called Hingol which means *sindoor*, as there was *kumkum* or vermillion on her forehead when it fell on this sacred spot. A cave temple with just a tombstone in its confines, it is a low mud edifice and it is this humility along with all the intriguing legends surrounding it that make it so special and valuable.

This shrine has also been given the Arabic name of *Mahal* (palace) as its natural environs are believed to have been built by

Yakshas (demigods). Another noteworthy mark of this edifice is a mark resembling the sun and moon upon a boulder on top of the hill, and it is said that this mark came into being when Lord Rama struck his arrow at this spot at the end of his fourteen years *vanvas* (solitude or penance).

Agni Devi, the Red Goddess, Bibi Nani (grandmother, so called by Muslims), Parvati, Kali or Mata, are some of Hinglaj Devi's other names. She is also called "Hingula Devi" as cinnabar or hingula (an Ayurvedic herb) is found in abundance there and used as a medicine since antiquity to cure snake bites, all kinds of poisoning, and illnesses.

The journey to this shrine takes upto twenty-four days and adding to its severity is the endless desert land surrounding it. It is also believed that only someone with a pure heart, free of ill intentions, and who has sought genuine forgiveness can step into her temple. Apart from Sati's self-immolation story, there is another important place linked with this shrine, surrounded by alchemy. David Gordon White in his book *The Alchemical Body: Siddha Traditions in Medieval India* has greatly researched this site for mercury deposits. While there's no mercury here, there is an important place of geothermic activity called Chandrakupa (The Moon Well) or Baba Chandrakup (Father Moonwell), which is incidentally Asia's largest mud volcano. It is said that its waters gush up like waves in a hot spring and even belch fire.

Interestingly, an important ritual associated with this place decides the fate of pilgrims, whether they can proceed to worship the goddess in her temple or not. Pilgrims make *roti*s or *chappati*s all night and have to put small pieces of that *roti* in the water. During this ritual, many devotees also put *ghee*, jaggery and sugar in the *roti*, tie it with a wooden stick and offer it to the waters. After this, each pilgrim has to honestly confess his sins and seek forgiveness for every wrongdoing however big or small. The fate of his confession and its acceptance by the goddess is decided by the waters of the sacred Chandrakup. It is said that depending on the bubbles rising on the surface, the waters decide whether the pilgrim is "pure" to proceed and enter the goddess's cave temple, or not. Hence, Hinglaj Devi is also called "The Goddess of Fate".

There is another surprising account of a Muslim devotee related to the shrine of Hinglaj. Related by Muslim jogis of Sindh, Jogi

Maula Baksh has described the tale as follows:

"One day Shah Abdul Latif Bhitai, Sind's great mystic poet, met Jogi Madan Vaniyo who taught him ablutions of the spirit and took him to Goddess Hinglaj. Shah saw the jogis feed Nani Hinglaj milk that she promptly vomited out. Nani ignored him the first time, but the third time she obediently drank the milk. Taken aback by Shah's success, the jogis decided that night that they would devour Shah so that his powers, as evinced by his success with Nani, would pass on to them. Shah overheard their plan and prayed to God for help. So Shah was swallowed by the earth instead and the good earth brought him to the safe haven of Bhit where he started to preach mysticism."

Hinglaj is also a place of pilgrimage for people from Baluchistan, and even for those on the banks of the Euphrates River, who often visit the Devi who grants boons to sincere devotees. She is the "Kuldevi" (Goddess of Origin) of Sindhi Hindu devotees residing in Sindh and worldwide, but most of them are unaware of this. An architectural beauty amidst rough mountainous terrain, with so many mysterious tales of devotion, it is indeed a sight to see.

There is also a *dhuni* of Gorakhnath here, called "Gorakhji ki dhuni" (fireplace of Gorakhnath) and gas vents are still maintained there. Another intriguing spot is a pit or hollow near the village of Khajuri where it is believed that the brother of Hinglaj Devi named Gaib Pir by Muslims, and called Mahadeo (Shiva) by Hindus, sank into the ground after being pressed by the Gabars and Zoroastrians of Persia.

On the Lakhpat River in Sindh, pilgrims often pay homage to a temple of Mahadeo at Koteshwar which is an ancient *Tirtha* by the borders of India. Here, Gorakhnathis get a yoni-linga emblem of Shiva-Shakti branded on the right upper arm to signify that they have gone beyond the confines of India and visited Hinglaj which is looked after by Muslims as their property. Many stories are related to these shrines of Sindh and go on to demonstrate how closely connected India and Western Asia were. Though Muslims have taken ownership of these holy places, they remain somewhat indispensable to Indian pilgrims on spiritual journeys.

Significant shrines include the monastery of Kanthadnath at Manphara near Kanthkot in Vagad (Kutch, Gujarat), and the monastery at Dhinodhar, also in Kutch. The Kanthadnathis worship Ganesh and Kanthadnath and the Dhinodhar is believed to be a sacred hill. It is also close to a temple of Hinglaj Devi which is accessible for devotees who cannot endure the long pilgrimage to Sindh. The Dhramanathi's founder was a disciple of Gorakhnath and this monastery has branches at Mathal, Baladhiya and Aral.

The Kanphatas of Sivaramandap in Bhuj belong to the Shantinath sect and are devout disciples of Goddess Shakti. Many places in Kathiawad are linked to Gorakhnath. The hills of Girnar are said to have been one of his favourite haunts. It is believed that it is here that Parvati sang praises to Lord Shiva and waited till he finally came before her.

Gorakhmadhi which is situated nine miles east of Patan has three images of Gorakhnath and one image of Matsyendranath in an underground cave. Situated in Kathiawad, at the top of Turanmal Hill, are remains of many temples dedicated to this yogi. Southeast of Shirala in Satara district is a grove called Gorakhnath named in respect of the presiding deity. Hills in the Deccan region north of Ahmedabad are also named after him. At Ganeshpuri in Thane, there are hot springs which have curative powers and one of them is named Gorakhmacchindar.

A monastery of the Bairag Panth of Kanphatas is cited in Trimbak close to Nasik near the holy Godavari River. A chief centre for the Kanphatas is at Pai Dhuni in Mumbai which is used by all twelve panths. The *mahant* (chief priest) is chosen here at the Kumbh Mela for a tenure of twelve years.

Few miles north of Udaipur is the Ekliganji temple in Rajputana, which has religious connections to Bappa and the Kanphatas. Two other vital places of worship in Kolkata are at the Cantonment of Dum Dum and Mahanad, in Hoogly district. Jagannath Puri is a seat (*gaddi*) of the Satnath sect of the Kanphata yogis. Each of these heritage places are visually stunning and have many legends and fables associated with them through the ages.

III

The Siddhas and the Buddhist Tradition

3.1 Yoga: Its Roots, Stages, and Principles

A system of intense mental and physical discipline, yoga is "a code of disciplinary practices". In his book *Yoga Philosophy* author Das Gupta writes:

> In order to be assured that our minds would not be attracted by worldly temptations, certain psychological exercises should be undertaken in order to move the mind in a direction, the reverse of ordinary experience. The yogi looks to the yoga practice for gaining a complete mastery over his mind. Throughout all the epochs of Indian culture we find the highest reverence paid to the (yogis) who were believed not only to possess a superior sense, by which they could know the highest truth beyond the ken of ordinary vision, but also to wield the most wonderful miraculous powers which Patanjali has described as the vibhutis of yoga, by which the (yogi) showed his control not only over his mind and the minds of others, but also over inert external objects.

Interest in yogic practices lies as much in their superior powers, as in their knowledge. Some of these practices date back to the non-Aryan sources and even the *Brahmanas* and *Upanishads* are familiar

Lord Shree Krishna

with this philosophy. The first mention of yoga is said to be in the *Taittriya Upanishad, Maitrayana Upanishad,* and the *Svetasvatara Upanishad.* Most sutras related to yoga are more than a thousand years old with a mention even in the *Rig Veda* which calls yogis "mad muni". According to Panini (500 BC), a yogi is one who practises religious austerities and the vows of celibacy. Life-long study and asceticism are highly valued to be able to gain higher powers.

In those times, however, ascetics were seen more as magicians with supernatural powers than as divine spiritual beings and gradually, bodily discipline gained a lot of importance, as much as mental control. In *Faqire and Faqirtum,* Schmidt has included an important quote by Swami Vivekananda which says, "The yogi proposes to himself no less a task than to master the whole universe, to control the whole of nature."

Attainment of the Supreme Brahman is the focus of the yogi. The *Maitrayana Upanishad* states:

"The seer sees not death,
Nor sickness, nor any distress.
The seer sees only the All,
Obtains the All entirely."

Closely connected to yoga is the concept of *Sankhya* which is also needed for mukti. The *Bhagavad Geeta* describes *Sankhya* as "the way of salvation of pure knowledge, the intellectual method, and it is understood as implying quietism, renunciation of action (*sanyas, vairagya*)." In contrast, yoga is a more disciplined and unselfish physical and mental activity that demands years of practice.

Karma Yoga (disciplined action) brings about a complete lifestyle change. On the other hand, *Sankhya* is an inactive and intellectual way which is slow and hard to practice. A beautiful example of this is Lord Krishna's words to Arjuna in which the latter was told that "in life action is inevitable, but it must be brought under a rule of conduct (dharma)". Thus, following the *Varna-dharmas* (customary duties) of the various orders of society is linked to every person's karma. A spiritual or transformational goal is always associated with yoga and right action is the foundation of all its practices.

3.2 Gorakhnath's View on the Constitution of the Individual Body

The disciplined lifestyle taught by Gorakhnath is the same as the Ashtangika–Yogamargika (the Eight-fold Path) taught by Patanjali in his *Yoga Sutras*. However, Gorakhnath and his Nath Sampradaya greatly elaborated on this system by adding various additional forms of asana, pranayam, mudra, *bandha*, *vedha*, *dharana*, dhyan, *ajapa*, *nadanusadhana*, Kundalini-shakti-*jagarana*, and more. According to both these expounders, samadhi was considered to be the fulfilment of yoga and hence many a times the word "yoga" is applied to refer to samadhi.

Patanjali, however, in his interpretation of samadhi, stresses on the "perfect suppression of all mental functions", i.e., *chitta-vritti-nirodha*. And it is said that the transcendent character of the soul is reflected in that state. Gorakhnath, on the other hand, emphasises on the "mastery over all mental functions and the cosmic forces along with the perfect illumination of the mind in that samadhi state". Gradually, this *Jeeva* Consciousness (individual consciousness) ascends to Shiva Consciousness (universal consciousness) and the mind transcends itself realising it is *Unman*, i.e., Supermind.

From the yogic viewpoint, Gorakhnath has comprehensively analysed the human body and described it as the following in the *Goraksha Vachana Sangraha*:

1. The material body called *Bhuta Pinda*.
2. The mental body is described as *Antahkarana Panchaka* or "The Five-fold *panchaka*".
3. *Kula-panchaka* or "The five-fold *Kula*".
4. *Vyakti-panchaka* or "The five-fold *Vyakti*".
5. *Pratyaksha-karana-panchaka* or "The five-fold perceptible determinant of causes".
6. *Nadisamsthana* or "The system of the *nadis*".
7. *Dasa-vayu* or "The ten prana *vayu* or vital forces forming the vital body".

Each of these has to be thoroughly grasped and their procedures practised sincerely by the yogi seeking the perfect body that can help attain enlightenment. Gorakhnath's procedures are usually very active and practical, and require the yogi to be constantly aware of his physicality. Following these procedures at every step is crucial to the seeker's sadhana.

1. *Bhuta Pinda*

The *Bhuta Pinda,* also called *Bhautika Pinda,* is the gross material body constituted of five gross material elements that appear in different proportions in different parts. In all solid parts, viz, bones (*asthi*), flesh (*mamsa*), skin (*twak*), tissues (*nadi*) and hair (*roma*), the elements of Bhumi or Prithvi appear dominantly. These are the five *gunas* or five manifestations of Bhumi according to Gorakhnath.

The element of *Ap* or *Salila* called "*Gunas* of *Ap*", appear in liquid substances of the body such as *lala* (saliva), *mutra* (urine), *sukra* (semen), *sonata* (blood), and *sweda* (sweat). Physical phenomena which are the manifestations of *Tejas* are *ksudha* (hunger), *trishna* (thirst), *nidra* (sleep), *kanti* (lustre) and *alasya* (sloth). According to him, the proportions of these differ depending on the influences and functions of the Agni or *Tejas* in the body.

The elements of air, called "*Gunas* of *Vayu*" are *dhavana* (movement), *brahmana* (fidgeting), *prasarana* (expansion), *akunchana* (contraction), and *nirodhana* (suppression).

The "*Gunas* of *Akash*" are *raga* (physical attractions), *dwesha* (repulsion), *bhaya* (fear), *lajja* (shame), and *moha* (delusion).

The human body is thus constituted of five gross *bhutas* consisting of twenty-five *gunas* as mentioned above, according to Gorakhnath. Through discipline, all these can be properly regulated as these have a major influence on our overall well-being, habits and temperaments, and it is for this reason that yogis lay great emphasis on the constitution of the body.

2. *Antahkarana Panchak*

The mental body or the nature of the mind forms the *Antahkarana.* For yogis, the mind is seen as an individualised self-manifestation of the cosmic mind which depends on the living body, as well. It is said that the cosmic mind and cosmic life evolve from the *Maha-Sakara-Pinda* (the cosmic body) of Shiva-Shakti. Hence, every individual is a manifestation or a reincarnation of Shiva-Shakti. Gorakhnath classifies all manifestations of the mind under the five names of *Manas, Buddhi, Ahamkara, Chitta* and *Chaitanya,* i.e., the *Antahkarana Panchak* (the five fold internal instrument of the empirical mind).

Each of these has special characteristics and is expressed variedly. *Manas* (the undisciplined empirical mind) appears in *Samkalpa* (desire/will), *Vikalpa* (doubt/hesitancy), *Murccha* (swoon/ temporary senselessness), *Jadata* (idiocy/confused thinking) and *Manana* (reflective thinking).

Buddhi which is the sense of reason and intellect is manifested in *Viveka* (discrimination of right from wrong, good from evil, valuable from valueless, and so on), *Vairagya* (voluntary restraint of desires and attchmnets or turning the mind away from what seems unreal, wrong, evil, ugly, and so on), Shanti (cultivation of calmness and tranquillity of the mind, or peacefulness of character) *Santosh* (cultivation of contentment) and lastly, *Kshama* (cultivation of the forgiveness for others). *Buddhi* is also called the higher mind which controls or regulates the lower mind which is *Manas*.

Ahamkar can be understood by *Abhiman* (sense of ego or "I"), *Madiyam* (sense of mine-ness, senses, mental, physical consciousness that is one's own), *Mama-sukham* (brooding over or planning one's own happiness), *Mama-dhukham* (brooding over and struggling against one's sorrow) and *Mama-idam* (sense of this is mine, possession, or monopoly). *Ahamkar* is significant to the mental constitution of a person and it controls each person's identity and individuality and manages it even amidst all physical changes and mental functions. Both *Buddhi* and *Ahamkar* are connected with higher stages of development of individual minds.

Chitta is constituted of *Mati* (disposition or instinctive and habitual tendencies), *Dhriti* (power of conservation of energy and experience), *Smriti* (memory or power of recollecting and reproducing past experiences), *Tyaga* (the capacity for renunciation, sacrifice or forgetting) and *Swikara* (capacity of accepting and assimilating or making one's own what is obtained from external sources). *Chitta* is said to be manifested in the revival of old *sanskara*s and in the sub-conscious operations of the mind.

Chaitanya can be explained by the phenomena of *Vimarsa* (rational reflection), *Silana* (systematic self-discipline), *Dhairya* (patience or self-control), *Chintan* (contemplation and meditation) and *Nihsprhatva* (cultivated desirelessness). These are the twenty-five forms of manifestation of the mind of the individual body according to Gorakhnath. The *Antahkarana* constitutes the *Sukshma Sharira* (the subtle body of the individual soul) while the physical body is constituted as the *Sthula Sharira* (gross body).

3. *Kula Panchak*

Kula Panchak is the most puzzling and technical aspect of sadhana. Defined in many ways, it is used in different senses and contexts. According to Gorakhnath, Kula is manifested in five ways such as, *Sattva, Rajas, Tamas, Kaal* and *Jeeva*.

Sattva is manifested through *Daya* (kindness or compassion), Dharma (righteousness), *Kriya* (pious habits or willingness to perform good and noble deeds), Bhakti (reverence or devotion) and *Shraddha* (faith). It is the attribute of *Sattva* that inspires the human mind to ascent and gain higher spiritual and moral ideals. It helps us direct our emotions towards realising perfect truth and beauty and goodness and freedom.

Rajas in manifested through *Daan* (charity made from an egoistic sense of one's superiority and not out of a spirit of humility), *Bhog* (hankering for more and more sensuous and mental enjoyment), *Sringara* (love for decoration and ornamentation and artistic luxuries), *Vastu Grahana* (love for more and more property) and *Swartha Sangrahana* (acquisition or accumulation of things for selfish purposes). The influence of *Rajas* makes a person enterprising and ambitious and makes him selfish, materialistic and immersed in artistic or pleasurable enjoyments of all kinds.

Tamas is responsible for the darker, evil and wicked forces in our nature such as *Vivada* (useless controversies), *Kalaha* (quarrelsomeness), *Shoka* (lamentation or melancholia), *Vadha* (killing), and *Vanchan* (deception).

Kaal is related to time and all the significant changes it brings about in our lives, such as the fruition of our actions, development of the body, so on and so forth. It is manifested in *Kalana* (calculation of periods regarding objects and events and perceiving the coexistence and succession among them), *Kalpana* (appreciation of regular temporal orders in the production of natural phenomena), *Bhranti* (confusion of thoughts), *Pramada* (periodical insanity), and *Anartha* (accidental misfortunes).

Jeeva is the *avastha* (changes of states) that is connected with the individual consciousness and existence amidst all these changes.

The states through which *Jeeva* is manifested are *Jagrat* (the waking state, in which mind comes in direct contact with external realities through the sense organs of perception and action), *Swapna* (dream state in which despite direct contact with realities the mind has various experiences at a subconscious level), *Sushupti* (state of deep sleep in which mind exists at an unconscious level without objective or subjective experiences and is at complete rest or sleep), *Turiya* (state of perfect concentration upon the transcendent character of the spirit, blissful state of illumination), and *Turyatita* (an elevated state in which perfect concentration is elevated to absolute union or identification in which the individual mind realises itself as one with the transcendent spirit, i.e., Shiva).

Thus all these states are detrimental to *Kula* which, in turn, directs the evolution of character, of aspirations, of spiritual goals of a person and makes him complex yet harmonious. *Kula* evolves from Shiva-Shakti and leads an individual at every stage towards highest fulfilment in the cosmic order.

4. *Vyakti Panchak*

Vyakti Panchak constitutes the five forms of *Vyakti* (self expression) according to Gorakhnath. These are classified as *Iccha* (volition), *Kriya* (action), Maya (pretension or illusion), Prakriti (temperament) and *Vak* (speech). Each of these further manifested in five various forms.

Iccha is manifested in *Unmada* (mad and unbalanced impulses and excitements found in children as well as in those who are intoxicated), *Vasana* (deep rooted desires which are due to instincts or past habits), *Vancha* (desires for alluring or covetable objects such as wealth, power, pleasure), *Chinta* (voluntarily thinking and planning about desirable objects and how to buy them), *Cheshta* (mental efforts or resolutions for attaining desirable objects or for accomplishing cherished purposes).

Kriya is manifested in the forms of *Smarana* (active contemplation upon desirable objects to be attained or the purposes to be achieved), *Udyoga* (making preparations necessary for pursuit of a desired objector purpose), *Karya* (active pursuit of an object or ideal), *Nischay* (pursuit of an object or ideal with a strong determination and perseverance), and *Swakulachara* (performance of duties and good deeds which conform to society and family values at the sacrifice of one's personal happiness).

Maya is the expression of each person's individuality and consists of giving undue importance to one's individual self and interests and dealing falsely with others. Maya is manifested as *Mada* (intoxication with a sense of pride or vanity and desires or actions originating from it), *Matsarya* (an attitude of intolerance, envy, malice towards happiness and good actions of others), *Dambha* (self-conceited expression of one's own superiority in other's presence and over-valuing oneself and under-valuing others), *Kritrimatva* (artificiality or duplicity in behaviour to create false impressions in other's minds), *Asatya* (having recourse to untruth or falsehood in speech and action). These active expressions of maya show the dominance of *rajas* and *tamas* in nature and these have to be transcended for individuals to ascend to higher planes.

Prakriti is the expression of individuality and even this is manifested in five forms of *Asha* (hopes for future prospects), *Trishna* (thirst for more), *Spriha* (desire for attaining objects), *Kanksha* (ambition for greatness), *Mithya* (dreaming of achieving things that are beyond one's aspiration, i.e., false hopes). All these build a person's temperament and indicate whether he is inclined towards material goals or higher ideals.

Vak is speech and is manifested in five forms according to Gorakhnath viz., *Para* (stage at which speech is wholly identified with consciousness), *Pashyanti* (stage at which consciousness perceives or sees subtle ideas), *Madhyama* (organised vibrations or some kind of upheaval in the physiological system which requires physical activity for the expression of the ideas), *Vaikari* (articulate speech or words uttered which are heard by others, communication of mental ideas) and *Maitrika* (ultimate phonetic constituents such as words, sentences, phrases, languages). *Vak* is essential for the yogi to be able to reflect and meditate on the sound embodiment of holy mantras and chants during the course of his practice.

5. *Pratyaksha Karana Panchak* (The Five Red Reasons)

According to Gorakhnath, there are material causes which are essential for developing and renewing the human body and to realise the ultimate goal of one's life. These are called *Pratyaksha Karana Panchak* and are further classified as: Karma, Kama, Chandra, Surya and Agni. Operating in subtle ways, their influence on bodily life is perceptible *(pratyaksha)*.

Karma means actions or deeds, and these are influenced by bodily limbs, mental thoughts, desires, and can have a beneficial or injurious effect upon the person's future as well as, his future birth. Gorakhnath has listed five-fold factors that constitute Karma and these are: *Shubh* (good actions which have beneficial consequences), *Ashubh* (bad actions which have negative consequences for the doer), *Yashah* (actions that are approved and praised by others and bring temporary or lasting fame and praise to the doer), *Apakirti* (actions that are condemned by others and create a bad reputation for the doer), and *Adristaphala* Sadhana (righteous and unrighteous deeds which produce *punya* (moral and religious merit) and *paap* (demerit) for the doer). All these factors are detrimental to the doer's happiness or misery and these conditions affect his mind-body-spirit in the present, and are also carried forward to the future incarnation.

Kama is the second *Pratyaksha Karana* for the birth and growth of living individuals in the cosmic system. Kama is used by Gorakhnath in a sexual connotation and plays an important role for reproduction of living creatures. It is a fundamental law of the cosmic play between Shiva-Shakti as we are are born through sexual intercourse. Five characteristics of Kama are *Rati, Priti, Krida, Kamana* and *Aturata*. *Rati* is sexual attachment between a male and female, *Priti* is pleasure or happiness enjoyed by both in mutual companionship that develops into love and attachment, *Krida* refers to sports and games that gratify sexual passions, *Kamana* is the desire for more intimacy and enjoyment, and *Aturata* is the exhaustion or loss of strength due to excessive gratification of lustful desires and a temporary reaction against it. Kama overall is instrumental in regeneration, as well as in the development of vital organs and mental attributes.

Chandra (moon), Surya (sun) and Agni (fire) exercise their influence over the evolution of life in this world. Life without these three factors would have been impossible. For yogis, however, these three have different meaning as they see the sun, moon and fire within the human body, and regulation and harmony of these three factors is needed for the healthy preservation of the body. According to yogic terminology, Chandra is the power within the living organism that makes *anna* (food) capable of being digested so that it can build the tissues, energy and organs of the body. It is also called soma which is the source of all rasa (essence of food materials). It is thus the source of all nourishment, delight and vivacity that constitutes the *bhogya* (materials that can be consumed or absorbed) in every living body. Surya and Agni are perceived as powers within the individual that assimilate, absorb, and convert the foods into the necessary ingredients needed for fuller growth. These are essential for building mental strength, spiritual powers, alertness, brilliance, and moral strength. Surya and Agni are thus called *Bhokta* (the consumer) and every living organism is seen as *Bhoktri-Bhogyatmaka* (consisting of the consumer, consumable, eater and eatable, power to absorb and power to be absorbed). *Agni–Somatmakam–Jagat* is a name given for the whole world which implies that the whole phenomenal world is evolved through the union duality of *Bhokta-Bhogya*.

Gorakhnath has listed Chandra as having seventeen *kalas*, Surya as having thirteen kalas and Agni as having eleven *kalas*. *Kalas* are diverse kind of shaktis (powers) that emanate from each of these elements and perform diverse functions for the preservation and development of individual living bodies, as well as, for the balance and beauty of the whole cosmic universe. Each of these has one *kala* in common that keeps them in direct spiritual touch with the Supreme Spirit. Essentially, Chandra, Surya and Agni are manifestations of the *Mahashakti* of Lord Shiva, and in their ultimate nature they are one and the same. (More on the Chandra, Surya and Agni relation within an individual is discussed in a later chapter.)

6. Nadi Samsthana

Knowledge of the *Nadi Samsthana* (nervous system) is crucial to yoga, and this system plays the most important role of demonstrating the oneness of the entire body. The thousands of nerves which constitute the human body carry out innumerable functions and they are the instruments through which the commands of the mind are carried out to the limbs and organs, of the body. Some nerves contribute to perception and knowledge while others are related to passions, emotions and excitements, some to movements and some to respiration, and so on and so forth. Their purpose however remains to maintain the harmony and unity of the psycho-physiological aspects of the individual.

Yogi gurus have identified that the common source of these *nadis* is the *Mula-Kanda* which is the most vital part of the body, located above the reproductive organs, and below the centre of the navel, within the spinal column. From this centre all the vital *nadis* have evolved and spread in many directions all over the body, in zigzag tracks. The brain and spinal columns are the most important organs in the nervous system; the brain is the location for the *Sahasrara* Chakra (the wheel of a thousand petaled lotus) through which moral consciousness and an

Brahma Danda

enlightened mind develops and influences the individual. This is the most supreme part of the entire nervous system. The spinal cord maintains the balance of the whole individual and it's often called "Brahma *Danda*" or "*Meru Danda*". Seventy- two of these *nadis* are prominent ones according to Gorakhnath, and these are named in the *Siddha Siddhanta Paddhati* as *Sushumna, Ida, Pingala, Saraswati, Pusha, Alambusha, Gandhari, Hasti-Jihvika, Kuhu* and *Samkhini*.

Sushumna is the *Brahma Nadi*, and plays the most important role in the development of our intellectual, moral, and spiritual life. It is the *nadi* which arises from the *Mulakanda* chakra, passes from the *Muladhara* through the Brahma *Danda* and upto the *Brahmandhra*, in the *Sahasrara* (cerebrum, crown area of the head). It is also the path through which the Kundalini Shakti ascends to meet Shiva in the head.

Ida and Pingala are connected with the two nostrils and are united in a vital centre just between the two visual organs, as the service of all the respiratory organs. The yogis speak of *Ida* as *Chandra Nadi* connected to the left nostril, and Pingala as *Surya Nadi* connected to the right nostril. Besides the two sides of the *Sushumna*, they are vitally connected with the movements of prana-*vayu* (the vital breath). Breath control and movements of *Ida* and *Pingala* are vital to yogic discipline.They can be unified in the *Sushumna* and their whole energy can be concentrated for realisation of the ultimate truth.

Saraswati Nadi, connected with the mouth, the organ of speech, connects all the vocal instruments with the brain and the rest of the body, making them responsive to wills, thoughts, emotions and sensations. *Pusha* and *Alambusha* are *nadi*s connected with the organs of sight, i.e., the two retinas and eyeballs. *Gandhari* and *Hastijivhikais Nadi*s are connected with the two ears and hence, are responsible for auditory sensations. *Kuhu* is connected with the anus or the organ through which waste is excreted from the body. *Samkhini* is the nadi connecting the organs of regeneration.

These *nadi*s are thus the *Mukhya Nadis* (the principal *nadi*s) and are always in *vahati* (the flowing condition). They are responsible for the physiological, mental, psychological, emotional, and even the spiritual growth of every individual.

7. *Vayu Sansthana*

Vayu (the vital breath) is responsible for all the functions of the body. It activates all the organs and ensures the proper functioning of all parts. It draws the energy of the environment and refreshes the bodily organs, helps in the assimilation of food and liquids, circulation of blood, processes of secretion and keeps the individual active at all times including the periods of waking, sleeping, and dreaming. It serves all *nadis,* and Chandra, Surya and Agni to keep them alive and fresh. This energy of *vayu* is also called Prana Shakti. Although *vayu* is essentially one source which flows through the whole body, it has been given ten different names as per the *vritti* (functions) it performs. These ten vayus are: *Prana, Apana, Samana, Udana, Vyana, Naga, Kurma, Krikara (Krikala), Devadatta* and *Dhananjaya.* The first five of these are primary, and the last five are secondary.

Prana is the most important of all these constituents and is said to be located in the *hridaya* (heart). It energises and activates all organs by breathing in and out. The breathing process is the main channel and there is continuous interaction between the vital energy in the body.This energy is also found in an inexhaustible amount, in the cosmic system. *Apana* is located near the *guda* (anus), and energises the lower parts of the body. It helps organs in clearing the impurities and unwanted materials that are produced in various forms. Its functions are linked with prana. Prana helps the body in taking in fresh air whereas *Apana* helps it remove the harmful or unwanted air.

Samana is located in the navel and its function is to enkindle or deepen the fire, i.e., Agni in the stomach and intestines, and increase the *pachana* (power of assimilation). *Vyana* moves about the entire body infusing fresh energy and agility to all the nerves and ensures equal distribution among them all. *Udana* is located in the *kantha* (throat region) and its function is helping the organs easily swallow food and drink. What we sometimes vomit out is what the body rejects. This *vayu* also helps in the spontaneous movements of the organs of the speech.

Naga is the *vayu* that is responsible for contributing to the strength and balanced movements of the body. *Kurma* is the cause of involuntary shaking of the body in particular parts in certain occasions, and also for the spontaneous opening and closing of the eyelids and movements of the eyeballs. It is thus responsible for helping delicate organs adjust to unexpected circumstances. *Krikala* is responsible for two purposes: pushing out unassimilated gasses from the stomach area through the throat and mouth and restoring normal conditions within the body. It also increases and generates hunger.

Devadatta relieves the body from abnormal conditions that sometimes happen such as spontaneous outbursts through the mouth and other channels. *Dhananjaya* pervades the entire physical system and produces *Nada* (continuous sound or a series of sounds), as if accompanying operations and interactions between various organs and forces that are occurring for the development and preservation of the body.

According to Gorakhnath, breathing is made up of three activities: *Puraka* (breathing in) *Rechaka* (breathing out) and *Kumbhaka* (a little suspension of breathin between the two). Between breathing in and out there is a momentary suspension. Through yogic practices, we can lengthen and regulate the time of suspension only with the guidance of a guru. According to Gorakhnath, we breathe out with the sound "*Ham*", and air enters into our body with the sound "*Sah*". Thus, every individual is unconsciously repeating *Ham-Sah* like a mantra, by a divine design. The deeper spiritual significance related to this is explained as: *Ham* implies *Aham*, i.e., "I" or the individual self, and *Sah* represents Brahma or the *Paramatma* Shiva. Thus, every time we breathe out, the individual *jeeva* frees himself from the limitations of the body and goes into the cosmos and meets Shiva. Every time we breathe in, the soul of the cosmos or Shiva enters the body and identifies himself as *aham* (the individual soul).

Interestingly, when the mind is calm and the body is tranquil, the sounds of "*Hum*" and "*Sah*" cease to exist and there is a rhythmical soundless, a wavelike sound of Om, called *Pranav*. This Om sound represents complete unification of *Aham* and *Sah*, of the individual self and universal self, and of *Jeeva* and Shiva. This sound is the Echo of the Cosmos, Absolute Spirit, Brahma, Atma, and the Supreme Spirit that transcends the universe.

Rules and Restraints

The sacred text *Maitrayana Upanishad* mentions some very important technical terms related to yoga: "The precept for affecting this (unity) is this: restraint of the Breath (*Pranayam*), withdrawal of the Senses (*Pratyahara*), Meditation (Dhyan), Concentration (*Dharana*), Contemplation (*Tarka*), Absorption (Samadhi). Such is said to be the six-fold Yoga."

But before delving into these restraints, there are a few more commands the yogi has to master before he can walk on this path. These five commands are: ahimsa (abstinence from injuring anything), covetousness (keeping away from deceit and falsehood, avoiding theft, controlling material desires and yearnings for excessive riches) and celibacy (abstaining from sexual intercourse).

Another set of rules is related to the purification of the body, which includes external cleansing of the body which results in attitude of disgust of the body, discouraging sexual intercourse which is connected to asceticism, and suppressing the senses of pleasure. Instead, what is encouraged is the cleansing of the mind, living in moderation and frugality, contentment, silence, learning to adapt the body to heat and cold, keeping the body still, philosophical studies, repetitions of chants, words and spells (including Om), fasting on important religious days, meditating to enhance concentration and complete surrender to God and his will. This forms the *niyama* (*yama*) of the yogi and this pattern of his daily life includes *tapas*, mantra and bhakti. In case the yogi's path is obstructed, he should use the principle of *pratipakshahara* which involves use of opposing qualities, and thinking of the consequences as deterrents. For instance, feelings of equanimity or indifference to other people's vices, placing the good over the bad in deeds and thoughts, feeling kind towards all those who suffer, and thinking of all beings as friends, among others.

According to Professor Radhakrishnan, *yama* and *niyama* encompass all the passive and active virtues. He says, "A practice of these two favours the development of *vairagya* or passionlessness or freedom from desire, either for things of the world or the pleasures of heaven".

Once the above disciplines have been mastered, the yogi can ascend to the daily and sincere practice of asanas, pranayam and *pratyahara*. The yogi first begins with asanas (postures) which are connected with the discipline of the body in stillness or rigidity. In a quiet andcomfortable place, the yogi must fix his attention by steadying the mind and controlling his breath and bodily poise (like the flame of the lamp in a windless place). Hatha Yoga propagates eighty–four *lakshas* (postures), the *Shiva Samhita* gives importance to four, while the *Gheranda Samhita* has named thirty-one chief postures.

After mastering the asanas, the next stage is regulating the *vayu* (breath or the vital wind), i.e., pranayam. Constant respiration can obstruct attaining perfect concentration, hence, it becomes essential to control and finally stop breathing at regular intervals. Interruptions and set patterns of inhaling and exhaling are integral to pranayam. Expelling in-held breath is called *rechaka*, and while doing so one has to concentrate on Shiva. Inhaling the breath is called *puraka* and this has to be done while concentrating on Vishnu. While one retains the breath one must concentrate on Brahma, and this is called *kumbhaka*. The main objective of this entire process is retaining the in-held breath, and it is believed that it must be carried out to extremes for it to be truly fruitful.

In Hatha Yoga especially, controlling the breath is vital as it is said to enhance the yogi's occult power and wisdom. Once this stage of breath is mastered, the yogi can ascend to the next level which is *pratyahara*, which involves suppressing the yearnings of the sense organs and, over time, completely withdrawing from them. This helps the mind concentrate better, increases the attention span and does not let it wander.

Thus *niyama, yama*, asana, pranayam and *pratyahara* are the five major principles every yogi must follow during his preliminary stages as these are the steps that will lead him to samadhi.

The last three stages are internal processes and these eventually help the yogi cease all unnecessary mental activity. These are *dharana*, dhyan and samadhi, wherein, *dharana* and dhyan are connected with illumination, whereas samadhi is connected with union. As a cohesive unit when focused on a single object or entity, these three practices constitute *samyama* (a stage of contemplative trance, concentration and conquest). When this *samyama* is focussed on internal activities, miraculous powers can arise.

Dharana is fixing or focussing attention on a particular object or position, such as the nose, tip of the tongue, the navel, space between the eyebrows (where the Third Eye resides), concentrating on Ishvara or just universal space. It is a "one-point meditation" which requires mental and physical restraints and once mastered, the yogi will never wander away from the object or entity in focus. An even deeper and more intense extension of this is dhyan or "one-pointed concentration" in which an object or entity can be focussed on for longer periods and is placed before everything else.

The third and final stage which puts an end to unnecessary mental activity is samadhi, which is a prolonged experience of release. After coming such a long way, the yogi is free to choose the focus of his object but most practitioners concentrate and immerse themselves in Ishvara. At this stage, the yogi is so absorbed in the object that he loses consciousness of self and of all existence, and becomes unified with the object itself.

In his book *The Yoga System of Patanjali*, James Houghton Woods describes four progressive qualities of this stage of samadhi:

> Concentrating on objects remembering their names and qualities; then on the five subtle elements (*tanmatras*) first remembering their qualities and then without any notion of their qualities; afterwards on the buddhi with its functions of the senses causing pleasure and then, leaving the feelings of joy behind; and upon pure substance divested of all modifications. Here memory is eliminated and mind (subject) alone is left.

The stages within this process of samadhi are *Samprajnata* samadhi, which is "the samadhi in which there is consciousness of objects" and *Nirodha* or *Asamprajnata* samadhi, in which "the mind is without an object", i.e., a stage of voidness or vacuum. Once the yogi perfects this, his yoga is gradually is perfected and eventually he experiences a final release. Samadhi is thus a union with the Brahman according to Vedanta, and an isolation of the soul according to *Sankhya*.

Apart from divine peace and beauty, mastering this stage grants many physical and psychical powers to the yogi. (More on these supernatural powers or siddhis is discussed later.)

According to the *Yogatattva Upanishad* there are four kinds of yoga: Hatha Yoga, Raj Yoga, Mantra Yoga, and Laya Yoga. The influences of all these types were crucial to the development of Tantra and other spiritual practices. Hatha Yoga is concerned with breath control, control of muscles and organs through postures, concentration and other exercises. Mastering this form of yoga can help the yogi achieve miraculous feats in every aspect of life. It is also connected with the power of the supernatural, healing diseases, and keeping the body immune against diseases and illness. Raj Yoga also called Jnana Yoga, encompasses intellectual processes and all the activities of the mind along with developing psychic powers. Mantra Yoga on the other hand makes use of sacred chants, syllables, symbols and religious books and is closely connected to the realm of magic. This form of yoga requires constant practice and repetition (*japa*). Laya yoga emphasises on quietening the mind or rather, eliminating all mental processes and inducing a trance like state, i.e., *Laya* (unconsciousness) which is the fourth state (samadhi) which ultimately leads to the permanent stillness in mind. Often connected with Kundalini Yoga, Laya Yoga is considered to be supreme among the *Shaktas* as it is through this process that complete union of Shiva and Shakti can be attained.

Each of these types of yoga is special and emphasises different kinds of discipline, which benefit every individual in some way. To become a perfect yogi it is important to master all these yogas deeply and sincerely. These practices can also be used in different combinations to achieve desired results. The book *Hatha Yoga Pradipika*, says that Hatha Yoga and Raja Yoga are interconnected and should be used together for the success of the other.

The Gorakhnathis primarily practise Hatha Yoga. According to the sacred book *Goraksha Paddhati*, it is said that *"Ha"* signifies Surya (sun) and the *"Tha"* signifies Chandra (moon), and their union is Yoga or Hatha Yoga. (More on the sun and the moon theory is discussed in detail in a later chapter.)

Hatha Yoga implies a great amount of discipline and difficult physical postures which have to be carried out sincerely. These include Asana, Mudra, Pranayam, Dhauti, Chakra, Kundalini and Nadi. Many a times Kundalini Yoga is considered to be similar to Laya Yoga. Interestingly, Kundalini Yoga requires dhyan, i.e., involvement of mental processes which is Raja Yoga, thus all these forms of yoga often overlap.

It is important to understand Kundalini Yoga as it is closely related to the attainment of divine bliss, liberation and nirvana. Kundalini Yoga is solely dependent on the union of Shiva and Shakti, and it is believed that every yogi aspires to experience this divine ecstasy that is born during their creative union. It is said that from the lowest chakra, i.e., *Muladhara* where the Shakti energy resides (coiled three-and-a-half times like a serpent) to the domain of Shiva in the crown, i.e. *Sahasrara*, each stage experiences a pure joy and at each stage, the god or goddess resides. During her ascent, Shakti drinks the nectar of the crescent moon. This form where Shiva and Shakti unite, and where there is cosmic balance of energies is also called *Ardhanari* (half-woman). However, Hatha yogis enable the individual to reverse or regress this natural process so as to conserve or protect the *Bindu* (immortal divine nectar).

It is important to note that for the mastery of this yoga, there is a disciplined routine that the yogi must follow or else his path will be very strenuous and difficult. The main concern here has to be the health and energy of the body and so a perfect diet and environment are crucial. The food he eats should be sweet, easy to digest and good to taste. He must drink milk and stay away from salty, bitter and acidic foods. Good food would be food cooked with rice, wheat, sugar, barley, butter, white honey, vegetables, fruits and ghee. Bad food would be food which is highly spicy, oily, containing liquor, meat, fish, curd, pulses, plums, fermented food, containing garlic and onion, and certain vegetables. The stomach should be full only two- or three-fourth as the one-fourth space is needed for prana (the breath) during the exercises of pranayam.

While practising Kundalini Yoga, the yogi's environment should be a small room which is clean and comfortable and one which offers him solitude. Some also emphasise that the yogi should practise in "a secluded place, in a country governed by a dutiful king, in a land of plenty and free from disturbance". The yogi must also give up pleasures and should shun fire, travelling, women and the company of evil men. He should also not rise too early or too fast, should not exert his body and should take a cold bath. It is important for a yogi to have a spiritual guide or guru on his path. According to the *Shiva Samhita*, only the instruction imparted by a guru by word of mouth is of use (3:11).

The main postures to be practised are *Padmasana* and *Siddhasana*. *Siddhasana* is often called the perfect asana and is considered the best to practise. Asanas and pranayam are closely connected and it is essential to control them both for the prana and *apana* to move freely through the *nadis*, so that the Kundalini or Shakti can ascend. Gradually with practice the *nadis* which are blocked with impurities get cleansed by either drying up, or by removing the substances collected in them. Thus, as all these channels of the chakras (energy centres) get purified and the *vayu* (breath) can be held for a longer time. Pranayam is the most common way to serve this purpose and the *shatkarma* (the six purification acts)—*Dhauti, Neti, Basti, Trataka, Nauli* and *Kapalabhati* are employed.These help in preserving health and building up a stronger immunity.

Gradually, this process helps the Kundalini to rise from chakra to chakra. During this breathing process the yogi also uses mantras for gaining the best results. When the Kundalini lifts to each chakra there is a peculiar experience associated with each of them. It is important to know that as she rises upwards, the bodily region below each successive stage becomes cold. In *Khechari* mudra (hypnotic trance) only the region on the top of the head stays warm and sometimes, at this stage, the yogi is also taken to be dead.

The Seven Chakras

Each of the seven chakras has specific *bija*s and functions. Kundalini has to ascend all these chakras to fully complete and cleanse the subtle body and prepare it for the powerful union of this energy with Shiva in the crown. In brief, these seven chakras can be described as follows:

1. *Muladhara* Chakra or the Root Chakra

Located at the base of the spine, this chakra forms the root foundation of energy centres. It has four petals consisting of four mantras: *vam, sam, sam* and *sam*. Its essence is of the earth element or the solid state of all matter, and its *bija* mantra is *lam*. The yogini that governs this chakra is Shakini, and at a physical level this chakra relates to the bones. It also governs the sense of smell, organs of reproduction, and the organs of action. Physically, it represents the ovaries/testes and the urino-genital system. At the mental level, it relates to the mind or *ahamkar* (ego /pride), and is associated with the *apana vayu* (downward moving energies) or prana. At an elemental level, it is a yellow square and its colour is deep red. At this level, the yogi's task is to get rid of his ego and personal identity through yoga so that the Kundalini can ascend upwards. (Frawley, p.164)

2. *Swadhisthana* Chakra or the Water Chakra

The *Swadhisthana* or the water chakra is also called "the sex centre" and it is located a little above the root chakra, near the space of the sex organs. This chakra is linked with the water energy and in Sanskrit it means, "The self-abode where the Kundalini resides". It consists of six petals and its mantras are *bam, bham, mam, yam, ram* and *lam*. It is the seat of the water elements of all matter and its main *bija* is *vam*. Kakini is the goddess presiding over this chakra,

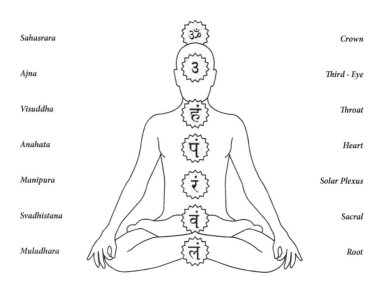

Sahasrara		*Crown*
Ajna		*Third - Eye*
Visuddha		*Throat*
Anahata		*Heart*
Manipura		*Solar Plexus*
Svadhistana		*Sacral*
Muladhara		*Root*

and on a physical plane she governs the fat or adipose tissue. It rules the sense organ of taste, the organs of tongue, and the main organs of elimination. It is also connected with the coccyx, urino-genital system, endocrine system and adrenals. On a mental plane, it is linked with the *manas* (emotional states) which operate through the senses and the prana *vayu* (vital energies) at this stage move inwards. Elementally this chakra is a white crescent and the colour of this energy centre is dark blue.

3. *Manipura* Chakra or the Fire Chakra

The *Manipura* Chakra or the Fire Chakra is located behind the navel. *Manipura* means city of gems, and this energy centre is like a radiant city of gems. This chakra consists of ten petals involving the mantras of *dam, dham, nam, tam, tham, dam, dham, nam, pam* and *pham*. The fire element resides here and its governing *bija* is *ram*. Lakini is the yogini governing this chakra, and physically, this energy centre is concerned with the tissues relating to muscle. It corresponds to the solar plexus and the functions of the digestive tracts mainly the liver and small intestine. Its counterpart is the pancreas. On a mental plane it's related with the *buddhi* (reasoning faculty) and the upward ascent of the *udana vayu*. Elementally, it's a downward pointing red triangle and its colour is dark blue.

4. *Anahata* or Heart Chakra/Air Chakra

Located along the heart region in the spine, *Anahata* chakra is also known as the Heart chakra or the Air chakra. In Sanskrit, *anahata* means "unstruck sound" and it is believed that it is from this space that the *nadas* (inner sounds or natural music) arise. It consists of twelve petals and its mantra is *kam, kham, gam, gham, nam, cam, cham, jam, jham, nam, tam,* and *tham*. The element of air and all gaseous matter is ruled by this chakra and its *bija* is *yam*. Rakini is the residing goddess and she relates to the tissues of blood. This chakra governs the sense organ of touch such as the skin and hands/grasping powers. It corresponds to the heart plexus and the circulatory system. It is linked with the thymus gland. Mentally, it corresponds to the *chitta* (conditioned consciousness) and it is the seat of the *vyana vayu* (vital energy that governs the pranas). Elementally, it is represented as a smoky six-pointed star, and its colour is deep red.

5. *Vishuddha* Chakra or the Throat Chakra

Located in the throat region, the *Vishuddha* chakra is also known as Throat Chakra or the Ether Chakra. In Sanskrit, *vishuddha* means "very pure". It consists of sixteen petals and its mantra consists *of am, am, im, im, um, um, rm, rm, lrm, lrm, em, aim, om, aum, am,* and *ah*. The element of ether or the etheric state of mind is ruled by this chakra and its *bija* is *ham*. Dakini is the residing goddess and she relates to the tissues of plasma. This chakra governs the organs of sound, the voice, the ears, and the mouth. It is where the individual soul resides and it is the source of all inspiration and the balancing of all *samana vayus* (vital forces). It is linked with the larynx and throat, and also the respiratory system. It corresponds to the thyroid gland. Elementally, it is represented as a dark blue circle and its colour is a smoky grey.

6. *Ajna* Chakra or the Third Eye Chakra

The *Ajna* or Third Eye Chakra is also known as the Mind Chakra. In Sanskrit, *ajna* means "command". This is the centre of command as all chakras are guided from here. The Third Eye chakra has two petals and consists of the mantras *ham* and *ksham*. It is the seat of the mind-space or mental ether and its seed syllable is *ksham* which means patience, peace and fortitude. Hakini governs this centre and relates to the nerve tissues. Physically, this chakra corresponds to the cerebellum and medulla oblongata and the involuntary nervous system and the pituitary gland. Mentally, it is the site of the cosmic or universal self and the place from which we have direct contact with the Divine Creator, who rules the universe. It is the seat of primary prana (life-force). Elementally, it is represented as a point and the colour of this chakra is silver-white.

7. *Sahasrara Padma* Chakra or the Crown Chakra

Located in the crown region, the *Sahasrara* chakra is the final and most important point for the Kundalini as this is where Shiva and Shakti unite in everlasting bliss.In Sanskrit, *Sahasrara* means "thousand petalled lotus". It is the seat of pure consciousness and it is symbolised by a crown. This is the seat of the atman (divine spirit) and its seed syllable is Om. The seat of consciousness and consciousness space, it is the seat of origin for all material ethers. Yakini governs this centre and it is related to the reproductive fluid in the seven tissues. Physically, it is associated with the cerebrum, controls the voluntary nervous system and functions through the pineal gland. Mentally, it is the seat of the *Parmatma* (supreme soul) and the true self that is the source or guide of all energies of the body, of the spirit and of life itself. Elementally, it is without any symbol or colour and its experience is indescribable and of pure bliss.

To sum it up, the Kundalini Shakti enjoys her union with Shiva in each chakra but the maximum bliss is experienced in *Sahasrara* (the crown).For instance, in the *Muladhara* there exist physical powers and here, the Kundalini enjoys physical fulfilment. Even knowledge and powers of experience are found here. While meditating on the *Svadhisthana*, sexual feelings are aroused and many a times the yogi can also hear divine sounds. In the *Manipura* are the powers of recreation and destruction. From here on, the Kundalini rises to subtle or higher forms of experience. In the *Anahata* (heart) rests the seat of desire, ego and compassion, and it is here that the soul must find freedom.

Next is the *Vishuddha* located in the throat which, with great concentration, can enable the yogi to become wise, peaceful, free from disease, creative and to even hear divine sounds. It is said that if the yogi confines his breath in this centre, in his wrath he could move the three worlds. He becomes invincible. When the Kundalini Shakti reaches the *Ajna* (the Third Eye), i.e., the mental plane, the yogi's psychic powers or sixth sense are enhanced. The yogi at this stage can also see a bright light like a lustrous flame, and becomes immortal.

From here he begins ascending to the highest stage of ecstasy and harmony in the *Sahasrara* (crown). When the *jeeva* or Shakti finally reaches this centre it is said to be at the *Satya-Lok*, i.e., the real world where there is a stream of nectar which originates from a blissful union. This is the fountainhead of all creation and here, the yogi enjoys *Parmataman*, i.e., where pain, birth, death and misery dissolve. It is bliss of the absolute kind or the place of *Brahmananda*.

From this high place, the Kundalini's Shakti returns again and again to the *Muladhara* despite efforts, and eventually rests for longer when she returns to the *Sahasrara* for her union with Shiva.

3.3 Hatha Yoga: The Gift of the Nath Siddhas to Mankind

Although there are many texts describing the body of knowledge of the Nath Siddhas vis-à-vis Hatha Yoga, the literature on their yogic practices and history is either obscure or insufficient to describe them in totality. However, the main texts of Hatha Yoga in Sanskrit are usually poetical texts, which are peppered with many legends and myths.

The wide-spread belief of this cult is that the practice of yoga can help a yogi attain occult power. All legends describe supernatural siddhis (gifts of yogic power) with incidents of magical feats and acts of sorcery. Indian religious history is surrounded with many occult beliefs and practices from the times of the *Atharva Veda,* and has many associations with the schools of Hinduism and Buddhism, among others. In the Pali literature there are many mentions of *iddhis* or *riddhis* (psychic powers) that can be attained through religious practices. There are also many references found to the *dasa-bala* (ten supernatural powers) and the *abhijna* (six supernatural faculties) that are easy for a Buddhist adept to attain.

Patanjali, who was mainly concerned with the psychological aspect of yoga, has mentioned different supernatural powers in the *Yoga Sutras* which are thought to be the eight powers of Lord Shiva himself. These can be attained through the concentration of the mind on different objects, or different centres of the body. These powers are: *Anima* (the power to become as small as an atom), *Mahima* (the power to become big), *Laghima* (the power to become excessively light at will), *Garima* (the power to become as heavy as one likes), *Prapti* (the power of obtaining everything at will), *Prakamya* (the power to obtain all objects of pleasure at will), *Isitva* (the power to obtain supremacy over everything), *Vasitva* (the power of subduing, fascinating or bewitching), and *Kamavasayitva* (the power to suppress desire, self-denial or mortification).

The yogi also becomes the master of prakriti (evolution) in nature and sees all processes as one, without any sequence. Such unusual powers are called siddhis. He also gains insight into the future, past lives, and can look into the minds of others. He can understand the cosmic laws and all the mysterious laws of the universe in general.

These supernatural powers are displayed in multiple ways throughout many legends and fables of the Naths. In one such fable, when Shiva blessed a princess and told her that she would get a husband like Gorakh, the yogi assumed the form of a six-month-old baby and expressed a desire to be breastfed by her. The princess got offended and insisted on having him as her husband, and since Gorakhnath could not accept this, he gave her his torn and rugged garments and told her to wash them in water and later drink that water. She then bore two sons as ordained by Shiva himself. There are many such instances which mirror the supernatural powers of Gorakhnath. It is said that once when the yogi was meditating under a bakula tree, Kanupa who was passing through the sky, and who couldn't discern which siddha it was, threw his magic sandals in the air to bind him and bring him down.

In the legend "Matsyendra's Fall" it has already been seen that Gorakhnath used various yogic powers to bring his guru back to his senses. Siddhas know everything through their dhyan (meditation) and *maha-jnana* (great mystic knowledge) and can do almost anything by a mere utterance, i.e., *Humkara* (sound of the mystic syllable "Hum"), or similar Tantric mystic syllables. During Mayanamati's initiation, Gorakhnath grew a full-fledged banyan tree from its seed within the span of just twelve *dandas* (less than five hours). Additionally, the people at her initiation were served with rice cooked from a single grain of paddy and even after every person had eaten to his heart's content, the food for one Siddha still remained in the earthen pot. Interestingly, the Naths hardly ever walked on earth—they moved in air and could cover the distance of more than a thousand miles within a second.

Goals of the Nath Siddhas

What was it that motivated the Nath Siddhas to lead a life of austerity? What were they truly seeking by leaving behind their homes, their lives and taking on a new identity? What was this force, this ultimate goal that drew them like a powerful magnet until the end? This goal in one word is—Shivahood.

The ultimate attainment for every Nath Siddha was attaining Shivahood within himself, discovering the immortal elixir of life, the endless nectar of divinity, and gaining complete freedom from the suffocating cycles of birth and death. The path to reach this blissful stage is Hatha Yoga.

Escaping death or living a life that is beyond the notion of death forms the essence of Hatha Yoga. As discussed earlier, it is different from the other forms of yoga such as Raja Yoga, Laya Yoga and Mantra Yoga. While these three schools are focussed on "the mental state" or "mind", Hatha Yoga is primarily concerned with the physiological practices or the physical states that help remove decay, disease and death.

Many ancient texts related to the "Doctrine of Immortality" or the *Amar Katha* of yoga, emphasise how yogis through their sadhana (dedication) could get rid of all diseases and rejuvenate their old physical bodies to become like a mountain—strong and changeless. A yogi is then said to be a deceiver and a victorious being over time, i.e., Kaal. Hence he is called *Mrityunjay* i.e., "He who is a victor over Kaal."

Liberation for the Nath Siddhas means immortality of the perfect body, i.e., Siddha *deha*, which eventually leads to immortality in a divine body, i.e., *divyadeha*. And it is this state of physical perfection in siddhi (yogic power) that the Naths aspire for. They seek liberation in a transmaterialised or transformed body that is perfect in every sense. This is an indestructible spiritual body that is free from *ashuddha*-maya (principles of defilement) and associated with *vishuddha*-maya (pure dynamic principles) that leads them to *para*-mukti (final state of spiritual evolution). Yogis who attain this perfect body through the path of *vishuddha*-maya are involved in benevolent activities of spiritual guidance and become gurus or spiritual preceptors who guide others seeking this path. Siddhas are thus considered to be the true preceptors in the world, and because they are free from all forms of *ashuddha*-maya, they are free from the world of suffering.

This state of the Siddhas that enables them to help other seekers and helps them to evolve too, is *para*-mukti which is similar in essence to the Bodhisattvahood of Buddhists. The Buddhist path, however, emphasises activity motivated by universal compassion which helps suffering beings rise to peace, helps the Boddhisattva achieve the ten stages of Bodhisattva-*bhumi*, and brings him closer to the final goal of Buddhahood.

The book *Yoga-vija* states that the human body is either *aparipakva* (unripe) i.e., not disciplined by yoga or *paripakva* (ripe) i.e., a body disciplined by yoga. A daily practice of yogic postures can transform the human body to become supramaterial, which has risen above sorrows and sufferings of ordinary people. Such a perfect yoga-*deha* is rare among the gods and is said to possess great powers and freedom from limitations, bondage and ills.

The yogi who possesses this body is omnipotent. He lives in the world according to his free will and since his body has already been strengthened by the fire of yoga, he does not fear the death of his physical body. Thus, while an ordinary person lives, the yogi is dead, and whereas the ordinary people die there is no (physical) death for the yogi. He is free of duties and liabilities and simultaneously active. He is thus liberated while he is alive and continues to live in his true body which is unbound by defilement. This deathless/timeless ripe body is essential for every Siddha and leads him to *para*-mukti.

All Siddhas are inherently Shaivites and attaining the state of Shivahood or Maheshvar is their ultimate goal. Thus, attaining *para*-mukti (immortality) is synonymous with attaining this divine state of Maheshvar. Hence, many sacred texts consider Matsyendra and Gorakhnath to be the same as Shiva/Maheshvar.

The ultimate power of all Nath Siddhas is their victory over death and decay that plague the lives of ordinary men. Even Yama, the God of Death, does not have any control over their lives. It is also said that whenever Yama forgets this fact and crosses his boundaries to seek the life of a Siddha, he is taught a very important lesson.

For instance, in the sacred text *Goraksha-vijaya,* or the *Min-chetan* it is said that when Gorakhnath found out about his Guru Matsyendranath's fall in Kadali, he picked his Siddha–*jholi* (magic bag), wore his robes, took his wooden sandals and staff, and entered the city of Yama. When he reached, he saw that Yama was seated on his throne and as soon as he saw him he got up and with great respect asked him the reason for his sudden appearance in the city of the dead. Gorakhnath then confronted him very sternly saying that once again he had meddled in the lives of the Siddhas. He even warned him that he would drag Yama to the creator of the universe, Brahma, and ensure that he learns the exact limits of his powers. Gorakhnath's anger was so great that he threatened the God of Death and told him that he would ruin his city. He stood up in anger and started chanting the *Humkara*, making Yama and his kingdom tremble in fear. Yama, in his helplessness, took all the official records and placed them before Gorakhnath who examined them and found the decree of his guru. Upset with his guru's name in the list of the dead, Gorakhnath left the city leaving behind a very stern warning. Even when Matsyendranath was dying in

Dharmapala or Yamaraja

Kadali and had forgotten all his knowledge (curse of Goddess Parvati) in the company of women, the only way of escaping that untimely death and being immortal was the path of yoga, which Gorakhnath reminded him of. It is important to remember that in all his texts, religious discourses and songs, Gorakhnath emphasised that yogic processes made the body perfect through *Kaya* Sadhana and it is this *Kaya* Siddhi that was the ultimate goal of each and every yogi. This ideal of an immortal life in the Siddha-*deha* is greatly influenced by the Orissa school of Vaishnavism of the sixteenth century. Though the essence of this school of thought was similar to the *Bhagavad Geeta*, the principles of Siddha-*deha* were present. There were many rules and instructions by which a yogi could make his body immutable. These practices were mainly of *Ulta Sadhana* (regressive process), the theory of the sun and the moon, and the ideal of *Sahaj*. The main foundation or practices of these means are briefly enumerated below.

Foundations of Hatha Yoga

Ulta Sadhana is the yoga practice adopted by the Nath Siddhas which involves an upward motion to the whole psychological and biological system which ordinarily possesses the tendency of flowing in a downward motion. This leads the Siddha to his original state where he is an immortal being in a perfect/divine body, and no longer fearful of decay or death.

As discussed earlier, Shiva is the aspect of perfect rest, and Shakti is the aspect of creativity, continuous change and the whirl of coming and going which leads to death and decay in the ordinary form. Thus, the crucial aim of every yogi is to help this Shakti rise upwards through physico-psychical efforts so that she can be united with Shiva, and be absorbed in him who is the "motionless immortal being". According to Hatha Yoga and Tantric practices, the area of the body below the navel is where the Shakti resides, and the area above the navel is where Shiva resides. Shakti's domain is also called *Pravritti* (activity in change), and Shiva's domain is called *Nivritti* (rest).

As described earlier, Shakti resides coiled three-and-a-half times like a serpent (nature of the world force) located in the lowest *nadi* of the spinal cord called *Muladhara*, and Shiva is located in the *Sahasrara* (thousand-petaled lotus) in the crown. It is within these two poles of *Sahasrara* and *Muladhara* that the entire creative process evolves. Yoga thus, continuously evolves raising this Shakti from the lowest region of the body to the highest region of Shiva, to transform an ordinary person into an immortal being. *Ulta* Sadhana is thus the slow and gradual process which brings a perfect control over the physical, biological and psychological process. All spiritual practices are based in its foundation as they raise us upwards and transform us into higher beings. In a popular Buddhist verse it has been beautifully written that "when an intense thirst is felt within for something higher, the mind becomes no more perturbed by desires and at that state one is said to be in an upward current". In the *Mahayana Sutra Lankara*, the *Pravritti* of the five senses is similar to *Ulta* Sadhana as it is the process of introversion of reversal, aiming to reach the state of *Nivritti*.

In the *Jnana Sagara* by Ali Raja, it is said that "the process of divine love is a reverse process, and he who does not know the secret of this reverse process cannot have eternal life". This quote can be connected to the forward and backward process, and the world is related to this inverted law. This way to perfection has been kept hidden like a secret by the Lord and only the *Asara* Panth, i.e., the unreal path, is visible to all of us creatures. It is because of this that after birth man takes the unreal path and stays absorbed in enjoyment and fulfilling desires. The reason for keeping this path hidden is that easy access to it would have made it cheap and reduced its true value, glory and power. This thought is in tandem with a saying from the *Upanishad* which says that "by giving the senses and outward tendency and turning them away from the inward truth the self created one (Brahma) gave proof of his jealousy, as it were ; it is because of this fact that man generally sees what is external, and not that which is within; but wise people there are, who, inquest of life eternal, have inverted their visual power and realised the self in and through a reverse process".

Control of urges is the most important function of yoga and is called "*Khemai*" in Bengali texts. It is said that this guard is placed in different centres of the body so that our inner wealth is not stolen away by *Kaal* (death/change). *Khemai* is often represented as a police officer who arrests evil tendencies and with his *ankusha* (hook) takes control of the undisciplined mind. The process of Hatha Yoga has listed important practices that purify and control our muscles, nerves and makes them stronger over time. These processes are Asanas (postures), *Dhauti* (cleansing of body tracts), Mudra (symbolic or ritual gesture), Pranayam (breathing) and *Bandha* (different kinds of arrest). Along with this, attaining full control over the mind is emphasised. Pranayam helps us hold the vital air which is the vehicle of the mind, and practising it helps us control the mind eventually. It is for this reason that the Nath Siddhas and all yogis in general, emphasise controlling the *vayu*, i.e., the vital air or wind of our breath.

The purifying processes of yoga (fire of yoga) burn away the ordinary and decaying body to purify and rejuvenate it into a divine body with great immunity. This is a slow and gradual process and to fully understand the secret of *Kaya* Sadhana we have to grasp the "Theory of the sun and the moon". In many Tantric and yogic literatures, the unification of the sun and moon is considered important. The sun refers to the right nerve and the moon refers to the left nerve, and their union is the union of two currents of the prana vayu and *apana* vayu, i.e., inhalation and exhalation.

In the book *Siddha Siddhanta Paddhati* related to Gorakhnath's teachings, it is mentioned that the physical body depends on five factors, i.e., karma (activity), kama (desire), Chandra (the moon), Surya (the sun) and Agni (fire). Karma and Kama are related to conditions of the visible body whereas the essence of which every human body is made is Chandra, Surya and Agni. Since Surya and Agni are similar in nature, the main elements are the sun and the moon. The moon is represented by the element of soma or rasa (the quintessence in the form of the juice). And hence, the body is said to be the result of Agni and soma. Fire is the *Bhokta* (eater) while rasa as soma is the *Upabhogya* (food). The whole creation depends on the balance and proportion of the consumed and the consumer.

Physically speaking, Agni is taken to represent the seat of the father (semen), and soma is taken to represent the ovum of the mother. In yogic texts, generally the sun is the element of change and destruction, whereasthe moon is the element of creation and preservation. The moon as the essence of immortality and non-change is present in the region of Shiva whereas the sun, as the essence of change and destruction, is present in the region of Shakti. The sun is *Kalagni* (the fire of destruction), whereas the moon is amrit (the nectar that grants immortality). The sun is located in the lower chakra that is the *Muladhara*, facing upwards, whereas the moon is located just below the *Sahasrara* (the thousand-petaled lotus). It is also believed that *Bindu* which is the main essence of the body is of two types, i.e., the red Bindu called "Lohita Bindu" and the yellowish white Bindu, called "Pandura Bindu". The red Bindu represents the *Maha-rajas* (ovum) whereas the yellowish white Bindu represents *Sukra* (semen). Since the ovum is contained in the sun, in the navel, it is the *Rajas* or Shakti, and since the semen is contained in the moon, in the upper region, it is the *Sukra* or Shiva.

The sun as *Kalagni* is also called "The Dire One" which contrasts to Shiva "The Benevolent One". In the *Kula Jnana Nirnaya*, Rudra in the form of *Kalagni* is connected with Shakti seated in the *Muladhara* within the mouth of the *Vadava*. In this text it is also mentioned that there are seven lower regions of this universe called *Patala*, and seven upper regions called *Swarga*. The process of creation can continue smoothly as long as *Kalagni* resides in the lower regions because if it rises upwards dissolution will begin.

According to Buddhist Tantra, the sun is in the *Nirmanakaya*, i.e., the plexus of the body of transformation, whereas the moon is the Bodhichitta in the Usnisa-Kamla. This fire force that resides in the navel is described as the Goddess Chandali.

The main sadhana of yogis practising Hatha Yoga depends upon combining the sun and moon after gaining a complete mastery over them. In practical yoga it is seen as returning to the original form of rest as Shakti awakens to rise and unite with Shiva in the crown. The sun and the moon elements also represent the union of the male and female energies and their combined substance is sucked by the yogi through some secret yogic processors. Even the process of purifying and controlling the nerves during pranayam involves the play between the sun and the moon.

Attaining the immortal body is also connected with the balancing of the sun and moon energies. The yogi has to avoid being stuck in any of the extremes of destruction (sun and moon) and for creation, has to adopt a principle of eternal conservation. This is when the yogi has to co-mingle the sun and the moon. In many of his songs, Kabir has spoken of *Banka nala* (the curved duct) which lies below the *Sahasrara* chakra upto the hollow in the palatal region known as *Sankhini*. It is through this *Banka nala* that the *maharasa* or the somarasa passes. The *Goraksha-vijaya* describes Sankhini as "The serpent with mouths at both ends". This mouth of the Sankhini from which the amrit (nectar) pours down from the moon is called the *Dasam Dwar* (the tenth door) which is the most important.

It is through this tenth door that the nectar of immortality is stored but ordinary people are unaware of this secret. Usually, this nectar trickles down and falls in the fire of the sun and is eventually eaten up or dried up by the sun. The body thus becomes a victim of *Kalagni* (fire of time) and dies. If this tenth door is well guarded and the flow of nectar is controlled, then the person can become immortal and even deceive *Kaal* (time). This nectar or *maharasa* is the greatest wealth in every person and if it can be saved from being consumed by the sun, and is instead consumed by the yogi himself, then he will definitely become immortal.

This amrit can be protected or saved in many ways. These processes are described in Hatha Yoga and Tantric books in great detail. One of these processes is the *Khechari* Mudra in which the tongue has to be turned backwards into the hollow above so as to reach the mouth of the *Raja-Danta* or the *Sankhini* (tenth door) and concentrating on the sight between the eyebrows. The tongue which is turned backwards shuts up the tenth door and protects the nectar to be later drunk by the yogi himself. This yogic process is so powerful that it has the capacity of controlling all types of secretion. It is also said that if a yogi continuously practices *Khechari*, his *Bindu* (seeds) will remain protected even if he is intimately embraced by a woman. The practice of mudras and the *bandhas* involved in the drinking of the nectar is the surest way to eternal life. Even in Kundalani Yoga, raising the Shakti to the *Sahasrara* (crown) is essential to the flow of nectar, and it is said that Shakti herself is the drinker of this nectar.

The nectar trickling from the moon is also referred to as "*amara varuni*" (the wine of the immortals) and it is said that the greatest of gods have become immortal by drinking this. Drinking wine and eating meat are part of a Tantric sadhak's lifestyle and are explained by the Nath Siddhas as the drinking of nectar from the moon and turning the tongue backwards in the hollow above.

Another theory compares the sun and the moon to a woman and man. It is even said that the moon must be saved from the destructive sun. In the grosser sense, man must be saved from the clutches of women who have been described as "tigresses" in Nath Literature. It is because of their charms and sex appeal that man loses his focus and in due course, loses his vital energy. Since the Nath Siddhas are strictly celibate, women are regarded as the greatest danger in their path to yoga. Once again, a reference has to be made to Matsyendranath's fall in Kadali where Gorakhnath rescued him from the temptations and sexual desires that ordinary men are caught in. In many poems, Gorakhnath has mysteriously said, "The breath of women dries up the body and youth vanishes day-by-day. Foolish are the people who understand nothing and make pets of tigresses in every house; in the day the tigress becomes the world-enchantress and at night she dries up the whole body. The milk is stolen and the tigress boils it, and the cat (death) is sitting by; the essence of milk is thrown down on the ground and only the vacant vessel remains in the sky." It is thus clear that Gorakhnath, and the Nath Siddhas in general, had an uncompromising attitude towards women and they were often termed as thieves, dacoits, pirates, thirsty tigresses and hypocritical cats. Thus, the sadhana of the yogis consists of saving the *maha-rasa* from any kind of discharge and he who has been able to give an upward flow to this fluid is no longer just a man, but is transformed into a god.

3.4 Nagarjun and the Buddha

The most esteemed Buddhist philosopher, Nagarjun, has no equal. His teachings of the "Prajnaparamita Sutra" (wisdom sutras or sermons regarding the perfection of wisdom) are said to be an account of his life. A few Tibetan sources claim that he had to leave his home as a child because his parents were devastated after an astrologer's prediction that he would die as a seven-year-old. However, it is said that he escaped this fate after he entered the Buddhist Order and practised the *Aparimitayurdharani* in accordance with the teachings of Rahulabhadra, also known as Saraha, at Nalanda. However, Kumarajiva, a Buddhist monk who studied his teachings in detail, says that Nagarjun was overcome by lust and passion in his early days and seduced women in the royal court using invisibility and at one such time he had even escaped death at the hands of the guards. This awakened in him the realisation that the origin of suffering is passion. He then entered the Buddhist Order and studied the sacred texts available to him and even wandered off in search of more knowledge, when he was not satisfied with the sources available to him.

His life's accounts thus came to be recorded in the *Prajnaparamita Sutras*, i.e., Kumarajiva's *Vaipulya Sutras* which he obtained from a Naga. These quenched his thirst for knowledge hence he devoted himself to the teachings of the Buddha to teach and propagate his profound truths. Many Tibetan books also share accounts of Nagarjun's deep compassion and care for the entire community at Nalanda.

Nagarjun's work and contribution to Indian alchemy, and his connection with it, is deeply intriguing. There are many historical figures with the same name, but it is difficult to trace his exact timeline in India, as well as the fields he mastered. "Nagarjun the Madhyamika Philosopher", "The Tantric Buddhist Commentator and Author", "The Hindu Tantric Sorcerer", "The Nath Siddha", "The Buddhist Alchemist" and "The Southern Hindu Alchemist" are some of his famous names. While he is called "Faust of Buddhism" by Albert Grunwedel, there is no denying that he was a prominent Buddhist figure based on the vast knowledgeable treasures of religious texts available even today.

Nagarjun is also deeply associated with the nagas (snakes) and it is said that he obtained the *Prajnaparamita Sutras* (Perfection of Wisdom texts) from them. Kumarajiva explains how the Mahanaga (naga chief) led him into the sea and opened the Saptaranakosa (Treasury of the Seven Jewels). Nagarjun picked the *Vaipulya* (Mahayana) *Sutras* for reading and after doing so, the meanings penetrated deeply into his mind. He then told the Mahanaga that what he had read was ten times greater than what he had read at Jambudvipa and he brought back a boxful of books with him. According to Tibetan sources, among the texts were 100,000 gathas of the *Prajnaparamita Sutras* which is said to often overshadow the Buddhist philosophies even today.

These sutras convey the teachings that in the ultimate truth, there are no divisions between the conditioned and the unconditioned, and the wisdom lies in realising this and in not clinging to the determinate. *Adaya* Dharma (undivided being) and *Anupalambha* Yoga (the skillfullness of non-clinging) are the essence of the *Prajnaparamita Sutras* and shunyata is the most important means of conveying their basic teachings in all aspects. Perfect wisdom and universal compassion are emphasised as the two integral courses of every life.

Nagarjun's Basic Buddhist Concepts

1. **Non-exclusive understanding as the root of the skillfullness of non-clinging**

   Nagarjun emphasised on *anupalambha* (non-contentiousness) which, according to him, was at the heart of Buddha's teachings. However, Buddha's followers were making the Enlightened One the object of their *upalambha* (contention) and *graham* (clinging), thus missing out on the richness present in his teachings and the fact that he taught the same truth differently to different people. The non-exclusive understanding is of being able to see the different sides of the same truth without clinging to any of them, which is what the root of Buddha's skilfulness is. However, his disciples set aside this basic truth before discovering its real meaning.

2. **The tendency to seize is the root of conflict and suffering**

   According to Nagarjun, this human tendency to cling and to seize has its basis in false imagination, not in right understanding, and hence it is the root of suffering, *anta* (dead-ends), and conflict in understanding. We often see reality as separate and not in its dynamic entirety or relatedness which encompasses the richness of all experience, and of life itself. This misapplied drive for the relative is called misplaced absoluteness. We thus can become confined to the level of fragmentaries and, in ignorance, cling to everything we come across as a safe refuge which limits our experience, leading to many frustrations and disappointments. In right understanding the indeterminate is revealed to be distinct and separate from the determinate.

This again must not be viewed as an absolute separateness. The determinate is thus not a self-being but only related to all other determinate entities, and is dependent on the indeterminate. Thus, according to Nagarjun, "While the indeterminate reality is the ground of the determinate entities, it is only the ultimate nature of the latter themselves and not another entity apart from them."

3. **The ultimate nature of man is the undivided being**
Man as an individual is related to the rest of the world. However, in his ultimate nature, he is the indeterminate, unconditioned reality—the undivided being. The sense of voidness or devoidness, i.e. shunyata, lies in the real nature of one's self according to Nagarjun. One's own imagination can limit one's ultimate nature, and a rise in awareness from the finite to the ultimate level can truly satiate the thirst in man. The way to realisation, according to Nagarjun, lies in preparing one's awakening to the absurdities and self-contradictions in one's own false imagination. His criticism lays bare these absurdities to reveal the conditioned-ness or shunyata of the conditioned, and also the truth that conditioned-ness of the conditioned, is not unconditioned, i.e., shunyata-shunyata.

4. *Prajna* **as the principle of comprehension is the Middle Way**
Every standpoint has a unique nature and value and yet is not confined to any one point of view. This is a comprehensive understanding that encompasses several standpoints at the same level as well as different levels of understanding. This comprehensive understanding forms the basis of the Middle Way by *Prajna* (intellect). Determinate entities as well as specific concepts are accepted and taken to be expressions of the real in man, and are also necessary for the complete realisation of the ultimate reality.
Nagarjun says, "The ultimate truth cannot be taught, except in the context of the mundane truth, and unless the ultimate truth is comprehended, nirvana cannot be realised."
The self conscious man, thus, expresses his standpoints through thoughts and actions to reflect the deepest in him, which is the sense of the real.

5. **To elucidate the sense of the real is the mission of the** *Madhyamika*

Every individual has within him the timeless truth, the eternal light and the self-consciousness which has to be "discovered" and not just realised. By active choice, each individual can discover it as the foundation of his very being. The *Madhyamika* (traveller on the Middle Way), has sought to lay bare the innermost core of this individual. The individual has no exclusive position of his own, rejects views to formulate his own, does not cling to specific views or concepts, and uses them to help others. This sense of non-exclusiveness makes this individual very objective and enables him to stay in rapport with all systems and see the truth in every position. As the *Madhyamika* says, "Non-exclusiveness (shunyata) is the very nature of wisdom (*prajna*)."

Basic Teachings of the Buddha

1. **Conditioned Origination and the Middle Way**

Considered synonyms, "Conditioned Origination" and "the Middle Way" are two important concepts. Conditioned Origination emphasises the import of relativity in regard to the events or entities that we encounter in mundane existence, whereas, the Middle Way stresses on the relativity regarding the views of the mundane nature of things.

2. **The Four Noble Truths**

These truths constitute the Buddha's main teachings and his preaching of the "Wheel of Dharma" and are the foundation of Buddhism. The cause of suffering is craving or desire which is rooted in ignorance. Thus one has to destroy the root of suffering to completely extinguish suffering and this is the truth of "Conditioned Origination" which forms the heart of the dharma (dhamma).

"He who sees the dhamma sees the conditioned origination and he who sees the conditioned origination sees the dhamma."

3. **The Middle Way**

Right View is the main element of the Eight-fold Noble Way and it consists in keeping away from extremes. These extremes also apply to correct understanding, living a life of moderation and in case of morals, these extremes apply to sensualism and asceticism. With regard to right understanding, this applies to the distinction of "is" and "is not". The Buddha reveals that *"things here are neither absolutely being nor absolutely non-being, but are arising and perishing, forming a continuity of becoming."*

4. **The Buddha's silence as the Revealer of Truth**
Individuals seeking clarity in the mundane nature often make the mistake of eternalism and annihilationism. A fable explains how the Buddha often revealed answers and truths in his silence. Once, when Vacchagotta (the wandering ascetic) asked Buddha whether there is Self, Buddha just kept silent.He then asked him whether there was no Self, but Buddha again remained silent. After Vacchagotta left, Ananda (disciple and chief attendant of the Enlightened One) asked him why he did not answer the question. To this Buddha replied that if he had answered that there is a Self, he would have expressed the eternalism view, and if he had said there is no Self, he would have expressed the annihilationism view. Also, the question asked by Vacchagotta was asked with a clinging mind and hence, was rooted in the "*is*" and "*is not*" which is a concept the Buddha did not support or encourage.

The "fourteen unanswered questions" which were never answered by the Enlightened One and kept aside, also follow the pattern of eternalism and annihiliationism and are about the mundane nature of things. These are also briefly discussed in the *Udana* where Buddha describes them as partial views which ignorant beings cling to and view as a whole, which again gives rise to quarrels. An example which explains this is the story of the six blind men and the elephant where all of them quarrelled over what the elephant really looked like. They all thought of him differently—as a pot, a winnowing fan and so on. Similarly, teachers who belong to different sects don't know what the goal is and what it is not, and hence they "wrangle, quarrel and dispute" as they have only partial and fragmented views of things and not a comprehensive understanding.

Pratityasamutpada (the Middle Way) is to view things the way they are in their totality, and to be able to see them differently from different standpoints and also to realise that these determinations are not absolute. This way one can realise the relativity of specific views and of determinate entities, which is the central philosophy of Nagarjun. The Middle Way is also the path which Buddha chose to answer questions, and in this regard he can be compared to the sun which illumines all things equally. He does not make the non-existent existent, or the existent non-existent. He always speaks the truth, and by the light of his wisdom illumines all things.

The Middle Way: The Non-exclusive Way

The *Prajnaparamita Shastra* is compared to *akasha* (space) as the principle of accommodation as it has room for everything and is all comprehensive. *Prajna* as the sense of the unconditioned is the basis of all conditioned specific views however, by itself it is not any specific view. This non-exclusive understanding is the all-comprehensive *prajna* which is similar to the Middle Way that is above extremes and beyond exclusiveness, revealing the mundane nature of things.

"*Prajnaparamita* is non-clinging (*anupalambha*) and cannot be seized either as existent or non-existent, either as permanent or as impermanent, either as unreal or as real. This is *prajnaparamita*. It is not (any specific entity) comprised in the (classifications), *skandha*s, *ayanata*s or *dhatu*s; it is not anything composite or incomposite; not any dharma nor adharma; it is neither seizing nor abandoning, neither arising or perishing; it is beyond the four *koti*s of "is" and "is not"; getting at it one does not find in it anything that can be clung to, being comparable in this regard with the flame that cannot be touched from any of the four sides. *Prajnaparamita* is also completely beyond the possibility of clinging, and anyone who would attempt to cling to it would be burnt by (his own) fire of perversion." (I39c) It is indestructible, undeniable, it is the highest truth, and there is nothing beyond it.

Often, individuals take their own stand and believe their own viewpoints to be true hence contentions arise. *Prapancha* is the root of contentions and it is born out of wrong notions. The Buddha also insists on individuals taking a firm stand on dharma and not on any particular individual, to emphasise on the meaning rather than the words, on *jnana* not *vijnana*, and to reflect on sutras of direct meaning, not on those with indirect meanings.

It is also important to remember that the Buddha's dharma abandons all passion, wrong views and all self-pride. An individual has to put an end to all of these and not cling to anything. (63c) According to Buddha, an individual can gain freedom by abandoning the false sense of self which is the root cause of the tendency to cling. Thus, *Bodhi* (knowledge) can be realised when one lets go of the notion of "I" and "mine" and does not cling or get attached to the diverse nature of things. Thus, even words have a pure nature, and so do concepts. The way we use them, and the way we perceive them makes all the difference. Thus, the Middle Way has to be adopted where we can see the right view as well as the wrong view, with objectivity.

Ignorance and Knowledge

According to the Buddha, ignorance is a power that creates objects of experience but is not an ultimate entity. It is neither existing nor not existing; it is "the root of all things as the common people conceive them". The Shastra observes that in their ultimate nature, both ignorance and knowledge are the same and "there is no difference in the ultimate truth between the world of the determinate and nirvana, the unconditioned reality". Streams of different rivers have different colours and tastes, but after entering the mighty ocean, they have one name, one colour and one taste. Similarly, stupidity/ignorance and knowledge enter *prajnaparamita,* blend and become of one essence. Even internal and external things enter *prajnaparamita*; they blend and share the single essence. This is because, *prajnaparamita* is naturally completely pure.

The real nature of stupidity and ignorance is also *prajna* and clinging to this *prajna* again would be stupidity. When seekers enter the realm of the Buddha, they are aware of the distinctions between stupidity and wisdom. Gradually, as their penetration deepens, there is no difference between the two. This shows that ignorance is present but it is not ultimate. So the sutra says, "(in its ultimate nature) ignorance is purity itself; and so even the *samskaras* (the products of ignorance) are (in their ultimate nature) purity itself."

The Shastra further explains that *prajna* as knowledge can be distinguished into the eternal (substantial) and functional (impermanent/temporary). The functional *prajna* can end the darkness of ignorance and fetch the true or eternal *prajna*. Whereas in the eternal *prajna*, even the distinction of ignorance and knowledge cannot be found. The eternal *prajna* thus has been called "eternal light in the heart of man", i.e., the permanent and ultimate principle of knowledge. Even nirvana cannot claim its absoluteness, it cannot be cancelled by the *prajnaparamita*, and transcends all things unimpeded. Therefore, if there is anything that excels nirvana, it is the power of wisdom as *prajnaparamita* itself remains undenied.

In contrast, the functional *prajna* is just an act of knowing, which consists of analysis, criticism, and comprehension. These are modes of the power of *prajna* and are based in the permanent principle of knowledge.

The Five Eyes of the *Prajnaparamita* Sutras

The five eyes of the *Prajnaparamita* sutras are simply the different levels of comprehension and understanding. Metaphorically, they represent the different degrees of removal of dirt from the mirror of the mind which enables it to reflect the true nature of itself, as well as of all things. The eyes yield views and these differ in the quality and depth of illumination. They are however, covered in the dust of limitations such as ignorance and passion and therefore, are unclean.

It is through the eyes that we see, view, judge and perceive the nature of things. As powers of sight, eyes are naturally very pure although they differ in the way in which they conceive and comprehend. They can persist in limited levels, or see the ultimate and the unconditioned.

The Eyes of the Flesh and the Deva Eye: These see only partially and by confining oneself to them, one could commit an error. All eyes and all kinds of sight have their origin in *prajna* and thus, even the sutra says, "All the five eyes of the Buddha arise from *Prajnaparamita*" (467C), further adding that "the Bodhisattva while cultivating *prajnaparamita* purifies his five eyes". (347a)

The physical eyes only perceive the objects of ordinary experience whereas, after the purification, the Boddhisattva can see "all the three thousand great worlds". Further, while the physical eyes become pure through one's moral deeds, the deva eyes become pure through dhyan (meditation) and samadhi (deep contemplation), and by leading a moral life.

The Eye of Wisdom: This is free from the errors which the eyes of flesh and deva eyes could commit, and all three can become pure through acts of merit, i.e., through love and compassion. The object of the eye of wisdom is nirvana, the true nature of things, and unconditioned dharma. The eye of wisdom can perceive the highest truth, non-duality of things and the middle path of all things. It abandons extremes, and this wisdom eye can put an end to all elements of perversion and ignorance. People often lose this eye of wisdom owing to doubts, ignorance, perversion, repentance, and false notions. However, when they realise the *prajna*, the eye of wisdom becomes clear once again.

The Eye of Dharma: This is concerned with the myriad ways in which people's minds function. This eye is inspired by its oath to save all beings and by the emotion of universal love and compassion. It also intensifies the knowledge of the individual to seek and aspire towards the sense of the real, to give up clinging to the determinate, to walk forward with insight and compassion, and to help others realise the true nature of things. Thus, "this knowledge of definite ways suited to specific individuals (*marganvayajnana*) enables the Boddhisattva to help everyone according to one's need that is called the eye of the dharma."

The Eye of the Buddha: This is the highest of the eyes; all other eyes have limited powers of sight. This eye is the one which is not exclusive or confined to any of the perceptions, yet comprehends everything in totality as an integrated form, and it is in this eye that the other eyes find their consummation.

It is described thus:

"When the Bodhisattva becomes the Buddha, (all other four eyes, viz.) the eyes of flesh, the deva eye, the eye of wisdom, and the eye of dharma (enter the Buddha eye where they) lose their original names and are called only the eye of the Buddha. This is like the four great rivers of Jambudvipa (India), losing their names when they enter the great ocean."(348b)

The Eye of the Buddha is the eye that is devoid of passion and is full of compassion for all beings, everywhere. Here there is no error, no perversion; no *klesha* . . . everything is pure.

Nagarjun shaped the Buddhist philosophical path greatly through the teachings of his Shastra. He also further developed the Mahayana philosophy of shunyata (emptiness) and proved that voidness or emptiness is at the core of everything in a small text called *Madhyamikakarika*. He also propagated the middle way to understand the true nature of things in totality. Tantrayana or the Buddhist School of Tantra emerged from the Mahayana and is deeply rooted in its foundation and philosophies. However, a Tantric teacher, active practices and certain disciplines have to be followed by the individual seeking nirvana.

3.5 Buddhist Tantra: A Boon to Pious Practices

What is Tantra?

Tantra essentially means scriptures or texts which contain knowledge about yogic practices, magical rites, mantras, and philosophy, for gaining spiritual illumination. Along with wise teachings, these contain liberations and tips for dealing with the ordinary goals of life. Traditional Tantric texts consist of knowledge related to the creations of the universe, destruction of the universe, worship of the Divine in various forms, attainment of the goals of life, and spiritual powers and ways of meditation to realise the ultimate truth. From youth to old age, rituals for charity, worship, yoga practices to sacraments, the Tantric knowledge runs the gamut of all these stages, and more. Tantra emphasises techniques or energetic approaches which include mantras, rituals and meditations that take us beyond techniques. It has a universal approach and uses all that is available, rejecting nothing. It honours the goddess in a very special way and her worship is vital for all seekers.

Tantra does not separate different areas of human knowledge. Instead, it brings them all together harmoniously to enhance life emotionally, mentally, intellectually and spiritually. It is thus like a tree of life itself and not limited to, or defined by, any single branch. Tantra seeks to understand dharma (the unifying law) which organises the diverse phenomena into maya (relative existence or illusion). It uses this knowledge to promote the evolution of individual consciousness. According to the *Kashika Vritti*, "Tantra is that knowledge which expands mind, body and consciousness."

Tantra's main goal is to expand our awareness in all our conscious states—while sleeping, while awake or while dreaming. For this, it adopts "re-programming" and "de-programming" of our human computer. From the time we are born, we have a primary programming that is influenced by heredity and the environment.

Time, situations, experiences and lessons, bring us to a point where we want to re-invent and re-write our program. Tantra becomes a path for this. It helps us break away from these limitations born out of ignorance, intolerance and attachment to selfish natures, by helping us refine our thoughts and feelings. Eventually, we learn to create peace, harmony and order within life and ourselves. This consciousness frees us from all suffocating limitations.

Tantra has practical solutions to re-program the brain stem, R-complex, and cerebral cortex. These are purification, pranayam, visualisation, mantra japa and Kundalini Yoga. A set of six practices can also help in finding total awareness. These are:

1) **Sama**: Subduing passions and attaining mental quietude.
2) **Dama**: Subjugating the five sense organs: ears (hearing), eyes (sight), tongue (taste), skin (touch) and nose (smell). Subjugating five organs of action—hands (grasping), feet (loco\motion), mouth (speech), genitals (generation) and anus (evacuation). Subjugating four internal organs—*chitta* (memory), *buddhi* (understanding), *manas* (cognition) and *ahamkara* (egoity).
3) **Uparati**: Completely halting the senses of perceiving and acting.
4) **Titiksha**: Inculcating patience and endurance. This means the power to be able to endure without any discomfort, extremes of heat and cold, joy and sorrow, honour and abuse, loss and gain and all other opposites.
5) **Samadhan**: Continuously concentrating the mind.
6) **Shraddha**: Having true faith, beliefs, devotion and conviction.

The yogi must also have six other attributes to excel in Tantra. These are: *Daksha* (intelligence); *Jitendriya* (control over the senses); *Shuchi* (purity); *Astik* (belief in truth defined as *Vidya* (knowledge), Veda (body of knowledge) and strong belief in God; *Sarva Hinsa Vinirmukta* (abstaining from all kinds of violence); and *Sarva Prani Hitrata* (concern for universal welfare).

The above attributes give a yogi control over the animal nature. The practices of *Sama* and *Dama* aid in coordinating the upper and lower brain during the states of consciousness and eventually lead the yogi to a state of extended consciousness, i.e., *turiya*.

In the twenty-first century Tantra has a universal quality that is greatly appealing to the modern mind which is curious, creative, intellectually stimulating and physically rejuvenating. However, it is one of the most misunderstood parts of yogic practice. For the people in the West, Tantra means sex, and this path is seen as one which involves many special sexual positions, powers and rituals, that can lead a person to enlightenment. There are some Tantric teachings which mention sexual practices, but they are not the main focus of Tantric Yoga. This again cannot be confused with the knowledge of *Kama Sutra* which is one of the most renowned Hindu manuals of sexual love.

Tantric Yoga like other pure yogic traditions is also composed of meditations, mantras and mudras. Many pious activities like breathing, eating and sleeping are also included in this path. It is an energetic approach to the spiritual path of enlightenment which also contains a devotional aspect that worships gods and goddesses and bestows great respect on their teachings. It is also essential to note that Tantric art appears to be erotic and sensuous, but this is just a depiction of the higher forces of consciousness that can be used to transform man's most primal instincts of sexuality. It does not glorify sex but simply accepts its power and sees the divinity in it. Tantra is also non-sexual in nature, and this can be seen through the examples of great teachers like Shankara, Ramakrishna and Nityananda who remained celibate all through their life but were masters of life-transforming mantras and energetic yoga practices. In contrast, there is another sexual school that emphasises transmuting sexual energy. This is because sex is the most basic force of our existence. Hence, we find two distinctive approaches. The first approach focuses on giving up all sexual activities, and the second propagates the "householder tradition" in which sex is practised in moderation.

The first approach is more direct in nature and can be very stressful and difficult for seekers in the modern world, especially the West as there is no cultural tradition to support it. It is important to note that yoga never encourages repression of feelings; instead it encourages a human being to inculcate self-discipline when faced with forces of desire. Over time, the person starts to look beyond those basic desires and tries to look for fulfilment in divine activities. This paves the way for true happiness that does not come from any outside person, material thing, identity, activity or sex, but comes from our own pure consciousness. The second approach of the householder tradition involves sexual yoga practices only with the aim to continue the lineage of the family, and indirectly inculcates the values of sexual purity and loyalty to one's partner. Interestingly, many Vedic rishis and yogis were married, and had children. This tradition, thus, believes that a married human being can fulfil all his family and social duties and yet achieve liberation.

Yoga in general does not tag sexual energy or its expression as bad, sinful or evil. It does not even see it as a shameful or disgusting expression. The reason why celibacy is recommended is because that energy can be channelled to other higher levels such as the intellect and the spirit. It is also important to remember that without the right meditations this unused energy of a celibate can become stagnant and cause various physical and emotional problems. The person might not have the power needed to concentrate and focus on higher meditative states.

Tantra: Body, Emotions, Spirituality

According to Tantra, the body should be respected as a temple that undergoes divine activity. According to this path, our small psycho-physical form is a reflection of the workings of the entire universe. It is for this reason that Tantra Yoga is a science of body spirituality, as it sees the body or the physical form as a mystic symbol. However, attachment to the body and its identity is not encouraged. An example of this is that ordinary people who consider their body their identity usually misuse and abuse themselves and their organs by over-indulging in pleasures that do not give them any contentment or fulfilment.

Our body stays with us till our final journey, so taking care of it and maintaining it through yoga and meditation is absolutely important. It is nature's vehicle that has been gifted to our soul to experience spiritual growth and understand the universe. Using it the right way can help us gain many cosmic powers that we can carry forward to our next life or to just dissolve into the Brahman. Most people do not understand that our body is not our true self as it constantly suffers, gets diseases, and ages with time. It cannot even give us long lasting happiness but can only help us learn many lessons. It is thus, just an instrument of experience. Using it with intelligence and care can help us develop unmatched higher awareness and it is in this sense that Tantra regards the body as a sacred vehicle through which we can discover our divine spirit.

Expressing emotions is another trend that has plagued the world. In many psychological circles it is encouraged to express feelings to gain relief or as a catharsis from traumas. However, Tantra considers emotions as important tools for spiritual growth and transformation. It does not encourage a person to express as it can cause attachment to feelings and one's attachment to the whole world at large. In fact, according to Tantra, emotions are trapped energy that can be released like a wave that blends with the sea of awareness. This happens when individuals recognise that their personal feelings are cosmic energies that are being limited and shattered by attachments. The gods and goddesses that are worshipped by Tantra in all their peaceful and angry forms, help us reconnect to the true meaning of the cosmic emotion as a natural force of nature. Individuals thus begin to see the Divine message or the play of consciousness which is the basis of their emotions. Soon, these emotions become a healthy way of relating to and realising the Divine that lives within each of us.

Tantra thus helps us transmute human emotions into divine energies by awakening devotion within us. Tantric Yoga also helps us kill our ego which is the most negative of all emotions. It does not tell us to suppress anything but, instead, helps us to naturally let go of all these suffocating attachments and negative dependencies that block our path.

The use of mind-altering drugs is often associated with Tantra. Consuming these intoxicants is found in Tantra, but this is not an important characteristic and it is not encouraged by most teachers. These drugs do alter our state of mind and take us out of ordinary consciousness, but their scope is very limited and can have dangerous side-effects. Instead, the bliss a person can experience through mantra and meditation is much more powerful and, alongside, beneficial to health and longevity of life.

Tantric gurus, especially in India, have had a very disreputable image owing to their explicit behaviour and actions, which in turn has often led people and society at large to question the true moral essence of Tantra. This ugly reputation or misconceived notion people have of Tantra is owing to the fact that some spiritual practitioners have indulged in excesses of magical practices, sex and the use of intoxicants to either gain pleasure, harm others, or take control and gain power over other beings. These are highly impure and incorrect methods that are in no way propagated by the religion. It is for this reason that many true spiritual practitioners practicing the Tantric way of life do not use the word "Tantric" to describe their work but instead choose to describe it as vedic or yogic, or vedantic school. For instance, Swami Vivekananda who brought yoga and Vedanta to the West a century ago was very careful about introducing these concepts to the audience.

As a science and as a way of knowledge for understanding the outer world and inner psyche, Tantra shares close connections with other Indian sciences viz. Ayurveda (Vedic medicine) and astrology (*jyotish vidya*). Tantra is also connected with alchemical traditions spread throughout the medieval world in countries like the Middle East, Europe, India and China. In fact, many scholars consider Tantra as a revival of old alchemical approaches that form the basis of European mysticism, and the global gamut of spiritual alchemy at large. This alchemical tradition exists in Ayurveda, which makes use of special preparations of sulphur, mercury, mica and other minerals. Ayurveda makes use of certain Tantric practices for treating mental health as well as for rejuvenating purposes. In the Hindu astrological field, many Tantric methods are adopted by spiritual guides such as the use of gems, rituals, mantras, planetary positions and symbolism among others. Forms of divination such as palmistry originated in India, and gradually spread across the world through gypsies who travelled far and wide.

Thus, in this global age, Tantra with its spiritual, occult, and material aspects is a holistic science that can be a great path for seekers to discover themselves, and find more meaning in life. Much more than the experience of sex and sensation, it is a path that is multidimensional and has spiritual, artistic, scientific and occult knowledge. Finding the higher truth and attaining moksha remains its final goal.

Tantric Roots of the Siddhas

In his book *Tantric Yoga and the Wisdom Goddesses*, David Frawley discusses Tantra in relation to various facets such as art, science, emotions, Kundalini, and the misconceptions around it as well as the ingenuity of this path. Tantra has been integral to the development of Hinduism, Jainism and Buddhism with relevant differences in its development.

He says that the timeline for the development of this yoga was as follows:

1) Vedic, when the Indus Valley Civilisation was at its peak in the famous cities of Mohenjo-Daro and Harappa. This civilisation was aptly called "Saraswati Culture" later, as it was situated on the banks of the river Saraswati.

2) Later when the Saraswati dried up (around 1900 BC) the civilisation moved to the banks of the Ganga-Yamuna rivers and then the Puranic teachings came into practice.

3) The Tantras were derived from the Puranas, in the medieval period.

Though the language and the forms have been changed in the course of time, the essence of all the three has persisted to be the same—that which deals with the unity of the individual self to the supreme spirit. The chief characteristics of Tantric texts are: creation of the universe, destruction of the universe, worship of the Divine in various forms, attainment of the goals of life, spiritual powers and ways of meditation to realise the ultimate truth.

The Hindu Tantra lore possesses the following characteristics:

1) Tantra emphasises techniques or energetic approaches, including ritual, mantra and visualisation, and should be employed as a means to reach the ultimate goal, and not as an end in itself.

2) Tantra has a universal approach that uses all available methods and rejects nothing. It includes methods that may be rejected in other teachings as "unspiritual".

3) Tantra gives a special place to the Goddess and her worship.

The diversity and the breadth of Tantra will continue to support this path; the world should recognise the full scope of Tantra with its many dimensions of spiritual, occult, artistic and scientific knowledge. The path of direct awareness and the path of technique are generally the two paths of achieving the ultimate objective.

Vajrayana Buddhism is synonymous with Tantric Buddhism and considered to be the final stage in the evolution of Indian Buddhist theory. It is also considered to be "a faster path to enlightenment" owing to its practical Tantric techniques and that can help a yogi attain Buddhahood in a shorter timeframe, often in a single lifetime itself. It is also important to note that this path is faster than the Mahayana and Theravada paths. The goal of the Theravada is liberation from the cycles of birth and death, whereas Mahayana also aims to help an individual gain enlightenment.

The origin of Vajrayana Buddhism is said to be in Udyana which is the modern day Swat Valley in Pakistan, while some sources claim its origin to be in southern India. In Tibet, it is believed that it was the learned Shakyamuni Buddha who taught the Tantra, and his secret teachings which were outside the teacher-student circles were written down as sutras, long after he was gone. These texts are said to have originated in the fourth century, and north India's Nalanda University was a centre for the development of the Vajrayana theory. It is from here that the journey of this school of thought truly commenced. India continued to be the source of Vajrayana practices until the eleventh century, but by the thirteenth century, most of these teachings were considered to have died out. However, many of its practices merged with Hinduism and both these faiths experienced pressure owing to the rising importance of Islam. It was then that the majority of these practices were carefully preserved in Tibet. In the second half of the twentieth century many Tibetan exiles broke free from the oppressive anti-religious rule of the Communist Chinese. They then established Tibetan Buddhist communities around Dharamsala and in other parts of north India. Today, these centres remain prominent practitioners of Tantric Buddhism.

Vajrayana Buddhism: Techniques and Process

The Vajrayana path is deeply rooted in Tantric techniques which are found in many ancient scriptures of India. The most important aspect of this path is "to use the result as the path", i.e., instead of placing enlightenment as a faraway goal of the future, the yogi has to identify with the enlightened body, mind and speech of the Buddha.

This Buddha form is called the *Yidam* in Sanskrit. To attain identification with this Buddha form, a lot of symbolism and visualisation is employed in Buddhist Tantric systems. An important basis of the foundation of this teaching is secrecy, mainly to protect others from being mis-guided and harming themselves or others, without proper guidance. The yogi practising this path needs to understand that the uninitiated cannot be explained the symbolism and psychology of this technique, as this could create unnecessary misunderstandings and dismissal. Initially, these practices may seem to appear to have many nonsensical rituals. However, these have to be practiced as per a thorough understanding of Buddhist philosophy and strict adherence to the traditions.

Some prominent Tantric techniques in Vajrayana include mantras (chanting of important scriptures and phrases), yantras (graphic presentation of the concept diagram carved on metal), mudras (use of special postures and hand positions), mandalas (use of cosmic diagrams, visual pathways that can teach and map spiritual enlightenment) and the use of symbolic tools and instruments such as the vajra, *ghanta* (bell), and *damaru* (hand drum). An important part of walking on this path includes giving reverence to the guru-disciple relationship wherein ritual empowerments and initiations are practised after permission.

Sex also forms an important symbolic aspect of Buddhist Tantra. Many practices include transforming or directing this sexual energy to a blissful consciousness for achieving higher states of wisdom and enlightenment through the act of sexual intercourse. Thus, more than the act itself, it is concerned with controlling sexual energies.

Sexual symbolism is also prevalent in the iconography and visual representations of Vajrayana, and these represent the marriage of wisdom and compassion. It is through this that Vajrayana also gets its alternate names of Mantrayana and Tantrayana, and its origin is from the Sanskrit word, "vajra" which means diamond, indestructible or thunderbolt, and also has a connotation of reality. This path is thus also called, "The Diamond Vehicle" or "The Adamantine Vehicle"

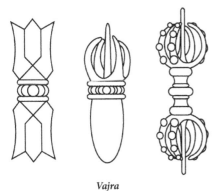

Vajra

(adamantine means diamond-like). The vajra, also known as the "dorje" in Tibetan, is important for rituals and it symbolises compassion. Another main component of the Vajrayana path is that it is esoteric in the truest sense of the word. Specifically, in this context, transmissions of certain accelerating factors occur directly from teacher to student during an initiation, and these cannot be just learnt from a book. Many of these techniques are said to be secretive. However, some Vajrayana teachers believe that secrecy is not important and that it is only a side-effect of the reality that these techniques have no validity outside of the teacher-student lineage. Since all these Tantric techniques are very powerful, if they are not practised properly, the yogi practitioner can harm himself/herself physically and mentally. To avoid these dangers, these practices are kept "secret" outside of this student-teacher bond. These esoteric aspects have resulted in several names for this school viz, Secret Buddhism, Esoteric Mahayana and Esoteric Buddhism which is most commonly used in Japan. This esoteric transmission framework has many varied forms and the Nyingma School of Tibetan Buddhism uses a method called "dzogchen" while other schools like Kagyu and Shingon use the alternative method called "*mahamudra*". Interestingly, even though Vajrayana is an independent path, it remains primarily a part of Mahayana Buddhism. Many sutras, the importance of Bodhisattvas, and the pantheon of deities in Mahayana are also a part of Vajrayana, and they also have in common the perspective that Buddhism is not just for the monks, but also for the layman.

Japanese Vajrayana teacher Kukai makes a very clear distinction between these two schools. According to him, Mahayana is mainly exoteric and provisional. Thus, according to this view, Vajrayana is the only Buddhist teaching that does not compromise with the limited nature of the audience to which it is being directed. Additionally, these teachings are said to be the "*Dharmakaya*", i.e., the principle of enlightenment in the form of Mahavairochana, engaging in a monologue with himself.

Both, the Hinayana and the Mahayana schools, consist of many aspects of Vajrayana, but in essence, many aspects of the Mahayana and Vajrayana schools are contrary to one another. For instance, ghastly and fearsome entities are found in weakened forms in Mahayana temples where protector deities are found glaring down at visitors.

Vajrayana Purification Process

Vajrasattva practice is an ancient Tantric meditation done to purify one's karma. As a practice in Mahayana, it is practiced along with a

Bodhichitta to cleanse all of one's karma to reach enlightenment in a short span, and to be able to help all sentient beings. Vajrasattva practice is essentially a non-conceptual meditation on voidness or shunyata, and on a provisional level, it requires repeated recitation of a hundred-syllable mantra which is often accompanied by some complex visualisations and extreme states of mind.

Vajrasattva mantra chantings and visualisation techniques are often carried out within the context of the sutra practice, and this is done before the onset of any kind of Tantric practice. Many a times, this is done with or without a set of formal "preliminary practices" for Tantra, during which the mantra is chanted 100,000 times. This chanting and visualisation forms a part of a formal Tantric "sadhana" practice that helps in actualising an individual as a Buddha-figure, and is carried out in any kind of Tantra class or level.

The sole aim of this practice however, remains purification of karma which is: "Uncontrollably recurring mental urges that bring us to act, speak, or think in a specific manner, or to the impulses with which those so-called 'karmic actions' are carried out." As with all actions, our karma leaves behind a "karmic aftermath" on our mental continuum. We are reborn in the future and these aftermaths ripen or bring about our experience of "karmic results" that are in accordance with those karmic actions. "Purification of karma" is thus "purification of karmic aftermath" and in this process, we eliminate the possibility of us experiencing karmic results that would come about from the ripening of this aftermath. It only in the Mahayana practices that the possibility of purification of karma is asserted before it gets ripened. In Hinayana schools, karmic aftermaths must ripen even though the experience has a minor result, and this must happen before we pass away in that particular lifetime, and become liberated or enlightened as a Buddha.

The stages of purification involve a detailed process wherein a person's network of karmic force, karmic tendencies, and karmic constant habits are purified. The stages of purification involve ridding mental continuums of their networks of karmic force and tendencies. We are liberated when we get rid of these networks of positive and negative karmic forces and karmic tendencies. Thus, even if we experience results of past actions, we no longer have feelings of happiness and unhappiness—we become free of past behavioural cycles. Vajrasattva mantra meditation is the next step which aims to help us avoid gross suffering and purify mental continuums of all karmas of all past lives as we strive to gain a better rebirth state as a human or divine being or a "god".

The forms used in Vajrasattva purification are practised with or without oral transmission of the mantra. When Vajrasattva is practised without any Tantric empowerment, or with any Buddha-figure from the first three classes of Tantra, Vajrasattva is a single figure. This single form is white, and composed of one face and two arms. When Vajrasattva is practiced with an Anuttarayoga Tantra figure, Vajrasattva is a couple. Both figures of this couple are white and have one face and two arms. The male has a peaceful mouth expression as depicted in Guhyasamaja and Yamantaka. Or contrastingly, he may have a semi-forceful, semi-peaceful mouth expression with fangs, similar to those found in Heruka Vajrasattva, practised in Chakrasamvara, Vajrayogini, and Hevajra. In Kalachakra Tantra, Vajrasattva is depicted in blue, and in this form, the female partner is in green, and both have three faces and six arms. If a yogi practises Vajrasattva without an empowerment for a Buddha-figure, he visualises himself in an ordinary form during the practice. In this scenario, all beings around us are visualised as having a Vajrasattva on his or her head, and each of them is being purified. If a yogi practises with an empowerment for a Buddha-figure, he visualises himself as the Buddha-figure during the practice, but maintains a very weak "pride of the deity". In the ordinary form, the yogi visualises a moon disc on his heart surrounded by all beings, with everyone being purified. "Pride of the deity" is a feeling of actually being the Buddha-figure.

Gorakhnath: An Expert Vajrayana Buddhist

It shouldn't come as a surprise that Gorakhnath is said to be a Vajrayana Buddhist. A very prominent Tantric element is found in all his teachings, and along with Shaivite Tantra, many beliefs and practices of the Nath sect have evolved in the pages of history. Accordingto Dr. B. Bhattacharya, in his book *Introduction to Buddhist Esoterism*, the Tantric culture presupposes Raja Yoga and Hatha Yoga. Historically speaking, according to him, the Buddhist Tantric preceded the Hindu version and the former forms the main foundation on which the latter is based. He also says, "The whole of the culture history of the eastern part of India from AD 700 to AD 1200 is locked up in the Tantras. Although the Buddhist cult disappeared under the Islamic advance, Hindu practice has continued down to the present time." Interestingly, Tantric practice is concerned with magic and erotic rituals which help it get in touch with supernormal existence and escalate its cosmic powers in totality. Shaktism is very intimately linked with Tantra and the worship of the goddess is considered highly important.

As a system, Shakta is practised in Bengal and Assam and in these regions the worship of Shiva's consort Shakti is prescribed in many Tantric texts with descriptions of various rituals and religious rites. According to Dr. Bhattacharya, Buddhist Tantra is mainly Vajrayana, and this system is a development of the Mahayana which contains elements dating back to the Buddha himself. Thus, certain important concepts which are found in the original Buddhism cult also contain the seeds and essence of Tantra. These concepts are yoga, mudra, mantra, mandala, dharani, and samadhi which eventually help an individual attain peace, prosperity and happiness. Dr. Bhattacharya also stresses that within the early stages of the cult, there were many followers who were unhappy because of the severity of the disciplines and regulations which were enforced. However, these concepts gained more liberty and license when they were allowed to search for supernatural power and also practise forms of enjoyment.

Historical Roots of Tantric Buddhism

During the period between the eighth century AD and the twelfth century AD, Tantric Buddhism truly emerged. During this period the ethico-religious rigorism of Hinayana sharply contrasted with Mahayana which was a religion of progress and liberalism. The Mahayana school was characterised by a very deep sympathy for the suffering beings of the whole universe along with a broad outlook. After the Buddha's death there was a great controversy among his disciples concerning the right interpretation of his teaching and the codes of conduct to be followed by a monk. To settle these controversies many councils were held and as a result, there was a schism that resulted in the emergence of two schools-the Sthaviravada (Orthodox School/School of Elders) and the Mahasanghika (School of a Big Group).

What make these two schools so different from each other are their thoughts and outlook. Hinayana seeks to attain "Arhathood" or "final liberation of the self from the whirl of existence", through a strict disciplined routine and ethical practice of dhyan (meditation). Mahayana on the other hand, aims to attain Buddhahood through different stages of Bodhisattvahood (based on the philosophies of Nagarjun), which is "a state of perfect knowledge about the void nature of the self and the not-self mixed up with an emotion of universal compassion". Mainly, Bodhisattvas work on redeeming suffering beings from samsara, and do not gain complete enlightenment like Buddha for themselves out of an intense selflessness towards fellow beings (like Avalokiteshvara).

Understanding Bodhisattvahood is crucial to Mahayana Buddhism as well as all forms of Tantra. The followers of Mahayana believe that every man or every being in the world is a potential Buddha, i.e., within him are all the qualities needed to become the enlightened one or the *Samyaksambuddha,*who can attain perfect knowledge, universal compassion, and eventually be on the path where he helps in uplifting other beings. Bodhisattvahood basically needs "the attainment of the Bodhi-Mind (Bodhi-Chitta) which is defined as a state of vacuity *(*shunyata*)* and universal compassion *(karuna)*". This ideal of being able to carry out missionary activities, is the ideal linked with attaining nirvana (final extinction).

Compared to other Buddhist schools, Mahayana was based on the ideal of redeeming the entire humanity from suffering and so, as a religion of all people, it made many provisions so that people from different backgrounds, castes, tastes and intellectual capacities could adopt it as a way of life. Hence, we find many heterogeneous qualities of faith and religious practices within its sect. Thus, gradually a new school developed within this province of Buddhism, which had more forward policies. This school introduced elements like mantras and dharanis and eventually, Mahayana got subdivided into *Paramita-naya* and *Mantra-naya.* *Mantra-naya* forms the introductory stage of Tantric Buddhism from which other smaller schools like Vajrayana, Kalachakrayana, and Sahajayana came into existence.

Many scholars have found references to sexo-yogic practices of Tantric Buddhists in the *Mahayana Sutra Lankara* by Asanga. The word "*pravritti*" has been found many times in the *Sutra Lankara* in connection with acts which include greatness of the Buddha. One of the verses in these texts says, "In the *Pravritti* of sexual union supreme greatness is obtained viz. in the enjoyment of Buddha-Happiness and in looking without impure thoughts at a wife."

In his book *An Introduction to Buddhist Esoterism* Dr. B. Bhattacharya writes: "Though Buddha was antagonistic to all sorts of sacrifices, necromancy, sorcery or magic, he is credited nevertheless with having given instructions concerning Mudras, Mandalas, and Tantras, etc, so that, by virtue of these, prosperity in this world could be attained by his less advanced disciples, who seem to care more for this world than for the nirvana preached by him. India in Buddha's time was so steeped in superstitions that any religion which dared forbid all kinds of magic, sorcery and necromancy could hardly hope to withstand popular opposition. A clever organiser as Buddha was, he did not fail to notice the importance of incorporating magical practices in his religion to make it popular from all points of view and attract more adherents thereby." Thus, it can be concluded that Tantrism was not introduced into Buddhism at a particular time, age or by a single person, or cult. Belief in mantras and the power of sounds of certain syllables are the heritage in which Indian scriptures are based, and similar beliefs are also found in early Buddhism. Worshiping the stupa, respect for the Bodhi-mandala, i.e. the circle around the famous tree beneath which Buddha attained the perfect knowledge (Bodhi), are popular features of early Buddhism. Many of his gestures and postures are also very important. These elements paved away for the mantra, mudra (posture and gesture) and mandala (mystic diagram) elements in Tantric Buddhism. Thus, tantrism is neither exclusively Hindu nor Buddhist, but a beautiful amalgam of both cults.

Asanga has been called the first propagator of Tantrism as a school in Buddhism, and the *Agamas* (religious texts/scriptures) of his times are a source of knowledge for all Tantric texts. Even in the early ages of Somananda and Utpala, many works existed which can be dated back to the ancient times. *Tantra Loka* by Abhinav Gupta (AD 10) is a collective work of many ancient texts and scriptures which were personally accessible to him.

The concept of "mantra" was introduced in Mahayana Buddhism in the form of "*dharani*" which means, "that by which something is sustained or kept up (*dharyate anaya iti*), i.e., the mystic syllables that have got the capacity of keeping up the religious life of a man". The *Bodhisattva Bhumi* by Vasubandhu lists four types of *dharanis*. The first two, *Dharma-dharani* and *Artha-dharani,* mean that a Bodhisattva remembers the texts and their meaning. The third, *Mantra-dharani*, means that a Bodhisattva can help reduce people's suffering by chanting mantras and the fourth is *Ksanti-labhaya-dharani*, the sadhana by a Bodhisattva needed for attaining transcendence.

Mantra-*dharani* consists of powerful chants composed of syllables which, through mystic power, help an individual attain perfection. The Dharma-*dharani* is linked to the mantras, which through their audio power or simply through hearing, help an individual gain *smriti* (memory), *prajna* (perfect knowledge) and *bala* (spiritual strength). *Artha-dharani* includes the kinds of mantras which through their *artha* (meaning) of the Dharma's are revealed to the individual in a spontaneous way, without the help of a teacher or shastra. In *Ksanti-Dharani*, the ultimate nature of the dharmas is revealed to the follower after he achieves the generosity of heart which gradually escalates into the attainment of forbearance.

Every mantra possesses a deep meaning which cannot be fully explained by any sutras/shastra, or by any preacher as each person interprets this for himself and its correct meaning is grasped at the right time. An example to explain this is an instance explained by Vasubandhu, who says that syllables such as "*iti, miti, kiti*, etc" have no meaning at all, but in this meaninglessness lies their real meaning, which the follower through his concentration, has to realise. Thus, by removing all possibilities of meaning, the pure void which encapsulates the mantra is revealed to the individual. Gradually, this individual also realises that the nature of the dharmas is actually essenceless. And with meditation, the unique, transcendental meaning of the mantra is revealed in the heart of the sadhaka as the real nature of all things.

Deeply connected with the practice of mantras, are mudras, which are different signs or gestures made using a particular position of the hands or fingers. Both these practices are vital to the yogic sadhana of the Tantrics as the mantras consist of the power of sound, while the mudras possess the secrecy of touch related to physiological realms and together, these can make the practitioner attain all his heart's desires. Along with these esoteric elements, the concept of mandala also came into being.

Early Tantric Buddhism mainly consisted of mantras, mudras, mandalas and *Abhisheka* (ceremonies of initiation and beginning) but gradually, may yogic practices involved sexual elements as being essential to attain the final bliss and thus, six other kinds of rituals—*madya* (wine), *mamsa* (meat), *matsya* (fish), *maithuna* (sexual intercourse) and those rituals related to women—also found their place in Tantric Buddhism. This path containing sexo-yogic principles and paths came to be collectively known as Vajrayana Buddhism (the Adamantine Path).

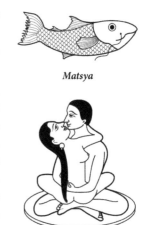

Matsya

Maithuna

Types of Tantra

The great Gautam Buddha spoke of Tantra himself, in his supreme manifestation as a monk. He also spoke in detail of the great *Vajradhara*, and in various manifestations of the central deity of specific mandalas. The great beings, Manjushri, Samantabhadra, Vajrapani and others, urged by the Buddha, also taught some Tantra.

There are different classes or types of Tantra, and although he appeared in many different manifestations, they were all taught by the enlightened teacher, Lord Buddha.

The *Kriya Tantras* were taught by the Buddha in the form of a monk, in the realm of the thirty-three gods on the summit of Mount Meru. In the human world, the chief hearers were Manjushri and other Buddhist devotees. The *Pung-Zang Tantras* were taught in the realm of Vajrapani. Others were taught by Buddha, some were explained by Avalokiteshvara, Manjushri and Vajrapani with his blessings, while others were spoken by worldly gods. The *Karya Tantras* were taught by Buddha in the form of his supreme manifestation in the celestial realms, and in the realm of Base and Essence, adorned with flowers. The *Yoga Tantras* were taught by the Enlightened One when he arose in the form of the central deity of each mandala in such places as the summit of Mount Meru, and in the fifth celestial realm of desire.

The *Anuttara Tantras* were also taught by the Buddha. Having manifested the mandala of *Guhyasamaja*, he taught King Indrabodhi this Tantra, in Ogyan. The *Yamantaka Tantras* were taught by Buddha at the time of the subduing of the demonic forces, and they were requested by either the consort of Yamantaka or by the consort of Kalachakra. The *Hevajra Tantra* was taught by Lord Buddha when he arose in the form of Hevajra in the land of Magadha at the time of destroying the four maras. The Tantra was requested by Vajragarbha and by the consort of Hevajra. Having been requested by Vajra Yogini, the Buddha, in the manifestation of Heruka on the summit of Mount Meru, taught the root Tantra of Heruka and, when requested by Vajrapani, taught the explanatory Tantra. As for the *Kalachakra Tantra*, the mighty Buddha went south to the glorious shrine of Dharnakotaka and there, manifesting the mandala of the *Dharmadhatu* speech surmounted by the mandala of *Kalachakra*, taught this Tantra to King Chandrabhadra and others.

A positive motivation that is made of the two-fold intention that seeks benefits for oneself and others is the goal of the Mahayana tradition of Buddhism. This can also be taken as a single intention that is based in ten virtues, to perform virtuous deeds and to achieve enlightenment—the ultimate realisation that benefits oneself and others. The preliminaries that each seeker practises i.e. the *Ngondro*, commence with the "Four Thoughts that Turn the Mind" towards the Divine or spiritual path. This forms the basis of the Hinayana tradition of Buddhism.

The Mahayana tradition comprises refuge, Bodhichitta, Vajrasattva, and Mandala. The practice of *Guruyoga* is linked with the tradition of Vajrayana. *Ngondro* is an extremely profound practice that activates all three vehicles simultaneously and since these are related, they activate compassion and contemplation of the Four Thoughts. When Shakyamuni Buddha had first introduced samsara he explained that it is a cyclic existence of suffering, delusion and turmoil. Hence, contemplating the Four Thoughts that "turn the mind" is essential before beginning any kind of practice.

Tantric practice consists of two levels—Outer and Inner. The Outer Tantras are—*Kriya Tantra, Karya Tantra*, and *Yoga Tantra*.

The Inner Tantras commence with *Mahayoga*. The differences in these two forms are many, from conduct, rules and practices, to views. Apart from this, crucial to the practise of any of these Tantras is empowerment given at the time of initiation.

The Outer Tantras

The Outer Tantras are considered to be more difficult, and to achieve results a lot of patience, hard work and perseverance is required. They also involve a lot of particularised activities. They contain both "*kye rim*" and "*dzog rim*", i.e., generation and completion stage practices. Performed separately, the generation stage is vital to the separation stage, and this is only found in the method of Outer Tantra. Moreover, the practitioners maintain very high standards of hygiene, a pure appearance, clean themselves several times a day, and change into clean clothes thrice a day. They are vegetarians who eat only three white and sweet things everyday, and drink from cups adorned with precious gems.

The realisations and results take longer with the Outer Tantra, for instance, it takes sixteen lifetimes for a Kriya yogi to achieve enlightenment. Practising diligently without any misses or lapses is recommended. The mandalas of deities are visulised as solitary figures wearing flowing silk scarves, skirts and jewelled ornaments. These practitioners practise in secluded and isolated environments like forests, away from people in places like the peak of Mount Meru.

Additionally, each of the Outer Tantras has different features and qualities. In *Kriya Tantra* (or activity Tantra), deities are visualised as external, and the main methods of practice involve rituals and ceremonies. Their main text is the *Susiddhi Sutra*, and the practitioner's lifestyle is defined by mantras, mudras, seals and cleanliness of the environment and himself.

In *Karya Tantra* (performance Tantra), the deities worshipped are identical and their practice involves rituals and internal methods. The training of "Body Tantric, oral Tantric, and mind Tantric in harmony" is emphasised. Their main text is the *Mahavairochana Sutra*.

In *Yoga Tantra*, the belief of the practitioners is that the power of deities arises from non-duality. In their worship, rituals and internal methods are equally emphasised.

The Inner Tantras

The Inner Tantras are slightly easier to practise as the time required to achieve the results is less, and they require less work. They are less contrived and combine "*kye rim*", i.e., the generation stage including activities and characteristics, with the completion stage "*dzog rim*", which is void of symbolism, elaboration and activities. These are joined and performed simultaneously. These practitioners experience everything equally and hence are not fanatic about cleanliness as they realise the real nature of things, and do necessarily need to distinguish the good from the bad. They wear animal skins for clothing and may never even change their clothing, hence at times, appearing to be beggars or peasants. The realisations and results are much faster to achieve compared to the Outer Tantras; for instance, these yogis can achieve complete enlightenment and full awakening in the same lifetime, in the same body. The results may also be achieved in half a lifetime or at the time of death or in the bardo (intermediate states). Their deities wear ornaments made of human skulls, bones and skins. The practitioners practise anywhere, especially in cemeteries.

The three Inner Tantras are *Mahayoga Tantra*, *Anuyoga Tantra*, and *Atiyoga Tantra*. The focus of *Mahayoga Tantra* is *kye rim*, of *Anuyoga Tantra*, transmission, movements and the dissolution of characteristics, while *Atiyoga Tantra* unites these two.

Additionally, each of the Inner Tantras has different features and qualities. In the *Mahayoga Tantra*, the visualisation of the deity is gradual and it mainly focuses on the development stage. It also lays emphasis on clarity and precision of visualisation as skilful means. The meditation practices are focussed on emptiness. In *Anuyoga Tantra*, the emphasis is on energy centres, wind and energy. The visualisation of the deity is generated instantly. In *Atiyoga Tantra*, the emphasis is on mind development.

In his book, *Shreechakrasambhara Tantra*, Kazi Dawa-Samdup has divided the Vajrayana path into four: *Kriya Tantrayana*, *Karya Tantrayana*, *Yoga Tantrayana* (*Yoga Tantra*) and *Anuttara Yoga*. Generally, Vajrayana has been divided in four classes: (i) *Kriya Tantra* and (ii) *Karya Tantra*, also called the "Lower Tantras" and (iii) *Mahayoga Tantra* and (iv) *Anuttara Yoga Tantra*, the "Higher Tantras". The Lower Tantras are concerned mainly with rituals, ceremonies and worship of different gods and goddesses, whereas the Higher Tantras are mainly concerned with yogic practices that lead the practitioner into divine realisation and contain discussions on the nature of the ultimate reality.

Kalachakrayana is often associated with a darker or rather a terrible aspect of Buddhist Tantrism. Commenting on this school, M.M. H.P. Sastri says, "What is Kala-Chakra-Yana? The word Kala [Kaal] means time, death and destruction. Kala-Chakra is the wheel of destruction, and Kala-Chakra-Yana means the vehicle for protection against the wheel of destruction." However, this explanation has not received any textual evidence or reference; hence this is just a probable theory.

The *Kalachakra Tantra* explains Buddha's description of how the universe with its objects is closely associated with the regions within our physical bodies and interestingly, time with its many divisions (day, night, minutes, seconds, years, and more) exists within the physical body in the form of *vayu*, i.e. breath of the vital wind, that keeps us alive. The concept of *Sahaj* has also been explained in detail along with sexo-yogic practices related to achieving it. Even the book *Tantra Loka* by Abhinava Gupta has detailed literature dedicated to the concept of *Kaal* (time), and the process by which one should keep himself above its influence. *Kaal*, with all its divisions, has been explained with reference to the *vayu* (vital wind) and it is said to be spread through all the channels of the body. Controlling the nervous system through prana and *apana* is linked with controlling time itself.

3.6 Shunyata: The Spirit of Tantric Vajrayana Buddhism

A Sanskrit word, "shunyata" means emptiness, voidness or nothingness. The essence of Zen, Tantric philosophies and Buddhism as a whole, it is an integral part of the Mahayana doctrine and essential to every spiritual seeker's path.

Among the greatest Buddhist philosophers, Nagarjun founded the Madhyamika philosophy of Mahayana Buddhism and this commentary is found in the rare Sanskrit book *Maha-Prajnaparamita Shastra* which is today available only in Tibetan and Chinese translation.

Madhyamika philosophy of the Middle Way is based on compassion to help sentient beings remove suffering. At its very core, like a pulsating heart, is the concept of shunyata. According to the Middle Way, the root cause of all suffering is clinging or holding on to things and people, ignorance of true reality, and mistaking the relative and conditioned for the absolute and unconditioned. K. Venkata Ramanan in his book *Nagarjun's Philosophy* says, "The error of misplaced absoluteness, the seizing of the determinate as itself ultimate, is the root-error." Shunyata thus, is the remedy, the medicine and the sweet antidote to relieve all suffering.

He further adds, "The intellect, owing to the operation of ignorance, wrongly transfers its sense of unconditionedness which is its ultimate nature to itself in its mundane nature." Simply speaking, our identity and concept of "I" comes from our physical and material world or our relationships, our achievements and everything that is external to our true essence, i.e., the spirit. This is where conflicts begin and the individual is lost in the illusion of the real and unreal. This gradually escalates and the individual can no longer connect with his being, his loved ones, the society or world at large. Thus the gap between the mundane and absolute widens as suffering grows, and we are lost in our own intellectualisations, dogmas, prejudices and thought processes. The result is a cluttered mind and a suffering heart beating inside a tired body.

Shunyata thus becomes a remedy as it helps us understand the relativity of all things. Simply speaking, shunyata helps us see and realise that all things are empty of inherent existence and it is we who label and categorise everything based our own points of view and experiences. It helps us to break away from false attachments of self to things and people and look at the world for what it really is. It removes ignorance and conditionings that block our divine path.

Thomas J McFarlane in his paper, "The Meaning of Shunyata in Nagarjun's Philosophy", sums this up as: "Shunyata, as emptiness, thus implies that the conventional world is not, as we fancy to think, composed of substances inherently existing; in truth, these entities are devoid of inherent existence—they are empty."

An important mode of spiritual transformation is the transformation of shunyata into the idea of *vajra* (the thunderbolt). In the *Advaya Vajra Samgraha* it is written that, "Shunyata, which is firm, substantial, indivisible, impenetrable, incapable of being burnt or perishable, is called the *vajra*."

This conversion of shunyata into *vajra* forms Vajrayana. In Vajrayana Buddhism, all deities, their different articles of worship, rituals, and all things related to pious customs get differentiated from their original nature after they are marked by *vajra*. *Vajrasattva* (vajra = shunyata, sattva = quintessence) is the supreme deity of Vajrayana and its nature is of pure consciousness *(vijnapti-matrata)*. In this form, shunyata becomes free of objectivity and subjectivity. Interestingly, all deities of this cult have a small figure of the *Vajrasattva* in their crest, and it has been described with endless attributes within the Tantras.

The reverence received by the Vajrayana cult in Tantric Buddhism is on par with the respect received by the *Upanishadic Brahmanas* in the Hindu religious order.

Described as "the self in the man" or the "ultimate reality in the form of the Boddhicitta", this Mahayanic concept also went through a metamorphosis centuries ago. Earlier, it was perceived as a mental resolve that was determined to attain *Bodhi* (perfect wisdom) along with universal compassion. Thus, the *Chitta* is an amalgam of two inherent attributes, i.e., shunyata (the understanding that the nature of all things is pure void) and *Karuna* (universal compassion).

The *Bodhichitta,* which is a union of these two qualities, gradually ascends upwards through the stages of *Dharmamegha* to attain perfection. This state is believed to be extremely blissful and is produced through sexo-yogic practices of Tantric Buddhism. Generally, in such practices, the union of the seed and ovum is also known as *Bodhichitta* and during this process it combines the essence of the five elements of air, fire, water, earth and ether, and becomes the ultimate substance of the entire universe.

Shunyata and *Karuna* as the Male and Female Principles

The history of the transformation of *Bodhichitta* is very closely linked to the idea of shunyata (as the female principle) and *Karuna* (as the male principle). The Mahayana texts, define shunyata as "*Prajna*" which is perfect knowledge of the void nature of the self and the Dharma's. *Karuna* (universal compassion) is known as the "*Upaya*" which is the means or the expedience for attaining the *Bodhichitta*. It is important to note that *Prajna* and *Upaya* were also mentioned by Nagarjun. In the sacred Mahayanic texts like *Bodhisattva Bhoomi* and the *Saddharma Pundarika* the concept of *Upaya* is explained as "missionary works which are prompted by universal compassion for the suffering beings."

Since antiquity, *Prajna* has been seen as perfect wisdom which is absolutely passive in nature. It is the negative aspect of reality and yet the innate source of all entities. In contrast, *Upaya* is dynamic in nature and is considered the positive and active essence of all reality. Thus, *Upaya* is the potential energy that exists in the phenomenal world of all beings and entities and this is manifested through the *Prajna* or the void. The Buddhist schools thus, conceived the negative/passive aspect of reality as perfect knowledge to be the female principle, and the positive/active aspect was conceived as the male principle. With the advent of these two principles the whole outlook of Buddhism started undergoing a radical change. Even the phenomenon of *Bodhichitta* which was seen as the union of the merging of void knowledge with universal compassion, was transformed into great bliss that could be attained by the yogic union of the male and female principles.

Thus, with the identification of *Prajna* as female and *Upaya* as male, the concept of Shakti and Shiva was established in the Buddhist Tantras. This evolved into a sexo-yogic practice which came to be associated with the Mahayana philosophy. Interestingly, the theories of all tantras believe that the human being is an epitome of the universe and so, all truth exits within the body itself. Therefore, Tantric Buddhists began to locate philosophical truths within the physical body. During the extensive research they found that *Prajna* and *Upaya* are linked with two important nerves in the left and right of the spinal cord, respectively. These nerves in yogic literature in general are known as the "Ida" and "Pingala", the moon and the sun, the left and the right, vowels and consonants, and so on and so forth.

In the Hindu Tantras, the middle nerve is associated with the *Sushumna* which is called *Avadhutika*, i.e., the channel through which the *Bodhichitta* passes. This *Bodhichitta* energy ascends from the Nirmana chakra (or the Nirmana kaya of Buddha) located in the navel to the Dharma chakra (Dharma kaya) located in the heart, then proceeds to the Sambhoga chakra (Sambhoga kaya) located in the throat region, and from here it passes to the lotus located in the crown. The person then experiences supreme and divine bliss.

Concepts of esoteric Buddhism, *Advaya*, i.e., non-duality, and *Yuganaddha*, i.e., the principle of union, are equally important to be considered in this respect. The principles of *Yuganaddha* are very well explained in the fifth chapter of "Yuganaddha-krama" in the *Panchakrama*. This state of *Yuganaddha* is defined as "the unity reached through the purging off of the two notions of the world process (samsara) an absolute cessation (*nivrtti*) through the realisation of the ultimate nature of both the phenomenal (*samklesa*) and the absolute (*vyavadana*), through the synthesis of thought constructions of all corporeal existence with the notion of the formless."

The *Panchakrama* further explains this phenomenon as the merging of the *Grahya*, i.e., the perceivable, with the *Grahaka*, i.e., the perceiver, as the union of the temporal with the eternal, of the *prajna* with the *Karuna*. *Yuganaddha* is thus, the immutable state where the final abode of *tathata* (that-ness) in body, mind and speech is reached, and one faces the world of miseries and realises the true nature of the provisional truth, i.e., *Samvriti* and the ultimate truth, i.e., the *Paramartha*.

In the sacred text, *Yuganaddha Prakasha* of the *Advaya-Vajra-Samgraha* the nature of *Karuna* and shunyata is thought of as being always in union. The *Prema Panchaka* has a different viewpoint of this. In this text, shunyata is said to be the wife, and *Karuna* is said to be the husband, and their relation is believed to be one of conjugal love which is "*sahaj prema*" (simply natural). They are thus inseparable and their love is so deep that shunyata without her husband's manifestation would have been dead, and *Karuna* without shunyata would have suffered bondage. The *Sadhanamala* describes this as "body of the ultimate nature which is the unity of both shunyata and *Karuna* is called the neuter (*napumsaka*) or as *Yuganaddha*."

Thus, we can see that the principle of *Yuganaddha* is similar to the principles of conjugal union of the Kama-Kala, of the Shaiva and Shakta Tantras. Even the male and female principles using the ideologies of the seed and ovum, negative and positive, and static and dynamic are taken to be real dynamics in the Hindu and Buddhist Tantras. We have thus seen the union of shunyata/*prajna*, and *Karuna*/*Upaya* into Vajrayana and the female and male, hence Tantric Buddhist gods and goddesses are also found in a state of union like the Hindu representations of the union of Shiva-Shakti into "*Ardhanari*".

We can also find similarities between the concepts of *Advaya* and

Yuganaddha, and the idea of *Samarasa* or the sameness and oneness of emotions. The deeper and more innate meaning of *Samarasa* is "realisation of the oneness of the Universe amidst all its diversities; it is the realisation of one truth as the flow of a unique emotion of all pervading bliss." The Hevajra Tantra explains that in this ultimate state of *Sahaj*, there is no difference made or sense of duality between *Prajna* or *Upaya*, and in this state, the lowest, middle or best levels are one and the same. The self is thus, neither passive nor active, nor static or dynamic but in fact, everything is seen as one and seen to possess the same cosmic power, character and function. All transcendental knowledge emerging from *Samarasa* is equal and non-dual in nature. This concept of *Samarasa* appears many times in many Hindu and Buddhist Tantric texts representing the union of Shiva and Shakti or the *Prajna* and *Upaya,* and mostly to help us understand the intense bliss that can be experienced through sexo-yogic practices which have the power to transform our psychical states into a healthy homogeneity.

3.7 *Sahaj*: Return to Simplicity

A fundamental school which is the basis of all spirituality, especially Buddhist Tantra, is the concept of *Sahaj*. *Sahaj* implies the inherent or innate nature of all beings and objects. Literally, *Sahaj* means, "That which is born or originates with the birth or origination of any entity *(saha jayate iti sahajah)*". All Dharmas thus possess this virtue and it forms the most intrinsic quality to attain spiritual goals.

In the Hevajra Tantra it is written that:

"The whole world is of the nature of *Sahaj*—for *Sahaj* is the quintessence (*svarupa*) of all; this quintessence is nirvana to those who possess the perfectly pure *chitta*."

This feeling of *Sahaj* in the form of *Mahasukh* (supreme bliss), though realised through the physical body, should not be seen as something belonging only to it; it is, in fact, an all pervading experience. It is spiritually transcendent.

Just as the *Upanishads* define Brahman as being the ultimate nature of self in which the external world transcends all intellectual and verbal expressions, in the same way, *Sahaj* nature cannot be defined or fully accessed by the mind, and can also never be expressed through speech. Just like the Brahman is realised within and there is no knower (*jnata*), knowable (*jneya*) or knowledge (*jnana*), the *Sahaj* nature is also comprehended only within oneself (*svasamvedya*).

In Hevajra Tantra it is explained thus:

"*Sahaj* can neither be explained by any man nor can be expressed by any speech; it is realised by the self through the merit of serving at the feet of the guru."

According to the *Guhya Siddhi*, truth attained through personal intuition can never be spoken by the tongue and it is an all pervading supreme state where there is no body, no mind, and no work.

In the dohas composed by Tillopada it is said, "*Sahaj* is a state where all the thought constructions are dead (destroyed) and the vital wind (which is the vehicle of the defiled *chitta*) is also destroyed—the secret of this truth is to be intuited by the self—how can it be explained (by others)? The truth (*tatta=tattva*) is inaccessible to the ordinary foolish people, and it is also unknown and unknowable to scholars, but it is never inaccessible to that fortunate and meritorious one who by services has propitiated the Guru."

This state of *Sahaj* is also called the "nirvana-dhatu" of Buddhism, and the "Vajra-dhatu" or "Vajra-sattva" of Vajrayanists. The *Mahasukh* has become the core belief of the Sahajiyas. Tillopada in his dohas also says, "When the *Sahaj* in the *Chitta* vanishes, the *Achitta* (i.e., negation) also vanishes; the state of non-dual unity (*samarasa*) is free from both existence and non-existence. This transcendental truth is free from all merit and demerit—for there cannot be any merit or demerit in what is realisable only within. It is bereft of all colour and form—it is perfect in the form of all. In *Sahaj*, the self is void, the world is void, and all the three worlds are void; in pure *Sahaj* there is neither merit nor sin."

Sarahapada describes this beautiful inexplicable state of *Sahaj* poetically as:

"In *Sahaj*, there is no duality; it is perfect like the sky. The intuition of this ultimate truth destroys all attachment and it shines through the darkness of attachment like a full moon in the night. *Sahaj* cannot be heard with the ears, neither can it be seen with the eyes; it is not affected by air nor burnt by fire; it is not wet in intense rain, it neither increases nor decreases, it neither exists nor does it die out with the decay of the body; the *Sahaj* bliss is only oneness of emotions—it is oneness in all."

Another important aspect related to *Sahaj* is that of totality. Just like a pure child relies only on the instructions of the guru without considering the positive and negative functions of the mind, so must a seeker. The mind remains inactive in *Sahaj* and even the cycles of birth and death come to a halt. Like a lotus whose essence can be expressed in totality not through its stem or petals or fragrance, *Sahaj* is a totality that has to be comprehended in a non-dual mind.

Even meditation and mantras become external forms and have to be seen as perfect void, and it is through this comprehension of *Dharma-nairatmya* (essence-less objects) and *pudgala nairatmya* (essence-less subject) that *Sahaj* is found in the heart of the seeker. This Supreme Lord that governs *Sahaj* is a waveless sea of perfect purity whose comings and goings are unknown. In this state there is no knowledge of without or within.

Like the lunar gem that brightens all things by its pure lustre, the supreme *mahasukh* experienced through *Sahaj* illuminates all darkness, and drives away all miseries of life in a moment. Kanhapada has described *Sahaj* as a state free of defilements, free from merit and sin, without any thought constructions, transformations, or corruptions and here, "mind has no function at all, this is what is called nirvana".

It is important to note that Buddhism as a religion was initially an uncompromising atheistic school that did not believe in god, self or the soul-substance. However, it gradually developed the theistic tendency and came closer to the Upanishadic conception of Brahman being the Supreme Being, which firmly established itself in Vajrayana. The *Upanishads* often describe Brahman as an all-pervading entity with hands, legs, eyes, ears and faces on all sides. *Sahaj* encompasses this, and it is thus the core of self which encompasses the universe, its transformations, and everything else. All the karmas (deeds) performed by us are also self-revealed or active *Sahaj* produced during mentation (*bodhanat*) in forms of the object and subject. And *Sahaj* plays the entire gamut of roles—it is the king, it is the lord, it is the *bharta* (sustainer) and the *karta* (performer). It is all pervading, resides in all bodies, vital process, existent and non-existent, and everything emerges from it. It is nature of pure consciousness, it is *jeeva* (individual personality), it is time, and it is ego.

In his *doha*, Tillopada perfectly explains the nature of self in *Sahaj*. He says, "I am the universe, I am the Buddha, I am perfect purity, I am the non-cognition (amanasiara), I am the destroyer of the cycle of existence."

Shree Gorakhnath

3.8 Moksha and *Mahasukh*

Moksha—Supreme Ideal

The Hindu spiritual system believes "moksha" or "mukti" as being the supreme ideal of life. Literally, it means freedom or liberation of a spiritual nature that frees the person from the cycles of birth and death. But what is it that we seek freedom from? This universal disease is "sorrow" that is caused by internal, as well as external causes. These causes are of all kinds—physical, emotional, mental and spiritual. Even if a person experiences temporary success or happiness, the roots of sorrows are very deep and binding. It is the basis of civilisation and of human culture. Even death cannot end its cycle as it is connected with the Law of Moral Justice, according to which, the world order ensures the continuity of life in the subtle body, and new births in new gross bodies, that serve and reap the fruits of our actions or misdeeds, i.e., karma. The struggles thus continue in the next life.

Sorrow is not just a negative aspect of existence but is also the stimulating force behind all life as it constantly motivates us to betterment and progress. Although sorrows keep generating desires in us and stimulate actions which help us gain relief from them, even the best of our actions cannot get us permanent solutions as this cycle is infinite. It is the scheme of how the world works, and its pages of history are full of struggles, strifes, and sorrows. We may have progressed with discoveries, inventions and powers. However, there is still a sense of dissatisfaction that plagues our being.

Fortunately, the mystics of India and spiritual masters around the world have a solution. According to them, this sorrow can be conquered and man can attain perfect freedom by turning wisdom, concentration, and energies inwards through yoga, which is the essence of all religions.

Around the world, all spiritual guides, masters, healers and mystics have proclaimed that the innermost essence of being of self and the universe is untouched by sorrow, and is perfectly blissful and calm. Thus, this positive attribute of life negates the sorrow and the illumination of the mind, and the experience of the ultimate truth is all that we need to be completely free. Thus, mukti (spiritual liberation) consists of this experience of truth which is called *tattva-sakshatkar.*

Another way to defy sorrows is through realising that the perfect and uninterrupted state of self-fulfillment in the normal plane of our existence, which is called Ananda. However, we fail to realise this inner state of peace because our desires which are endless create a host of other sorrows—hunger, thirst, ambition, pleasures, need for materialistic things, and more—and we get caught up in a web that has no end.

According to the Enlightened One, Gautama Buddha, all existsence is sorrow and to get rid of this sorrow and all its possibilities, one must get rid of existence and all possibilities of future existences. His teachings also convey that desires and attachments to temporary objects that give us momentary happiness along with seeking permanence and our permanent hankerings for objects can make life even more sorrowful. Thus, it is in the absence of attachments and desires that the mind would be illumined by the light of consciousness which has transcended all distinctions such as good and bad, virtue and vice, and we would thus transcend all sorrows. In such a state, even the law of karma would have no influence upon the person and there would be no rebirth as such a mind would be free of individuality and ego. This perfectly sorrowless and illumined state of being is what Buddha calls nirvana, which is synonymous with the Hindu concept of moksha and mukti.

According to Gautam Buddha, "existence means impermanent everchanging sorrowful phenomenal existence". The illumined mind has to pass through the stage of "non-existence" called *maha-parinirvana*, i.e., a transcendent existence that is not bound by limitations of time and space, and is peaceful, calm and blissful. This liberation from phenomenal existence and the attainment of a transcendent state is the highest ideal of human life.

Linked with this is the concept of Atma or "the soul that is the permanent existing phenomenon of this phenomenal mind". It is behind *Mana*, *Buddhi* and *Ahamkara*, and remains the luminous centre of every creature. According to Hindu saints and philosophers, this soul which is the core of our being, is pure, untouched by all sorrows and remains untarnished and unaffected by the experiences of *mana*, *buddhi* and other concepts that our existence wraps us up in.

Our nature is of pure consciousness and Atma, which is the seer, is our true self. Atma remains a spectator, non-participant and a witness to this everchanging cycle and it also watches our journey of ignorance and knowledge. When we have learnt the lessons we are born for, when we have completed our journeys of sorrows, of karma, and have risen above them through detachment, when our true self has emerged without aversion, attachment, ego or anxiety, we realise our soul's real, raw and untouched character. This is the process of *jivan mukti* (mukti or moksha as realised in the living embodied condition).

Many Hindu religious-philosophcal schools belong to the cult of Bhakti, i.e., devotion, and encourage the personality or super-personality of the Brahma who is the Absolute Spirit. He possesses innumerable qualities in infinite proportions such as infinite wisdom and knowledge, detachment and calmness, beauty and sweetness, love and mercy, strength and prowess, activity, tranquillity and self-enjoyment, and he is above all temporal and spatial limitations. Devotees who cultivate their faith through deep levels of concentration believe that after death, their soul enters the spiritual realm of Brahma and enjoys an immensely blissful spiritual relationship. Different forms of mukti described by such devotees in tandem with their sadhana are: *Sarsti*, i.e., blissfully dwelling in the kingdom of Brahma, *Salokya*, i.e., enjoying the proximity of Brahma, *Sayujya*, i.e., becoming consciously united with Brahma, *Sarupya*, i.e., enjoying the likeness of Brahma, and *Ekatwa*, i.e., attaining perfect identity with Brahma.

In contrast, the non-dualistic Vedanta school of thought and many other similar schools, have different fundamentals. According to them, there are two forms of mukti. The first, *Sadyo Mukti* is "absolute liberation or union with the Absolute Spirit (Brahma) immediately after the dissolution of the physical body." This mukti is attained by those souls whose consciousness in the physical body is illumined and liberated from root ignorance and who are longer bound to the idea of an ego or an individual self, beyond the Brahma. The second, *Krama Mukti* is liberation in gradual stages, i.e., "ascent to higher and higher worlds and higher and higher planes of existence and experience in more and more refined illuminated supra-physical bodies, till the absolute liberation or union with the Absolute Spirit is realised." This mukti is experienced by individuals whose consciousness has been freed from all attachments and earthly desires. It gradually rises to higher spiritual planes and experiences non-material embodiments and ultimately merges with the Absolute Spirit.

According to the Hindu cosmic order, *Bhuh* is our world, where we live, work, and have experiences at physical, mental, spiritual and emotional levels. Above this *Bhuh Lok,* the six worlds or planes of existence in order of superiority are *Bhuvah, Swah, Mahah, Jana, Tapah,* and *Satya.* Among these, the planes of *Bhuh, Bhuvah* and *Swah* are interconnected and known as the *Trilokee* or *Trailokya* as a group. *Bhuvah Lok* is the plane where departed souls pass on to and experience pleasurable or painful experiences according to their good and evil deeds, in its different regions. After their karma is determined, these souls are reborn in new physical bodies in *Bhuh Lok*. Those souls, who have noble deeds and selfless acts to their merit, enjoy higher orders of happiness in *Swah Lok*. After reaping these rewards, they are reborn here, and again after superior spiritual merits ascend to the realm of mukti and again enjoy progressively gainful experiences of these higher *lok*s till they

Lord Brahma

attain final mukti after which they are free from the cycles of birth and death.

Gorakhnath agrees with all these philosophies of mukti or moksha, and says that it is indeed the ultimate goal of human life and it lies in realising the transcendent character of the Self or Soul. His belief was that, the Absolute Spirit (Shiva or Brahma) has an innate power, i.e., *Nija Shakti* that manifests itself in the system through innumerable bodies in various orders as well as the cosmic lord and the infinite souls connected to it. Through his illumined yogic mind, Gorakhnath is said to have seen Shiva-Shakti *Vilasa,* i.e., playful and free manifestation of the Absolute Spirit in all planes of world experience.

In this Shiva-Shakti cosmic play, every individual spirit has an innate potentiality and urge to realise this oneness with Shiva and to get rid of all limitations, bondages and imperfections of this existence. Sorrow is an important factor that determines this journey and impels the spirit to break free from all restraints and struggles to seek Shivahood. The final aim is thus gaining this oneness after several births and sorrowful experiences, and ultimately uniting with Shiva or Brahma. This perfect realisation of Shivahood or Brahmahood by each individual soul through many births, purifications and experiences of sorrow is what Gorakhnath calls, "the supreme ideal of human life" and this is yoga in its truest core.

Thus, yoga is not only the means but also an end. Described beautifully by the Mahayogi himself as:

"Samyogo yoga ityahuh kshtrajna paramatmanoh"

This simply means that, the term yoga for the enlightened yogis means the union of the soul of the body with the soul of the whole cosmic system, i.e., the union of *"Jeeva"* and *"Shiva"* and of *"Aham"* and *"Brahma"* which defines yoga as the end. The various purification exercises, meditational states, physical disciplines, and its final elevation to the Shiva consciousness encompass the means of yoga.

Gorakhnath's school of yoga is in tandem with the Eight-fold Path (i.e. Ashtang Yoga) by Patanjali in his *Yoga Sutras*. His Siddha cult expounded this with additions of various forms of asana, Pranayama, mudra, *bandha, vedha, dharana* and dhyan among others. Even the moral principles of *Yama* and *Niyama* were defined in detail by them. For all these yogis, samadhi was the fulfilment of yoga and the ideal of all humans seeking self-fulfilment and liberation from bondages of sorrows, and cycles of birth-death.

Patanjali, however, lays great emphasis on *chitta-vritti-nirodha* which is suppression of all mental functions, a state in which the transcendent character of the soul is revealed. Even Gorakhnath lays great emphasis on the mastery over mental functions, along with cosmic forces and perfect illumination of phenomenal consciousness related to this state. Eventually, this single individual or *Jeeva* consciousness is elevated to universal consciousness, i.e., Shiva Consciousness and the mind transcends itself realising it is an *Unmani* (supermind).

All yogic teachers have explained that samadhi can be complete or partial, and it depends on the suppression of the mind. However, for spiritual illumination and truth realisation, samadhi along with yogic practices has to be guided by an adept guru who can instruct and save the disciple from any probable dangers or misunderstandings. Related to this, Gorakhnath says,

"*Durlabho vishaya-tyago durlabham tattwa-darsanam Durlabha sahajavastha Sad-Guroh karunam vina.*"

(For an ordinary seeker or aspirant it is very hard to gain true success at renouncing all objects and sources of sensual pleasures and enjoyments, and to establish himself in the state of absolute peace and freedom without the help of an enlightened guru.)

In the *Siddha Siddhanta Paddhati*, Gorakhnath defines samadhi as:

"*Sarva-tattwanam saavastha nirudyamatwam anayasa-sthitimattwam iti samadhi-lakshanam*"

(The unity of all planes of existence, effortless and simple state of consciousness, and leading a life of ease and equanimity is the nature of samadhi.)

An ideal superior to samadhi according to this Mahayogi is *Samarasakarana* which involves enjoyment along with a sense of ease and tranquillity in the normal waking state and in all states of the absolute spirit. It is thus, a permanently illumined spirit in which the mind does not withdraw itself like it does in deep meditation, and is always aware of the oneness of the self with the Shiva/Brahma consciousness, unity of diversities along with the identity of each individual soul. This is a heightened state of awareness and merging.

Such an enlightened yogi actively enjoys this stage of *Samarasa*, sees and takes pleasures in the similarities and differences, deals with the plurality of material objects, participates in the joys and sorrows of people, inwardly enjoys supreme bliss amidst transitory states of sufferings, and constantly dwells in the relam of spiritual unity that is non-dual and peaceful. He thus sees himself in all and sees all in himself. This is called *Sahaj samadhi* or *Jagrat samadhi* by Gorakhnath, i.e., a samadhi of an aware and normal waking state, which is the true character of a Nath and *Avadhuta*. This is the state that every yogi seeks.

The *Goraksha Siddhanta Sangraha* defines mukti and moksha as "*Natha Swarupena Avasthiti*", i.e., the perfect realisation of Nath-hood which is the same as realisation of Shivahood and attainment of *Avadhuta*.

The Siddhas believe that there are many goals on this way to samadhi. The yogi or Nath has to first become a complete master of his physical body and the physical forces of the world that affect his daily experience. He will thus have the power to transform his physical body as he pleases or needs, into an atom, a mountain, make it impregnable to deadly weapons, experience different pleasures, exercise hypnotic influence on other people's minds, enter other bodies, elongate the span of his life, and even ultimately conquer death through sadhana.

Man possesses the power to change the course of his destiny and also the power to experience the Divine Spirit in its pure state. However, these yogic powers and shaktis remains inactive or dormant owing to the sorrows and struggles of human life. The yogi's challenge is thus, to first master his body to attain mental equilibrium and objectivity, to be one with his spiritual self. All this can be achieved through an active and disciplined practice of yoga.

The aim of yoga is thus to help each individual explore his complete potential, enlighten the mind, and unite the individual soul with the Supreme Power of the Absolute Spirit.

Mahasukh—Supreme Bliss

The cult that practices *Mahasukh*, which is a branch of Tantric Buddhism, lays great emphasis on realising the *Sahaj* nature of the self and of the Dharma through practical methods, and aims at achieving the state of supreme bliss "*Mahasukh*" through this sadhana. The most important of these aspects is discussed below.

The Guru or Preceptor

Selecting the perfect preceptor comes foremost and like the Indian religious practices a lot depends on the *guru-vada*—the doctrine of the preceptor. Just like light is transmitted from one lamp to another, truth and knowledge is passed from the guru to the disciple. Thus, the oath is to discover the truth and to understand that it is the guru's grace that can make us realise the Supreme Reality. In a non-dual state the guru can guide and spiritually uplift the disciple who is an instrument in his hands. In most Hindu spiritual paths, the guru is held in very high esteem and at times, even substituted for God. God, it is said, can only be realised through the guru who is seen as his living example.

Being a more practical aspect of spirituality, Tantrism too, lays great emphasis on the guru's guidance and includes many secret practices that involve complex processes of esoteric yoga. These intricate rituals and activities of worship need the constant help of a guru at every step and if not directed or followed methodically and in the right manner, they can even lead a devotee to the dark abysses of hell. Owing to their stringent nature, these practices are called "*guhyad guhyam*" or the secret of all secrets in Tantra. It is only with the practical help of a guru that the disciple can get initiated into this method and hence, gurus are praised very highly even in the Tantras.

The Perfect or Mature Body

The human body is of utmost importance in practical aspects of both, yoga and Tantra, and it is considered to be the microcosm of the universe. The *Hevajra Tantra* has a beautiful story to explain this. In this book it is written that the lord was once questioned by a Boddhisattva on the necessity of a human body and physical reality, when all that exists in reality is actually just pure void. The lord then replied that "without the body there was no possibility of the realisation of great bliss and here lies the importance of the body. But though the truth arises out of the body, it should never be confused with something physical."

The *Shreekalachakra* states that without the body there cannot be perfection and even supreme bliss can never be realised without it. Hence, the body, especially the nervous system, is of great importance and if the siddhi or perfection of the body is attained, all kinds of perfection in the three worlds can also be attained. Saraha, in his dohas, explains this as: "The truth is neither to be meditated nor to be held in the body as a Dharani, neither is it to be muttered as a mantra." The Buddha thus, is within the body.

The human body, therefore, came to be recognised as "the abode of all truth" and the Mahayana principles were transformed into Vajrayana, and came to be identified within the physical system. The *Sat-chakra* or the six nerve plexuses are also identified as the six lotuses along the spinal cord in the Hindu Tantric and yoga system. The Buddhists identify this as three plexuses or lotuses which are identified with the three *kaya*s.

The lowest chakra in the navel region is the lowest *kaya*, i.e., the *Manipura* or the *Nirmanakaya* (the body of transformation). The Heart chakra is identified as the *Dharmakaya*, i.e., the body of ultimate reality or the principle of cosmic unity. The chakra just below the neck is the *Sambhogakaya*, i.e, the body of bliss. The *Vajrakaya* or the *Sahajkaya* also called the fourth *kaya* according to Tantric Buddhists lies in the *Usnisa Kamala* or the *Sahasrara*, i.e., the crown of the head. This is known as the Mahasukh chakra or the Mahasukh Kamala—the seat of supreme realisation.

The principles of shunyata and *Karuna* have already been discussed and out of the various nerves in the body, thirty-two are significant and among these three are the most important. Two of these nerves correspond to the principles of *Prajna* and *Upaya* and are located on either side of the spinal cord, and one is located in the middle which is the meeting place of the other two nerves. This is the path for the Sahaj called the *Avadhutika* or *Avadhutika Marga*. *Avadhuti* is defined as "the effulgent nature of which all sins are destroyed or that which washes away beginingless thought construction of existence or that which removes the evils of afflictions very easily." These two nerves are the representation of duality and the middle nerve which is the *Sushumna* or *Avadhutika*, is the principle of absolute unity.

The Patient Practice

The process of *Kaya* Sadhana is the most important process to strengthen the body and to build its capacity for higher spiritual realisations. Even the Nath Siddhas emphasised this practice and it is crucial to all yogic and Tantric schools. In general, yoga features both psycho-physiological practices and hence the higher stages of this practice should not be entered into without a perfect and mature body. To make it mature or perfect, Hatha Yoga has to be practised and hence many Buddhist Siddhacharyas are also adept at its practice.

Many *Karya* songs make several references to strengthening the "*skandhas*", i.e., "elements whose aggregate constitutes the body." Unless *skandhas* are strengthened or body is made ripe through Hatha Yoga, *Mahasukh* for the unprepared will be a lulling sleep of the senses. This state is far removed from the supreme bliss that yogis patiently wait to experience and even the *Rati-vajra* says that if the mind and body of the seeker fall into a swoon, he cannot be perfect in yoga. Hence, having a perfect body is crucial to attain *Mahasukh*.

Bodhichitta is the bliss found in the merging of the female (principle of *prajna*, the female organ or lotus) and male (principle of *Upaya*, the male organ, the thunder). The main objective of the Buddhist *Sahajiyas* is the production of this *Bodhichitta* in the Manipura Chakra (or the navel region) and gives it an upward motion through Hatha Yoga. Through these practices they have to make it ascend through the Dharma Chakra and the Sambhoga Chakra; make it motionless in the *Usnisa Kamala* where the Sahaj nature of the *Mahasukh* is produced.

Bodhichitta in general has two aspects: the ordinary restless aspect in which it is called *Samvrta* "the form of gross sexual pleasure which accompanies the discharge". The second aspect is the *Vivrta* or *Paramarthika* "the motionless aspect of intense bliss". The *Samvrta* and *Paramarthika* of the *Bodhichitta* is the "*Samvrti-satya*" defined as "the phenomenal or provisional aspect of reality

Prajna or the lotus

and the Pramarthika, i.e., the ultimate reality of Mahayana Philosophy."

The period of attaining the perfect body and then the sadhana is long and the bliss produced by the union of *upaya-prajna* remains in the Manipura or the gross physical plane where all the bondage and suffering is stored. According to the Mahayana Philosophy, after it is produced it must ascend upwards through ten stages called the *Bodhichitta Bhumi*s and reach the *Dharma-megha* or the highest state to attain Buddhahood. According to *Sahajiyas,* this flow of bliss must ascend through the *kayas* (connected to each of the ten *bhumis*) and reach the region of *Sahaj-kaya.* Throughout this process, this bliss acquires a higher status and when it finally reaches the *Usnisa Kamala* it becomes *Mahasukh*, where all kinds of duality disappear and only a unique realisation of supreme bliss remains.

The Middle Path in Sadhana

An important part of the Mahayana school is the emphasis on the middle path, i.e., to avoid the opposite extremes of views. Nagarjun's system is thus the Madhyamika System or the middle course, which denies the views of positivists and negativists. Even the Mahayanists opposed the idea of nirvana and the existence of samsara or *bhava*, i.e, the world of suffering, and according to them the final state is neither of these. For them this state is one of non-duality in which nirvana and *bhava* become one. The middle nerve is the middle path which leads to the non-dual state of *Sahaj* and the flow of *Bodhichitta* has to be regulated through this middle nerve. This is the most important and difficult part of every yogi's sadhana. Hence, many Buddhist Tantric texts stress on being guided by the right preceptor and following the correct practical suggestions. The yogi has to ensure that the *Bodhichitta* does not flow right or left, but through the middle path. Many *karya*s suggest several ways to secure the right and left nerve to gain perfect control over them, to merge them and operate them together, in the middle nerve.

According to yogic views, the river of existence is the nervous system with three principal nerves (*abhasa-traya*), i.e. *shunya, Ati-shunya* and *Maha-shunya*. These are the principle of defilement and also the cause of all existence. The left and right sides are muddy and hence these represent the principles of defilement.The middle nerve which leads to the depth of the truth is unfathomable. The bridge that experiences this unity is the way to realise how *Bodhichitta* can be transformed through the practice of yoga.

The process of ascension or the upward motion of the *Bodhichitta* is the most significant part of all sadhana. The seeker has to hold the *apana* (wind) which has a downward motion, and prana which has an upward motion. The yogi has to arrest this course and instead make them flow through the middle nerve. Thus, with the flow of the vital wind within the middle nerve, the *Bodhichitta* will ascend upwards and gradually reach the *Usnisa Kamala* where *Mahasukh* will be experienced. The yogi has to then steady his breath, and this state is the ultimate state of yoga.

In accordance with these four chakras and lotuses, the *Bodhichitta* has four mudras which are Karma mudra, Dharma mudra, Maha mudra and Samaya mudra, which are also the four stages of yoga practice. There are also four mental states—*vichitra, vipika, vimarda* and *vilaksana*—and four kinds of bliss which are Ananda, *Paramananda, Viramananda* and *Sahajananda*. These mental states correspond to the chakras in the following way: Ananda is the bliss when the *Bodhichitta* is in the Nirmana chakra, *Paramananda* in the Dharma chakra, *Viramananda* in the Sambhoga chakra and *Sahajananda* which is the most intense and powerful. Here, *Viramananda* is detachment from the worldly pleasures whereas *Sahajananda* is the final bliss.

The Female Force

For the Sahajiya Buddhists, the female force is another important aspect to be considered. Called many names in the *karya* songs viz, Chandi, Savari, Yogni, Sahaj-Sundari and Nairamani among others, references of the yogi in union with the personified female deity are also found. This yogini should not be confused with the woman of flesh and blood. An internal force of nature of vacuity, i.e., shunyata, she is essenceless, i.e. *nairatma,* and resides in different plexuses in different stages of the yogi's body during his practice.

In the Hindu Tantras, the Kula Kundalini Shakti which lies dormant in the Muladhara chakra has to be awakened and has to unite with Shiva in the *Sahasrara*. Similarly, in the Buddhist Tantras, Shakti corresponds to what Buddhists call "the fire-force" in the Nirmanakaya, and she is described as Chandali.

The *Hevajra Tantra* describes this as: "The Chandali burns in the navel and she burns the five Tathagatas and the goddesses like Lochana and others, and when all is burnt, the moon pours down the syllable hum." Chandali is the goddess Avadhutika or Nairatma, and when she is awakened through yogic practices all the five Skandhas and their related goddesses and Tathagatas are burnt away. What remains after this is the pouring of the *hum* which is symbolic of ultimate knowledge, i.e., *Vajra Jnana*.

Gunjaripada describes this in a song as:

"The lotus and the thunder meet together in the middle and through their union Chandali is ablaze; that blazing fire in contact with the house of the Dombi. I take the moon and pour water. Neither scorching heat nor smoke is found, but it enters the sky through the peak of Mount Meru."

Thus, when the lotus and thunder unite through *mahasukh* which is like a gush of wind, Chandali is a fire in the Nirmana chakra in the navel. When this *mahasukh* is contacted, the house which is metaphorically the house of desires, complexities, and root instincts also burns away, and only the moon, i.e., the *Bodhichitta*, pours water in the fire. This fire is without smoke or heat and enters the vacuity through the Mount Meru, i.e., the spinal column.

According to the text *Sadhanamala*, *Mahamudra* who produces *mahasukh*, resides in the navel. She possesses an intense scorch and her nature is like fire. She is also said to be the first vowel, the first wisdom of the Buddhas and remains pervading the *tridhatu* (the three elements) and is unknown by *prthag jana* (lay people).

The *Samputika* describes Chandali as the female counterpart of the *Vajra-sattva* who is absorbed in him. When awakened by yogic practice, she is ablaze in the navel region. Goddess Nairatma and Vasanta-tilaka are her other names and her lustre is similar to lightning and thousand heaps of fire. When the yogi makes himself a God, this Shakti is said to pass through the whole body in all her power, burning away the Dharma chakra, then the Sambhoga chakra before finally entering the *Sahasrara* (head), and after burning away everything it returns to the navel once again.

Goddess Chandali, thus, is an internal force produced through yogic practice and in her rising to the crown she becomes the pure nature of the *Mahasukh*. The Shakti force described by the Buddhists is related to the Tantric conception of Shakti mingled with the principle of destructive fire in the navel as defined by the yogis. As she ascends, she gradually detaches herself from the qualities of defilement and grossness, and reveals the pure nature of bliss once she reaches the crown where she embodies *Mahasukh*. In her upward movement, the Chandali is called "Dombi", and in the *Mahasukha-kamala* she is called Sahaj Sundari, with whom the yogi becomes united forever.

The Final State

The real *Mahasukh* is created only when Shakti reaches the *Sahajakaya*, becomes shunyata, and the perfected *chitta* becomes the *Vajrasattva*. They then unite to create supreme bliss that is untouched by dualities or impurities. When this final state is reached, there are five signs observed by the yogis in the following order—the form of a mirage, the form of smoke, the form of firefly, burning lamp and the stainless sky. Each of these signs is extremely crucial to observe and understand for the devotee. The Marma-kalika Tantra explains that the sign of the mirage represents the knowledge about the nature of the world. When we realise the illusory nature of the Dharmas, there is no *pratibhasa* (appearance) and everything appears to be smoky, like collected causes and conditions. Just like the firefly shines for a single moment, similarly the perfect knowledge that appears through the void nature of the Dharmas is momentary. As we ascend, our knowledge deepens and intensifies, shining bright like a burning lamp, hence the fourth sign. And in the final state, it becomes like the clear blue mid-day sky of autumn, resembling a stainless sky. These signs are also included in the Shri Kalachakra Tantra.

The *Vyakta Bhavanugata Tattva Siddhi* describes the condition of the yogi who has experienced *Mahasukh*. It says that "at that time all the senses are absorbed within, all thought-constructions are destroyed, all seeds of existence are annihilated; it is full of lustre of bliss—it is like the vacant sky and yet cool and congenial." The yogi may even feel as if all his senses are asleep and the mind enters within, and the body is without any function, completely absorbed in this blissful state.

There are many songs in the *Karya Padas* that describe this state. Mahidharapada in a song compares himself to three wooden boards, i.e., the three kinds of bliss that belong to the mind, body and speech and identified them all with the self. When this happens, a spontaneous *anahata* sound like a roar arises and on hearing this, the arch enemy *mara* and all desires and afflictions related to the body vanish away. All principles of duality, sun and moon, vices and merits vanish, and the *chitta* marches on towards nirvana. This *chitta* neglects the three worlds, drinks the nectar of *Mahasukh*, and is intoxicated by it. The yogi becomes the lord of the five objects and becomes the *Vajrasattva* himself, and no enemy is found near him.

The Final State of *Bodhichitta* or the State of *Mahasukh*

From our previous discussion it will be clear that the question of the production of the *Bodhichitta* and its upward march through the different *kayas* to the *Usnisa-kamala* so as to be transformed there into *Mahasukh*, is closely associated with the question of raising the Shakti from the lowest pole of phenomenalism to the highest pole of absolute truth. When the Shakti reaches the *Vajrakaya* or the *Sahajakaya*, she becomes Shunyata herself, and our prefected *chitta* becomes the Lord Vajrasattva; real *Mahasukh* follows only when this Shunyata is united in the *Sahajakaya* with the *Vajrasattva*.

Thus, just like darkness vanishes with the appearance of the luminous pure moon, the darkness of ignorance is removed through the ascension of *Bodhichitta* and through this divine experience of *Sahaj* bliss the ultimate and absolute reality of underlying objects is also realised.

3.9 Tantric Alchemy of the Siddhas

The Siddhas and Buddhas have a secret. A secret that contains the knowledge of the elixir of life. They have the knowledge of alchemy, and not just the physically present substances but the ones contained within the body. If discovered and used in the right way, these can make the seeker the master of his destiny and turn him into a Siddha, a Buddha, an angel, and a purified soul that is one with the Divine.

Vajra Sattva

The Siddhas (the perfected/realised ones) through their sadhana realised that the human body could achieve siddhis (superhuman powers) through yogic practices, and could also attain *jivanmukti* (body immortality). The alchemists of medieval India are the Rasa Siddhas, the ones mainly from north India are Nath Siddhas, and from the Western Transmission are Pascimamnaya which is a Shakta sect that worships Goddess Kubjika of Nepal. All these groups greatly overlapped one another and their Tantric, yogic as well as alchemical knowledge and discoveries, were part of the same practice.

These Siddhas developed a concrete and coherent method through which an individual could attain the Siddha status. Their mystic practices and doctrines listed male and female sexual fluids as the elixir. "Rasa" means the fluid element in the universe, human beings and sacrifice, and these elements are seen as "the fountain of life" in the Vedas as well. Rasa is also manifested through vital fluids in plant resins, animals, humans, rains, water and sacrificial oblation. Early Tantrism also conceived the fluids of semen, uterine blood, and sexual fluids of males and females to be "power substances". However, around the tenth and eleventh centuries, the theories began to evolve, and humans were seen as androgynous beings with "sexual intercourse an affair between a female serpentine nexus of energy, generally called the Kundalini and a male principle, identified with Shiva, both of which were located within the subtle body". For the Nath Siddhas, taught by Matsyendra and Gorakhnath, siddhis and *jivanmukti* (final liberation) were seen as direct results achieved through the internal combination and transformation of sexual fluids into the Divine nectar that grants immortality, i.e. amrit. Rasa Siddhas perceived this as "*yatha lohe tatha dehe*", i.e., as in metal so in body from, their classic text called *Rasarnava*. Thus, there were similarities being drawn in the fluids of human sexuality and sexual valences and fluids of the mineral world. For instance, the sexual discharge of the goddess is seen in the form of mica, and her uterine or menstrual blood is seen as sulphur. Mercury is another important element as it is said to possess miraculous properties.

The origin of mercury is wrapped in intriguing tales and Agni plays an important role in its origin. According to legend, Shiva and his consort were in a hidden cave in the Himalayas when the gods pleaded with them to produce Skanda to avenge Traka, who had set out to destroy the universe. However, Agni in the form of a pigeon was watching the Divine couple from a window. Upon seeing Agni, Lord Shiva was ashamed and shed his seed which had a bright brilliance and fell into the mouth of fire. Fire was also unable to contain it and it was spit into the Ganges who was also overwhelmed by it and with the power of her waves, pushed the semen ashore. From this seed, Skanda was born and the places where Agni (fire) dropped this seed from his mouth, formed into five wells of mercury that were nine hundred miles in depth. It is believed that the god's semen is found here even today.

According to a twentieth century scholar alchemist: "The central idea upon which the whole structure of the Hindu Chemistry is erected is the fact that mercury can be made to swallow, by special processes, a considerable quantity of gold or other metals, without any appreciable increase in the weight of the swallowing mercury."

It is also compared to being similar to the "All absorbing Shiva as he is the God who at the end of cyclic time has the capacity to absorb the entire universe in his perfect yogic body and transform mere existence into essence—just like mercury that absorbs a seed or drop of gold and silver, multiplies itself trillions of times in mass in base metals and

Agni

transmutes it into gold."

Often called "wizards of alchemy", Gorakhnath and his clan of Siddhas were yogis who had perfectly fit bodies with excellent digestion, and very long lives. It is believed that this was because they ingested mercury and sulphur as part of their daily regime. Yoga and alchemy are closely linked and are complementary and interpenetrating disciples that were perhaps the secret of longevity and immortality of these enlightened yogis.

The number "five" is especially significant and the Brahmanas describe the universe as being a five-fold one and explain the significance of their great five-layered fire altar, Agnicayana. These five layers as per the *Saptapatha Brahmana* are the five body constituents of the deity Prajapati and also the five seasons, five directions and more. In fact, the *Taittiriya Upanishad* represents these five elements in equation with the universal and microcosmic man as: "From this atman verily ether arose; from ether air; from air fire; from fire, water; from water, earth; from earth, herbs; from herbs, food; from food, semen; and from semen, Man."

This notion is part of the beliefs of metaphysical systems of ancient and classical India in particular, the Samkhya system, the Vedanta system and the Buddhist Dhamma system, and is relevant even today, especially in the nature of life and death. The phrase *Panchatvam Gamana,* which means going to the fiveness, the five elements encompasses this view. Even the Buddhist premise of deconstruction of a perceived unity called "self" was an ever-changing configuration of five *khandha*s or aggregates. According to this theory, existence is a series of evanescent recombinations of sensations, conceptions, mental formations, consciousness and appearances. The end of suffering, i.e., nirvana lies in dissociating these five aggregates from the notions of "self", for it is this that keeps one trapped in existence.

Both, the Vedanta and Samkhya systems shaped reality into five sets of categories headed by the preternatural pentad of *purush* (man), *prakriti* (nature), *buddhi* (intellect), *ahamkara* (ego), and *manas* (mind). Below this are four parallel pentads which interpenetrate and correspond to one another:

1. **Five *buddhindriyas*** of, i.e, sense capacities of of hearing, feeling, seeing, tasting and smelling.
2. **Five *karmendriyas*** i.e., action capacities of speaking, grasping,

excreting, generating and walking.

3. **Five *tanmatras*** i.e., subtle elements, i.e, sound, touch, taste, smell and form.

4. **Five *mahabhutas*** i.e., gross elements of air, fire, water, earth and ether.

In the Hindu system, the metaphysical differentiations or the cosmic principles, i.e, the *tattvas* of Samkhya were perceived as the "twenty-five faces of Mahasadasiva". After initial resistance, even Buddhism yielded to the yogic experience. In Ashvaghosha's (AD 80) theory of *tathata* or "suchness", the gap that Buddha taught between samsara (existence) and nirvana or (cessation) was yielding to yogic experiences. Later, as the Mahayana school emerged, the *Dharmakaya*, i.e., the "Buddha Body" which consisted of Buddha's teachings as a universal concept, was equivalent to the Vendantin's Brahman system that helped the seeker enter into a mystic union with the Divine.

Buddhist Tantrics also theorised that the Buddha had five emanated Buddhas or Tathagatas: Amitabha, Vairochana, Ratnasambhava, Akshobhya, and Amoghasiddhi. Each of these five emanated Buddhas were equated with the five elements. Additionally, each of these five Buddhas presided over five lineages of five Boddhisattvas which totalled to twenty-five divine beings when added to the *Dharmakaya*, which is similar to the Samkhyan categories.

The *Jnanasiddhi* very aptly states that:

"Since they have the nature of the five Buddhas, the five constituents of the human personality are called *jina*s (conquerers): and the five *dhatu*s (elements) correspond to the Buddhas Shaktis.... Therefore our body is a Buddha body."

This radical change of thoughts and beliefs was crucial to the rise of the Buddhist Tantra, and Hindu Tantrism too expanded into *kulas* or lineages of divinities. Soon, there were many Samkhyan categories and Buddhist transcendent categories (thirty-seven in the Trika Kaula synthesis). The supreme Hindu gods Shiva and Shakti had a sexual reinterpretation as the Samkhyan pair of Purusha and Prakriti.

These reformations of the Samkhyan System had many practical applications in the fields of Hatha Yoga and alchemy, and together, these emphasised the five elements. The former system identified the five elements with the five lower chakras whereas in alchemy mercury—the semen of Shiva—was seen as containing all the five elements.

The Gupta age in particular was the period in which there was an intense syncretism between Hinduism and Buddhism. Most of the alchemical tales are found in Buddhist literature, and sources like Bana's *Kadambari* contain accounts of Hindu alchemical heroes. Immortality and transcendence of the body are the goals, and the means to these is said to be serendipity. *"Rasa-rasayana"* is the intriguing and deeply mystical aspect here. A mercurial elixir and philosopher's stone, it is said to be among the eight magical siddhis or yogic powers of Mahayana Buddhism, medieval Hinduism and Jainism. Interestingly, this is a power or object that has to be won or wrested from the gods, demigods, or demons, and not produced in the laboratory. Ultimately, the goal of Tantric alchemy is to help the seeker gain the secrets, knowledge and path to immortality, invincibility, and transcend the human condition. Through the practice, the Tantric alchemist, like the yogis and tantrics, wants to eventually be able to render himself a godlike Shiva.

What makes Tantric alchemy different from magical alchemy are the therapeutic uses of mercurials proper to the Ayurvedic tradition. In Alberuni's text, the procedure is that the alchemist has to first "test out" his mercury on metals and then throw himself into the alchemical cauldron. Only mercury can be used here as it has the capacity to transmute ten million times its mass of base metals into gold. Dual focus is the necessity here which the *Rasarnava* describes as *"yatha lohe tatha dehe"*—as in metal so in body... first test (mercury) on a metal, then use it on the body." The two elements, metals (*loha*) and bodies (*deha*) define these two branches of Tantric alchemical synergy—*lohavada* (transmutational alchemy) and *dehavada* (elixir alchemy). The transmutation to gold is not the end result here, but the means which is necessary to reach the ultimate end of bodily immortality.

Tantric alchemy is consistent with the broader Hindu traditions and features many references to Tantric formulae or chants (mantras) and diagrams (mandalas). It also contains many descriptions of divine hierarchies, yogic, meditative, sexual and ritual practices. Central to the beliefs is the Shaiva-Shakta devotionalism, which has become the hallmark of this tradition. Many Hindu roots such as the teachings of Shiva in his Tantric Bhairav form, and forms of the goddess as Kali and Tara, reflect the Hindu roots connected to this science. However, many Buddhist elements are connected with all these Hindu aspects as discussed earlier, and Tantric alchemy and magical alchemy are a synthesis of both these cultures and cults.

There are many instances of shared ancestry or homology between the symbols and instances found in Tantric texts and the alchemy of the human body. The Matsyodari-Yoga, i.e., the fish-belly conjunction is an important reference point of yogic practices. This practice has been described by Gorakhnath in the *Amaraugh Prabodh* as: "Holding the breath when it is restrained by force (*hathat*)... in the fish belly (*minodare*)".

This is an important fundamental aspect of breath control called *kumbhaka* which is the "potlike diaphgramatic retention of the breaths". In this process, the channels of *Ida* and *Pingala* are pumped heavily until they open through breath control until the channel of the *Sushumna Nadi* suddenly opens up. At this point, these two channels empty out and remain collapsed. After this, automatically the vital breath rushes into the *Sushumna Nadi* and ascends upwards against the downward flow of bodily fluids, and the yogi attains liberation.

According to a Puranic legend, the god Bhairav while bathing during the "fish-belly conjunction" had attained freedom from the skull of Lord Brahma which had clung to his hand for twelve years. Thus, when he completed this *kapalika vrata* or the skull bearer's vow, Bhairav became the guardian deity presiding at Benares, at a shrine near the banks of the *Kapalamochana* (Liberation from the Skull) tank. This liberation experience by the god is similar in nature to what a liberated yogi experiences using the fish-belly practice. This practice of Matsyodari-Yoga is thus a Hatha yogic practice founded by Matsyendranath himself.

The Moon Island, the shore where Matsyendranath gained the secret knowledge of yoga from Shiva, is another intriguing symbol in alchemy. The island is believed to exist in the left side of the human body where the lunar *Ida Nadi* passes. *Kaulajnananirnaya* by Matsyendranath explains this as the oozing of the nectar through the *brahmarandhra* as the "gladdening of the moon" and it is interconnected to the lunar posture or the Chandrasana with the Hatha yogic power of the Khechari mudra, believed to be in the cranial vault. This explains why so many alchemists and even the teachings of the Western Transmission lay emphasis on the "western" or the left side of the body for major spiritual transformations of the subtle body.

The Mare's Mouth or the inner linga which is believed to be hidden by the mouth of the sleeping Kundalini is another important structure for the alchemical body. According to some legends and scholarly sources, this is located in the left side of the abdominal cavity called the *paschima-linga* or simply, the western linga. It is important to note that the sleeping Kundalini is identified with *Kalagni* (the fire of time) that eventually through the aging process, leads all creatures to their death. However, *Yogagni* or the fire of yoga, can destroy this fire of time through "Rudra of the Fire of Time", i.e., *Kalagnirudra*. This fire is greater than that of time itself and can even totally consume it. The passage of time of the sleeping Kundalini is determined by the movements of the sun and moon in the physical body whereas when the Kundalini is finally awakened, the *Ida* and *Pingala nadis* or the sun and moon become immobilised and the Kundalini energy which ascends through the *Sushumna Nadi*, consumes time.

Related to this is the concept of the "Mare's Mouth". When the Kundalini rises, a column of ambrosial fluid moves upwards from the *Sushumna Nadi* and floods the cranial vault in the brain. This is called the Mare's Mouth where the upward channelling of the seeds causes the *badava* or the downward fire to flare up from the place where it is submerged in the subtle body. A fifteenth century poem by Kabir asks the yogi to, "reverse the (flow of the) Ganges, and dry up the ocean".

The *badava* also has other Tantric and alchemical purposes and uses. Basically, this "fire in the mouth of the submerged mare" is identified with many pilgrimage sites and historical places. The Kamakhya, an important Shakti peeth, has a gas vent which is called *badava kunda*, i.e, pool of the submarine (mare) fire. In Himachal Pradesh, a similar place that is linked with the goddess is called *Jvalamukhi* i.e the mouth of a volcano. These places of geothermic and volcanic activity are important areas where deposits of mercury and sulphur occur naturally.

Apart from gas vents and volcanic mouths, other fiery mouths indentified in Tantric alchemy include the *adhovakrta*, i.e., the lower mouth—the yoni or the vulva of the yogini. A text of the Western Transmission dating back to the twelfth century identifies the *vadavanala* or the submarine fire with the Muladhara chakra of the subtle body. The vulva, like the Kundalini energy, is a source of great pleasure, power and danger for the yogi/yogini who can master it with practice. The exact result of this is explained by Gorakhnath as:

"Penis in the vulva's mouth, mercury in the mouth of fire, he who can retain these, (volatile substances of semen and mercury), him I call my guru."

It is also important to note that like Matsyendra's Yogini Kaula, there are various sects who incorporate sexual intercourse and activities into their practice. However, the Nath Siddhas led by Gorakhnath remain strictly celibate, are misogynists and consider sexuality to be a trap in which the yogi may lose all the precious knowledge of his sadhana and devotion (in the form of his precious semen).

Another homologous instance in Siddha and the Buddhist tradition of alchemy is of drums. The mridang or the two headed drum that Gorakhnath used to awaken his guru Matsyendranath from his state of maya from the Kingdom of Kadali is similar to instruments used by Tantric Tibetan Buddhists in Mongolia and Tibet. These damarus are made of "two human skulls joined together near the fontanelle with a rectangular hole drilled between them which, establishing communication between the two hemispheres allows the instrument to breathe and thereby have a better sound." This opening or hole is called the "Nada". The player during ceremonies usually holds a bell or *ghanta* in his left hand that complements the *damaru* in the left. In the Vajrayana context, these are said to symbolise the sun and the moon, the right and left channel and skill in means (*Upaya*) and wisdom (*Prajna*) which corresponds to the Buddhist concepts of Shiva and Shakti.

Many archaic divinities are also seen in both Hindu and Buddhist legends and iconography, and an example of this is snakes or serpents. In classic Hinduism, it is mentioned that "it is a serpent that serves to support the entire universe atop his bejewelled hood and at times when the Universe is non-existent (exactly half the time), he supports the sleeping God Vishnu and the Buddha too is sheltered by the hood of a serpent..." A great proof of this is a third century AD sculpted image of the Buddha on a serpent couch which is found in Nagarjunakonda (Andhra Pradesh) in south India. It is also in this region that the Buddhist text *Gandavyuha* dating back to the third century AD locates the seat of the Boddhisattva Manjushri who converted many indigenous serpents to Buddhism. This region was also where Nagarjun, the esteemed philosopher hailed from and who is identified as being a Siddha alchemist hailing from Sriparvata.

There are many instances that try to decipher whether it was Nagarjun who brought mercury and Goddess Tara to India. However, her two forms of Vajra (diamond) Tara and Ekajata (One Lock of Hair) suggest that she came to India through her connect with Nepal around the seventh century AD. Tibetans believed this mysterious philosopher was a siddha and his longevity was thanks to his amazing alchemy. The fourteenth century historian Bu-ston states that Nagarjun had procured gold-making elixir from the intermediate continent which had eventually saved Nalanda from famine. Additional references include notes by Taranath from the early seventeenth century that state that "with the help of the art of alchemy, he maintained for many years five hundred teachers of the Mahayana Doctrine at Shri Nalendra [*sic*]." He further adds, "From the time he became a Rasayana Siddha, his face shone like a gemstone." Late Tibetan sources also affirm this, stating that Nagarjun had received his initiation from his guru, Siddhacharya Saraha-pa and he "attained success...especially in the Rasayana" which was so immense that his body is said to have become as hard as a diamond (*vajrakaya*-siddhi).

By the twelfth century, historical records suggest that Buddhism gradually disappeared from the Indian subcontinent and the early alchemical traditions mirrored a syncretistic trend with clan lineages, mantras, and divinities converging with one another. Some instances of these pious overlaps are, Tara and Akshobhya, Avalokiteshvar and Shiva Lokanath, Vajrasattva-Adibuddha and Adinath, and also Mahakala. There are traces of Buddhist alchemical traditions in early Taoist practices and contemporary Hindu erotico-mystical techniques as well.

Even the Siddhacharyas, i.e., the teachers who were the founders of the Tantric Buddhist path between the seventh and twelfth centuries AD have mentioned obtaining elixirs. For instance,

Karnari-pa obtained his elixir from urine, Vyadi-pa produced an alchemical elixir with the help of a prostitute, and Carpata-pa gained the power to transmute and obtained an elixir of immortality from the penis and anus of a boy respectively.

The Buddhist alchemical tradition, in particular, offers the most penetrating view in the early eleventh century of the Kalachakra Tantra, which was was headed in the "internal direction" as opposed to the Hindu alchemical tradition that was mostly "external". Thus, the Kalachakra Tantra mentions that the external manipulation of mercurials and metals, which is called gold-making (*Kimaya* or *gser' gyur*) is "mundane" and is considered inferior to the "transmundane" inner alchemy (*rasayana*) of "channels and winds" which can lead to direct enlightenment. The Vajrayana alchemical practice consists of fixing the *Bodhichitta* by combining the ambrosial essences *(bhud rtsi)* of *prajna* (the female aspect, The Goddess of Wisdom) and *Upaya* (the male aspect, the Skill in Means), and the cultivation of a "Rainbow body" *(ja'lus)* or a "body of light" *('od lus)*.

It was in the eleventh and fifteenth centuries that Hindu Siddha alchemy truly emerged which was a fusion of Tantric alchemy and Hatha Yoga. These lists included Naths who were exclusively Hindu, and Siddhas who were Buddhist and Hindu. Siddha was the term used to acknowledge them extensively. One of the major ways these Siddhas came to be classified was the *Peeth*s and *Amnaya*s.

*Peeth*s usually refer to pilgrimage sites of the goddess in Shakta devotionalism and around the ninth century AD during the time of Brahmayamala Tantra, commenced a tradition of four literary *peeth*s. Here major texts were divided under simplistic headings like *vidya*, mantra, mudra, and mandala *Peeth*s. The most crucial texts of this period fell under the classifications of *Vidya Peeth* and *Mantra Peeth*.

The classification system of the *Amnaya*s emerged a little later and this was used to arrange the Kaula sects and texts, in a more geographical manner. Thus, the four *Amnaya*s are the eastern (which includes Trika centered on the three goddesses), western (includes worship of Goddess Kubjika, the "Contracted One", who is a form of the Hatha yogic Kundalini), northern (includes Krama which worships Goddess Kali) and southern (includes Srividya which worships the Goddess Tripura Sundari).

These classifications offer an overview of the heritage of the medieval mystics of India—the Buddhists, Hindus, Jains, Muslims, yogis and alchemists from Tibet to south India. Giuseppe Tucci sums this as: "Siddhas are the most eminent personalities of medieval India's esoterism and represent the ideal link between Sivaism and Vajrayana, indeed the expression of the same religious and mystical endeavour, translated through analogous symbols."

Another intriguing group that deserves mention is the Mahesvara Siddhas. This term is generally used for alchemists who do not seek *jivanmukti* (bodily immortality) but instead, their final goal is another kind of liberation called *paramukti*. They aspire towards achieving a *divya-deha* (divine body), rather than a perfected Siddha-*deha* (adamantine or a vajradeha physical body).

The *Rasarnava*, dating back to the eleventh century, is acknowledged as the greatest alchemical work. This book has cosmopolitan references to the alchemical histories, and even though it is penned in Sanskrit, it has a homogeneous and geographically widespread tradition. The lineage described in this book is that of many other Tantric sects and is said to be transmitted through female sexual emissions termed *siddhadravya*. The author also mentions that erotico-mystical worship and sexual intercourse is essential to alchemical transformation. Interestingly, the sexual and menstrual fluids of a female lab assistant are considered crucial for the alchemist's practice. This fluid called *"dravya"* is said to be withheld from other women, i.e., *paradarat*.

A Tantric alchemist is also said to control his Tantrism, and tone down certain Kaula erotico-mystical practices with Kapalika techniques which include both Hatha Yogic and laboratory techniques.

Basically, the goal of Buddhist alchemy is to help the individual produce the ambrosia or the nectar of immortality and wisdom, through a yogic and sexual combination of semen and uterine blood. Hindu alchemy has similar objectives, but relies on external substances like minerals to achieve these results. Erotico-mystical practices of Tantra came to be called the "Vajroli mudra" by the Hindu yogis and were simply called "Alchemy" by Tibetan Buddhists.

Rasa, in the Vedantic terms, means waters and liquids in general, including animal juices, vegetable soups, animal juices and more.

The application of this term extends to Ayurvedic medicine, Hatha Yoga, alchemy, and Indian aesthetics in general. It can also be taken to mean the fluid of the universe's great pulsating flow and essence. In the Vedas, rasa is considered similar to water, i.e. *ap*, soma as the moon or Chandra, semen, i.e., *retas*, and the mythic liquor of immortality. In general terms, rasa can be applied to any oblation offered into Agni (fire), and the essence then reaches the gods through *vayu* (wind) right upto heaven. This combination of rasa-Agni-*vayu* permeates all Indian practices and in the Aryankas and Upanishads, rasa was called the "body as oblation" whose fluids were transformed over fires of Tapas, i.e., ascetic ardour, and fanned by the breaths of the prana (vital breaths).

Internal Hatha Yogic practices are largely based on the dynamics of lunar (chandra), solar (surya) and vital (prana), which are considered to be on par with the rasa-Agni-*vayu*. Specifically speaking, in Hatha Yogic practices, the rasas are often taken to mean male and female *Bindus* (drops), which are said to be lunar and solar, seminal and sanguineous, and Shiva and Shakti, respectively. However, realising a state of equilibrium between the members of this pair is equal to forming a "great drop" or *Mahabindu* from which an all-powerful and immortal self of *jivanmukta* emerges. The male and female sexual essences are sublimated into mineral essences by the alchemist. These are described by Shiva as:

"You, O Goddess, are the mother of all beings, and I am the eternal father, and that which was generated from the great sexual union of us two, that is rasa."

In the ancient Indian science of Ayurveda, rasa was signified as a bodily fluid, and in Samkhya, as the element water, rasa was taken to signify the sense of taste. Hence, in Ayurveda was born the system of six rasas or tastes—sweet, bitter, acid, saline, hot, pungent and astringent, which arose from a mixture of water along with the other four gross elements, in different proportions. Apart from this ayurvedic interpretation, the Indian theory of aesthetics, of rasa (taste), was portrayed in the forms of dance, drama, literature through bhava (raw emotion). Ayurveda also considers rasa to be the support of all bodily constituents (*dhatus*), and digestion is said to be the serial cooking (*pachana*) of bodily constituents on the constituent fires (*dhatvagnis*).The end product of this process is semen in men and uterine blood in women.

These combine during conception to form the human embryo.

In the Siddha medicine of south India, the five elements are identified with five metals, viz., gold with earth, lead with water, iron with air, copper with fire, and zinc with ether. This is explained in Hatha Yogic terms in a simple way: When the Kundalini rises from the Muladhara chakra (base of the spine, earth) to the Svadhisthana chakra (organs of regeneration, water), the earth element gets absorbed into fire in the Manipura chakra (navel region, fire), fire then turns to air in the Anahata chakra (heart region, air), and air then transmutes into ether in the Vishuddhi chakra (throat region, ether).

The awakening of the Kundalini marks the commencement of the yogi's withdrawal into his/her trance or sleep into a totally integrated state called samadhi. The poles of the Kundalini's mode of being are sleeping and waking which are also metaphorically said to be her poison and her nectar. When she remains asleep in the lower abdomen the Kundalini is poison, and when she rises up the medial channel she is nectar to unite with the Absolute— Shiva. In Hatha Yogic practices, this phenomenon is said to make the yogi immortal because of the outpouring of nectar that occurs with the union.

Speaking of *Rasayana*, the *Charaka Samhita* states: "Long life, heightened memory and intelligence, freedom from disease, a healthy glow, good complexion, a deep powerful voice, great bodily and sensory powers, the capacity to see one's pronouncements realised, respectability, beauty, all these does one obtain from *rasayana*. It is called *rasayana* because it is a means to replenishing the rasa and other *dhatus* of the body."

Interestingly, the term "*rasa-rasayana*" was used in the second century AD in Hindu and Buddhist philosophies, to represent siddhis (supernatural powers) of alchemical transmutation and bodily transubstantiation. There is no reference of this siddhi in early texts. However, it was one of the eight magical powers, listed alongside *padalepa*, in which the feet were smeared with a cream that produced the power of flight that was often fantasised by Hindus and Buddhists during the first century CE.

Even the Vedic ritual of soma-sacrifice, of drinking the soma-juice, is believed to rejuvenate the body of the drinker, and is also offered to the gods. It is prepared from sacrostema viminalis, a plant which is said to grow abundantly in Indian and Persian soil, and is also mentioned many times in the *Avesta* and the *Vedas* in connection to sacrifice. Interestingly, the link between the soma plant and moon is very special. The soma plant is also called the moon-plant as it was believed to have been born of the moon itself, which is seen as the source of its reinvigorating juice. In fact, the moon was believed to be the force behind the powers of all medicinal herbs, even possessing the capacity to grant longevity to the person.

The *Vishnu Purana* has an important fable related to this. It mentions that Brahma had appointed the moon as the monarch of planets, plants and penances, and one of its names was "*Osadhi-pati*" or "*Sadhisa*", i.e. "The Lord of Herbs". The soma plant is also said to possess sixteen leaves that are connected to the digits of the moon and according to a Puranic legend: "At the churning of the ocean after all sorts of medicinal plants and healing herbs are thrown in, three of the precious things said to be produced are soma 'the moon', amrit 'the nectar', and *sura* 'spirituous liquor'. In other fables, it is believed to be preserved in the moon's body and this can be taken as the reason why yogis of the Vedic and post-Vedic times, had the ritual of drinking soma to gain eternal life."

Another important alchemical element is mercury. Alchemical mercury was seen as divine semen and it principal reagents, i.e., sulphur (*gandhaka*) and mica (*abhraka*) were the uterine blood and sacred emissions of the goddess. The yogic and alchemical traditions in India identify mercury (rasa, *parada, suta)* to be the semen of Shiva, and red arsenic (*manahsila*) or sulphur (*gandhaka*) with the menstrual blood (*khapuspa, rajas, sonita, artava*)or sexual emission (*virya*) of the goddess.

In the Indian context especially, *sindur* (or vermilion which is red mercuric oxide or synthetic cinnabar), is taken to be a substitute for, or a complement to, blood offerings. Blood is often seen to be closely linked with fertility and procreation and hence, married Indian women wear vermilion in the parting of their hair as a sign of connubial felicity. Red arsenic or *manahsila* is also identified with the uterine blood of the goddess and this can be related to Kamakhya Peeth in Assam where, according to the myth, when the goddesse's yoni fell in this region it is said to have taken the form of a great block of red arsenic where it fell on the earth.

There are five sacred alchemical places in India—Hinglaj Devi, Gauri Kund (near Kedarnath), Kamakhya, which are mineral manifestations of the goddess with a mercurial source, and Girnar in Junagadh district of Gujarat and Srisailam in Kurnool district of Andhra Pradesh, which have what is called a more "masculine mercury". Hinglaj is similar to Kamakhya and consists of many caves and wells, and most importantly the Moon Well or Baba Chandrakupa known for its geothermic activity.

Ca-ri in Southeast Tibet is considered the abode of Shiva and the goddesses, Chakrasamvara and Vajravarahi, and is deeply revered by Hindus and Buddhists. A narrow fissure of this temple is the entrance of its cave which is identified with the goddess' yoni and it is believed that the lake of sindur (red mercuric oxide) is contained in it. This is said to be co-mingled with the sexual fluids of the Divine spirits, dakinis, gods and goddesses that reside in the "womb cave" of this Tibetan goddess, and these are identified with *nadis* and chakras in the Buddhist subtle body. Thus, it is said that the pilgrim who follows the subterranean passages of this "womb-cave" to its very end is following the path that ascends to the Goddess Vajravarahi's medial channel, i.e., from her yoni (organs of regeneration) upto her *brahmarandhra* (crown area). Thus, the pilgrim ascending upwards seems to be following the streams of divine blood, semen and *sindur* (mercuric oxide), and following the course of the prajna and Upana which are the Buddhist terms for the Shiva-Shakti supreme realisation of the self.

Interestingly, pilgrimage sites of the goddess or Shakti Peethas have been considered as centres within the subtle body by Indian texts, as well as Buddhist Tantras. The four peethas of Buddhism such as Kamarupa, Jalandhara, Purnagiri and Uddiyana are seen to complement the four chakras within the Buddhist subtle body. Additionally, Shiva-Shakti sites like the sacred places of Srisailam, Hinglaj Devi, Kamakhya, Kedarnath and Girnar have deep-rooted alchemical traditions connected with them. Lord Shiva's Mount Kailash, especially, is described as "an alchemical wonderland" in the introductory pages of the *Rasarnava*. Thus, both Hindu and Buddhist alchemies are Tantric and very similar in essence as both cults place a great deal of importance and reference to bodily and concrete experiences which are liberating and greatly knowledgeable.

The Tantric universe is a "pulsating, vibratory universe", because of the exciting and enigmatic ways in which matter, souls and sounds are the outpouring of godhead, i.e. Shiva, and his manifestation or reflection that occurs in the form of the goddess. It is also considered to be a "bipolar, sexualised universe" wherein changes are seen as interpenetration of male and female principles. It is a hierarchised universe wherein sources higher in nature are capable of encompassing, penetrating and reabsorbing in itself, those sources which are of a lower plane. This Tantric universe is also a "radiating universe", wherein the source of the manifest world is seen to be in the centre of a huge network of metaphysical categories, divinities and more are interconnected in a complex interplay of energies. Over and above, the Tantric universe is said to be an "emancipating universe" wherein all beings, souls, bodies, matters are free and everything is a play of divine consciousness. Thus, Tantrism encompasses all planes of experience (physical, practical, and concrete), and along with knowledge, liberates each and every part of the entire cosmology.

3.10 Tantric Symbols of the Siddhas

Endless Knot

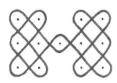

Endless Knot

Called "Beloved One" or "*Srivatsa*" in Sanskrit, this endless knot is an auspicious symbol for both Hindus and Buddhists. It represents the Buddha's endless wisdom and compassion. It also represents the "twelve links of dependent origination" which is the foundation of the reality of cyclic existence. In Hinduism, this knot is said to resemble the hair curl on Vishnu's breast and the devotion he has for his wife Goddess Lakshmi. Since the goddess is a manifestation of

Sun

good fortune and prosperity, this symbol represents wealth and abundance. It is also a graphic presentation of the sun and of how it looks from earth.

Lotus

A flower that grows in muddy waters and yet remains untainted, the lotus is a Buddhist symbol of purity and renunciation. The lotus is often seen in many spiritual iconographies as the seat of gods and goddesses upon which they stand or sit, and are considered absolutely pure in heart, mind and body. In Hinduism, the lotus is called "Kamala" or "Padma", and Surya (the Sun God) is said to hold this flower in both hands representing the sun's path across the heavens. It is also often seen as a symbol of potency, symbolic of the Divine womb or vagina and used as a metaphor in both Hindu and Buddhist Tantra. The Lotus in Tantric studies represents "the female vagina which is soft, pink and open" and the *vajra* represents the penis which is "hard and penetrative". Together, they form a sexual symbol of form and emptiness, or skilful means and wisdom. In an internal level, this signifies the penetration and ascent of yogic/Kundalini energy into the central channel that pierces and opens the channels or chakras of the subtle body.

Lotus

Thunderbolt/*Vajra*

In Sanskrit, *vajra* means "the hard or mighty one" and in Tibetan, it is called "*dorje*", which means "Lord of Stones". This signifies the hardness and brilliance which is similar to a diamond which cannot be cut or broken. The Buddhist *vajra* thus, represents the immovable, immutable, indivisible and indestructible force of absolute reality that the seeker attains with the enlightenment of Buddhahood. In the Vedas, the *vajra* was the weapon or the thunderbolt of the rain god Indra. It is said that he used it to control the thunder and lightning of monsoons and to slay dragons. The single-pointed *vajra* represents union of

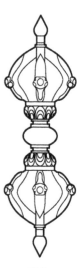

Vajra

polarities. The three-pointed *vajra* represents overcoming the three primary poisons of desire, aversion and ignorance, and also control over past, present and future,and control over the three realms of below, upon and above ground. It also symbolises attainment of the three *kaya*s or the Divine bodies of the Buddha, and the three main psychic *nadi*s or yogic channels. The five-pointed *vajra* represents the enlightened wisdom qualities of the five Buddhas, five purified elements, five sensory perceptions and five sense organs. The nine-pointed vajra represents the complete realisation of the nine yanas of the Niyama tradition, Buddha and his Eight-fold Noble Path, the Vajradhara surrounded by eight great Boddhisattvas, and the Mandala which is the principal of the centre of eight directions.

Six-Pointed Star

A universal symbol of divinity, the six-pointed star carries the message "As Above, So Below". It symbolises the connection of heaven and earth through the physical/human body. Also called "*shatkona*" in Hindi, it is an important yantra associated with Shiva-Shakti.

Shatkona

Trident/*Trishul*

Called *Trishul* in Sanskrit, the origin of the trident can be dated back to the Harappan civilisation of the Indus Valley, and it is a prominent symbol and weapon of Lord Shiva as asserted in all sacred texts including the *Vedas*. It represents Shiva's three powers of *Iccha* (will), *Jnana* (knowledge), and *Kriya* (action), and his mastery over the three realms. It also signifies his form of "Triveni" or the "The Lord of Three Rivers" viz., the ancient rivers of Ganga, Yamuna and Saraswati. The trident also represents the qualities of creation, preservation and destruction associated with the Holy Hindu Trinity of Brahma, Vishnu and Mahesh, respectively.

Trishul

In early Tantric Buddhism, the trident is among the first representations to appear as the insignia of the crown of Brahma, on Buddha's footprints. It is also symbolic of the trinities of the "Three Jewels" of the Buddha's teachings of wisdom, ethics and meditation. In Vajrayana Buddhism, the trident is often found in deities associated with Shiva, viz, Chakrasamvara, Vajrabhairava and Mahakala. It also represents the Mahayana trinity of Buddha, Dharma and Sangha, and the Vajrayana trinity of guru, yidam and dakini.

Wheel

Dharmachakra

Since ancient times, the wheel has been seen by Hindus as a solar symbol of creation, protection and sovereignty. The "chakra" or wheel is considered to be the main attribute of the Hindu God of Preservation—Vishnu, whose fiery six spiked Sudarshana chakra symbolises the wheel of the phenomenal universe, continuity, change, motion, and the continuous circling of the universe.

The wheel is also an important symbol for Buddhists who call it "The Golden Wheel" or the "Dharmachakra". It is the emblem of Vairochana and its eight spokes symbolise the Eight-fold Path of the Noble Truths, as instructed by the Buddha. It literally represents the wheel of transformation or spiritual change and its motion is symbolic of the rapid transformation that Buddha's teachings bring. It is often compared to a *chakravartin,* and shows the ability to cut through all obstacles and illusions.

Damaru

The origin of the *damaru* can be traced back to the early Harappan civilisation where it was first seen as a picture, in the ancient Indus Valley script. A Shaivite emblem, it is often depicted as being held in the hands of Shiva's form of Nataraj, the "King of Dance", who uses it while dancing. The drum creates the vibrant sound of the male rhythm (*taal*) which underlies the female rhythm (*raag*).

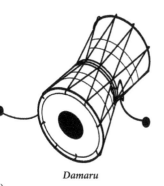

Damaru

The Tantric or Kapalika *damaru* is often shown as being held by wrathful deities and semi-wrathful Buddhist deities, and are said to be made from human craniums or skulls obtained from burial grounds. Always held in the right hand, the purpose of the *damaru* is to invoke all the Buddhas, Boddhisattvas, and dakinis, and fill them with supreme joy. The *damaru* is held in the right to signify the sound of great bliss and in the left to signify the female hand or the sound of emptiness.

Mridang

A famous musical instrument used throughout India, the *mridang* is a large barrel shaped drum that is often iconographically represented as being in the hands of the attendants, of deities. Also used during festivities and many auspicious occasions, this instrument has a distinct sound and

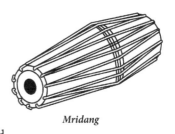

Mridang

vibration that pleases the gods and can even awaken those afflicted by maya, as shown in the legend of Matsyendranath's fall when his student Gorakhnath uses this drum to awaken his master in the Kadali kingdom.

Conch (Shankha)

Shankha

The white spiralling conch shell was used as a battle horn to emit the sound of valour, victory or *vijaya* by heroic gods as represented in many Hindu epics. In the depictions of the Hindu God Vishnu, the conch is shown as being held in his upper left hand and the wheel of chakra is held in his upper right. In early Buddhism, the conch shell was a proclamation of the Buddha's teachings which fearlessly resounded in the ten directions. It symbolises the Buddha's powers of speech and is said to terrorise and drive away all evil spirits. It proclaims the power and truth of the Dharmas and is seen as a call of awakening for helping others. It is usually held in the wisdom hand or the left hand of deities.

Bowl

The begging bowl or *bhikshapatra* is an important Buddhist and Hindu iconographic symbol.It is used by the yogis who follow their teachings and beg for food. This bowl is often a simple and humble earthen brown with rounded base and edges. It is either made from dariya narial or from brass, and is called *Tomri*. It is carried by almost all wandering yogis who have to go door to door to beg for food and water. Hindu yogis often chant "*Alakh! Alakh!*"or

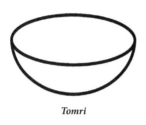

Tomri

"*Alakh Niranjan*", singing praises to the mahayogi Lord Shiva while begging.

Shield

The shield called *Khetaka* is a protector from evil influences. It is often depicted in epics and fables related to wars and battles, as a weapon of protection. It symbolises protection from evil influences and is seen as a symbol of Dharma by the Buddhists.

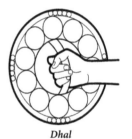

Dhal

Mantra and *Bija*

Mantras are chants or verbal charms which possess great vibrations. When properly uttered and repeated with faith and concentration, they possess great mystical powers to do good and bad. These are ancient texts taken from the *Rigveda,* the *Yajurveda*, the *Atharveda,* and other similar sacred scriptures texts. These are also used during important ceremonies, initiations, and in the practice of yoga and meditations. In Sanskrit it is taken to mean, "That which protects (tra) the mind (man)."

Practised majorly in Buddhism, they are believed to embody the power and attributes of particular deities, and are used repeatedly during dhyan or meditations. Mantras are often used for protection from evil and misfortune. They are chanted in large public places as well as private rituals, to protect individuals against illness or other misfortune. These protective chants are integral to Mahayanic principles and are widely used in exorcist and protective rites.

Bijas are mainly syllables or important sounds with spiritual benefits often elated to different deities, and the fifty letters of the alphabets are connected to the seven chakras. "Om" or "Aum" is among the *bijas* used by yogis for concentration or dhyan during meditation.

Yantra

Yantras are combinations of many mystic diagrams and symbols possessing great occult power. All goddesses held sacred by the Shaktas have a special yantra associated with them which is sometimes placed in the middle of a lotus diagram. These Yantras are often used along with mantras to generate positive energy and enhance consciousness. The Shri Yantra or the Shri Chakra is especially important for Buddhists and it is used by the Kula sect in Tantrism. It consists of nine intersecting isosceles triangles of different sizes: five "female" triangles that point downwards to represent Shakti, and four "male" triangles that point upwards to represent Shiva. In its centre is the power point or *Bindu*, the highest, elusive, invisible centre from which the entire cosmos expanded. The triangles are enclosed by eight and sixteen petals that symbolise the "lotus of creation" and the vital force of reproduction.

Kavacha

Kavachas are talismans or amulets used to achieve a desired result, usually for an offspring, or for protecting self and dear ones from the evil eye. These often contain a piece of paper or stone with mantras and yantras written on them. Used by people for many purposes, these are worn around the arms, neck, breast and even loins.

Mudra

Mudras are symbolic gestures, largely used in Hatha Yogic and Buddhist practices. They are gestures and bodily postures with deep occult and spiritual meaning, used to reduce ailments and increase the body's power, strength and longevity. These postures are said to improve concentration and align the practitioner to the spiritual realm with more ease. Buddhist mudras represent the identity of a Buddha and are used in meditation regularly. There are five main mudras that are associated with the five dhyani mudras. *Abhaya* mudra (the gesture of fearlessness and protection) which represents spiritual power and is often seen in standing Buddhas. *Bhumisparsha* mudra is seen as the "gesture of earth witness" and is believed to have been made by the Buddha when he attained enlightenment. The *Dharmachakra* mudra, the "Wheel Turning Gesture", is said to represent the Buddha's teachings, and the *Dhyan* (meditation mudra) is commonly used by practitioners while concentrating during meditations. The *Varada* mudra or the Gift-Giving Gesture is the symbol of bestowing gifts.

Together all these symbols are used by practitioners and yogis in particular, to gain spiritual powers and self-realisation.

3.11 Conclusion: Yoga and Tantra—A Heterogeneous Cult with Hindu and Buddhist Roots

The Buddhist Sahajiya yogis are commonly known as Siddhacharyas and the main leaders of the Nath Yogis are called Siddhas. Hence, there is confusion in the chronology of the Siddhas. A list of eighty-four Siddhas is found in the *Varna-Ratnakara* where names of seventy-six Siddhas have actually been found. A list of Yogis called Maha-Siddhas is found in the first chapter of the *Hatha Yoga Pradipika*. This tradition of eighty-four Siddhas is also very well known in Tibetan Buddhism, and is popular in the south.

What is important is that this tradition of eighty-four Siddhas is mentioned in the *Sant* literature and the Sufi literature of western and northern India, and also in the Nath literature of Bengal. The number eighty-four is considered to be a mystical and historical number. The Ajyvikas believe that "the soul must pass through eighty-four hundred thousand stages before attaining the human state". The mention of eighty-four thousand stages of birth is found in the *Naitrayani Upanishad*. In some *Puranas* and Tantras, there is reference to eighty-four lakh yonis or births, in different states. The number of Buddhist Dharma-Skandha i.e., branches of doctrines or division of the Dharma is eighty-four, or rather, eighty-four thousand.

In the Pali text *Gamdha-Vamsa* it is said, "Those scholars, who will write commentaries, notes etc. on the Pali texts containing the eighty-four thousand Dharma-Skandhas, or will cause others to write such works, will gather immense merit equal to the merit derived from building eighty four thousand shrines, constructing eighty four thousand images of Buddhas, establishing eighty four thousand monasteries. It has further been said that he who makes a good collection of the sayings of Buddha, or causes others to do it, and who scribes, or causes to be scribed the sayings of the Buddha in the form of manuscript, and who gives or causes others to give materials of preparing such a manuscript and to preserve it, will amass immense virtue equal to that which is gathered by building eighty-four thousand shrines and erecting eighty-four thousand monasteries."

In the religious Pali text of "*Anagata-Vamsa*" it has been prophesised that when the future Buddha, Maitreya, will renounce the world, moved by universal compassion, eighty-four thousand friends, kinsmen and princesses will follow him, and eighty-four thousand Brahmans, versed in the Vedas will also accompany him. Eighty-four is also the accepted number of asanas (yogic postures), which are said to be written in yogic and Tantric texts. Sometimes, the number of beads in the rosary of a Gorakhnathi is also said to be eighty-four. There is a detailed description of eighty-four Shiv-Lingas in eighty-four consecutive chapters of the *Skanda Purana*.

Hinduism and Buddhism in general, have many similarities. Names and terms of their yogic practices are very different; however, the essence and foundation is the same. For instance, the concept of "I" or *Ahamkara* (ego) is described by Lord Krishna as: "The wise man who abandoning all desires lives free of craving, who has no sense of ego (*nirahankara*) or of mineness (*nirmama*), attains to peace."(*Bhagavad Geeta*, II.71)

This concept is also found in Buddhism. Terms such as "Atman" appear as "self-nature", which mean the same. Terms such as "non-duality" and "absolute" are found in both texts. Similar to Atman, the Buddhist "*Bodhichitta*" refers to "the enlightened consciousness which dwells within the heart". Thus, both schools identify discrimination between ego and enlightened awareness. Further, both express that truth is beyond all worlds, dichotomies of the mind and ideas and are best reflected in silence in the absence of technical terms and theories. Just as the Buddhist scholar and Mahayanic Buddhist Nagarjun has emphasised shunyata (voidness) in the oldest Upanishad *Brihadaranyaka*, Brahman is described as "*neti-neti*" or "not this, not that". Truth is thus, beyond all concepts and complications. For Buddhists, "Mind is Buddha" and for Hindus, "Brahman is the Atman" or the pure consciousness. Thus, both Buddha and Brahman epitomise supreme reality.

Even the Tantric goddesses worshipped by both schools are

like "soul sisters" in essence and magnitude. Goddess Kali and Tara particularly, are similar in appearance and in the religious ceremonies associated with them. In fact, if their forms of worship are combined, there would be no violation to their essence or sacred meaning. Ritual worship (i.e., *puja*), Mantra Yoga (i.e., chanting of sacred verses), devotion to the forms of gods and goddesses (i.e., bhakti), and the focus on the practical aspect of yoga are common to both Buddhism and Hinduism.

Apart from practices, even the places of worship and pilgrimage, of both Nath Panth and Tantric Buddhism are similar and shrouded with many folk tales and myths of their deities, which are said to be incarnations of each other, appearing in different countries and castes across time. For instance, the Rato Macchendranath Festival mentioned earlier is held in honour of the Nath Siddha Matsyendranath who is identified with the Buddhist deity Avalokiteshvar, and is sometimes also called Luipa who is taken to be the first among the Buddhist Siddhacharyas. In fact, MM H.P. Sastri has said that Nath Yogis were present before the Buddhist Siddhacharyas composed Bengali songs which had great similarities to those of the compositions of Buddhist Siddhacharyas. S.C. Das in his index of *Pag Sam Jon Zang* has even said that "Gauraksa, a cowherd, who being initiated into Tantric Buddhism became the well-known sage Gauraksa, whose religious school survives in the yogi sect, who go under the designation of Nath." Thus, confusion of their heterogeneity can be attributed to their origin and genesis. In fact, in many researches, Nath Siddhas like Matsyendranath, Gorakhnath, Chauranginath, and Jalandhari are all counted amongst the Buddhist Siddhacharyas, and have even been credited with works of esoteric Buddhism in the Tibetan language. All these Naths are given the place of demi-gods. It is believed that they still live in the Himalayan peaks and are regarded as its guardian spirits.

As described earlier, Gorakhnathis or Kanphata yogis have many links and connection to Buddhism. In fact, their Hatha Yoga path is a fusion of Brahmanistic essence and late Buddhist Tantra. According to some Bengali texts, Gorakhnath was essentially a Buddhist saint named Ramanavajra belonging to the Vajrayana cult. Lord Shiva is said to be a pioneer is some ways for bringing Shaivism to the east and some of his spiritual teachings are found in Tantric Buddhism.

The Siddha cult is often described as an ancient religious cult which highlights the "psycho-chemical process of yoga" or "Kaya Sadhana' which relies on processes and a way of life to make the body immutable and attain an immortal spiritual life or moksha. Its historic roots are in many ways influenced and intertwined with the Indian region as well as other Eastern parts of the world, viz, Nepal and Tibet.

Surrounded by many folk tales, myths and legends, the origin as well as the spread of the Nath philosophies is mysterious and does not have any clear or definite point. However, there are many speculations by historians that characterise it by both Yogic Shaivism and Tantric Buddhist lineage that is essentially heterogeneous in nature. Simply speaking, it is neither just Indian nor solely Buddhist, but a confluence of both these mystic philosophies and heritage values. Let us see the many similarities between these two religions with regard to yoga and its practice.

For instance, in the Himalayas, namely Tibet and Nepal, many customs of the Nath Siddhas merged with rituals of the Buddhist Siddhacharyas. This is because all esoteric schools revolve around the cosmic activity and divinity of Shiva-Shakti. Yin-yang, sun-moon, masculine-feminine, are other general terms used to describe the balancing of these two opposite energies that lead us to salvation.

Historically, Shiva is the original instructor or "Adinath of yogis" in Hinduism. Tantric Buddhists believe that Lord Buddha or Lord Vajjrasattva (who is regarded and respected as Shiva) was the foremost yoga teacher. The Hindu Tantric systems stress on the union of Shiva-Shakti on a spiritual plane, and Tantric Buddhists call this ideology *Prajna* and *Upaya*, which is a reflection of the former.

Many Buddhist Tantras are often cited as being a spiritual/ philosophical dialogue between the Lord and a compassionate lady. Similarly, we have already traced Hindu Tantras and how Matsyendranath gained the secret knowledge of yoga directly through Shiva while he was disguised in a form of a fish.

The sun and moon theory of the Buddhists is also in tandem with the ideologies of the Nath cult. Another common theory is of the process of the final stage of yoga called "Sahaj samadhi" or "Shunya samadhi" by the Buddhist Sahajiyas which is also found in *Akula Vira Tantra* by Matsyendranath who describes "the same state of equal equilibrium" which goes beyond our perceived awareness of positive and negative qualities. In the Hatha Yoga text *Hathayoga Pradapika,* the Buddhist fundamental of Shunya or voidness (Shunya, Ati-Shunya, Maha-Shunya, and Sahaj-Shunya) is connected to the four stages of sound in Hindu yogic practices. Most importantly, both cults hold the "process of Kaya Sadhana" as the most important stage of finding supreme love and bliss.

The final aim of the Naths is attaining immortality while *Mahasukh* is the final goal of the Buddhist Siddhacharyas. While the Siddhas believe in the cycles of birth and death, the Buddhist Sahajiyas instead try to realise the void nature of the self and avoid these cycles and of all Dharmas, with the conclusion that *Mahasukh* would help them in the ultimate realisation of all. While the aim of the Naths is on the yogic process to transform the corporeal body of death and decay, the Buddhists are focussed on sexo-yogic rituals that can transform ordinary pleasure to an elevated and deeper state of bliss. Drinking of the Divine nectar and the conception of *Varuni* (the ambrosial liquor) are the same in both cults. However, while the Naths opposed association with women and posed them as distractions and temptations on their path to sadhana, the Buddhist Sahajiyas celebrated the feminine, and perceived them as incarnations of shunyata and *prajna,* whose presence was necessary for achieving spiritual goals. It is important to again take note that despite this general attitude, the Naths often practised yogic processes of Amarauli, Vajrauli and others in female company, but never really idealised them. The similarities between the Ajivikas and the Naths, according to Dr. Barua, are:

1) Both sects recognised three supreme personalities in their religious tradition:
   The Ajivikas: Nanda–vatsa, Krsa Samkrtyayana, and Maskarin Gosala.
   The Naths: Minanath, Matsyendranath, and Gorakhnath.
2) Both sects admitted singing and dancing as two important modes of religious expression.
3) Both sects believed that in order to reach the human state a soul must pass through eighty-four thousand stages.
4) Both aspired for *Ananta-manasa* or *Sahasrara* as the highest condition of the soul reachable through Hatha Yoga in which Pranayama or control of the vital wind is the essential feature.
5) Both were Chaturangis (Chaurangis) in the sense that their

religious life was to stand the four-fold test of ascetics, viz., *parama-tapassita* (great privation), *parama-lukhata* (great austerity), *parama-jegucchita* (great loathing for wrong-doing), and *parama-pavivittata* (great aloofness from the world).

The Nath Siddhas also have many similarities with the *Rasayana* school especially in ideology, as their sadhana is essentially one of transubstantiation and transfiguration. Both schools share the belief that a yogi's perfect body is superior in all planes and he is believed to be able to take any form as he pleases through his power. The *Rasayana* school is based in the principle of *jivan-mukti* and involves the transubstantiation with the chemical element, to make the body immutable. These ideologies were greatly influenced by the alchemist Nagarjun, Vyadi and Vyajapyayana. It is thus said that those yogis, demons, gods and men who have achieved the immutable divine body through rasa have become *jivan-mukta*. This was also the aim of the Nath Siddhas and formed the basis of the yoga they preached and practised. The Nath Siddhas and the Rasa Siddhas thus aimed at making the body proof against death and decay and their goal was the liberation of the soul from the cycles of birth and death.

Gorakhnath, as the link between the Shaivaites and the Tantric Buddhists, and his teacher Matsyendranath, were the chief facilitators of the Siddha cult in Nepal. Matsyendranath and Avalokiteshvar are often considered synonymous in many parts of the world, as are Goddesses Kali and Tara. Mirroring the same principles and paths, these gods and goddesses run parallel through history, and have inter-connected places of worship and principles. However, only the timeline and the appearances across generations and places around the world differ. As established throughout the book, there is sufficient archaeological, religious, and mythological information that strengthens common roots and the strong links between these two schools. We can thus conclude that the Siddhas and Buddhas are essentially *dharma-sathis/karma-sathis* or spiritual companions, and their final aim is to help seekers gain moksha and nirvana and show them the true and pious path to Om.

~~ ß leled meled ~~

~~ Om Tat Sat~~

Bibliography

I: Yogic and Tantric Gods and Goddesses

1.1 Adinath: The Founder of the Nath (Master) Sampradaya, the First Guru of the Siddhas (The Proven Ones)

Andrews, Karen M., "Avalokitesvara and the Tibetan Contemplation of Compassion", 31 May 1993. http://www.sacred-texts.com/bud/tib/avalo.html

Bhattacharya, B., *The Indian Buddhist Iconography*. Calcutta: Firma K.L.M, 1968.

Briggs, George Weston, *Gorakhnath and the Kanphata Yogis*, Calcutta: Y.M.C.A. Press, 1938; New Delhi: Motilal Banarasidass, 1982.

Dowman, Keith,*Masters of Mahamudra: Songs and Histories of the Eighty-four Buddhist Siddha*, State University of New York Press, Albany, NY, 1985.

Farrand, Thomas Ashley, *Shakti Mantras: Tapping into the Great Goddess Energy Within*, Ballantine Books; 1st edition, 2003.

Frawley, David, *Spiritual Secrets of Ayurveda: Tantric Yogaand the Wisdom Goddesses*, 5th Reprint, Delhi: Motilal Banarasidass, 2012.

Jackson, Roger, *The Journal of the International Associationof Buddhist Studies*, Dept. Of Religion, Carleton College,Northfield, MN, Volume 13, Number 2, 1990.

Johari, Harish, Tools for Tantra. Inner Traditions India Home Office, 1986.

Khatry, Prem K., "Rain for the drought: An Anthropological Inquiry into the structure of a Buddhist festival in Kathmandu", *CNAS*

Journal, Vol 2, No. 1, January 1996.

Kinsley, David, *The Ten Mahavidyas: Tantric Visions of theDivine Feminine,* Reprint: Delhi, 2003, 2008: Motilal Banarasidass, 2003, 2008.

Kripal, Jeffrey, *Kali's Child: The Mystical and the Erotic in the Life and Teachings of Ramakrishna*, University of Chicago Press, 1995.

Koester, Hans, "The Indian Religion of the Goddess Shakti", *The Journal of the Siam Society*, Vol.23, part 1, 1929 July, pp.1-18. Retrieved from http://ccbs.ntu.edu.tw/FULLTEXT/JR-JSS/shakti.html

Matsyendranath. In Google Sites. https://sites.google.com/site/nathasiddhas/matsyendranath

Dhavalikar, M.K., "The Origin of Tara", *Bulletin of the Deccan College Research Institute*, Vol XI. 1963-64.

Natha Sampradaya. In Google Sites. https://sites.google.com/site/nathasiddhas/natha-sampradaya

Regmi, Jagdish Chandra, "Goddess Tara: A Short Study",*Ancient Nepal: Journal of the Department of Archaeology*, Number 100, June-July 1987.

Sankalia, Hasmukh D.,

Shrivastav, Ramlal, *Siddhsiddhant Paddhati*, Gorakhpur: Gorakhnath Mandir, 2000.

Tara. (n.d.) In Religion Facts. http://www.religionfacts.com/buddhism/deities/tara.html

Tara. In Khandro.net. http://www.khandro.net/deities_Tara1.html

The Great Natha Siddhas. In Google Sites. https://sites.google.com/site/nathasiddhas/

Tripathy, Ram Prasad, "Taratarini Shrine through the Ages", http://www.orissabarta.com/

Pratima Kamat's article, (http://www.orissa.gov.in/e-magazine/orissareview/2012/nov/engpdf/33-44.pdf)

II: Gorakhnath: the thread that binds Shaivism and Vajrayana Buddhism

Banerjee, Akshay Kumar, *Nath Yoga*, Gorakhpur: Gorakhnath Mandir, 1886.

Banerjea, Akshaya Kumar, *Philosophy of Gorakhnath with Goraksa–*

Vacana–Sangraha, 6th Reprint, Delhi: Motilal Banarasidass, 2014.

Barthwal, Pitamber Dutt, *Siddha Sahitya.*

Briggs, George Weston, *Gorakhnath and the Kanphata Yogis,* Calcutta: Y.M.C.A. Press, 1938; New Delhi: Motilal Banarasidass, 1982.

Dwivedi, Hazaari Prasad, *Natha Sampradaya,* Uttar PradeshHindustan Academy, 1950.

Frawley, David, *Spiritual Secrets of Ayurveda: Tantric Yoga and the Wisdom Goddesses*, 5th Reprint: Delhi: Motilal Banarasidass, 2012.

Guru Gorakhnath. In Art of Living Blog. http://artoflivingblog.com/guru-gorakhnath/

Gorakhnath. In Gorakhnath.net. http://gorakhnath.net/

Guru Gorakhnath. In Art of Living Blog. http://artoflivingblog.com/guru-gorakhnath/

Muktibodhananda, Swami, *Hatha Yoga Pradipika*, Munger (India): Yoga Publication Trust, 2006.

Hinglaj. In Glorius India.http://www.gloriousindia.com/places/temples/hingula_shakti_peeth.html

Kinsley, David, *The Ten Mahavidyas: Tantric Visions of the Divine Feminine*, Reprint, Delhi: Motilal Banarasidass, 2003, 2008.

Lévi, Carlo, *Le Nepal,* 3 vols., Paris: Ernest Leroux, 1905.

Mahahradanatha, "The Cult of Maysendra-Mina and Gorakhnath in Nepal", http://www.shivashakti.com/werner.htm

Natha Sampradaya. In Google Sites. https://sites.google.com/site/nathasiddhas/natha-sampradaya

Pashupatinath Temple. In Nepal Tourism Site. http://nepal.saarctourism.org/pashupatinath-temple.html

Pashupatinath Temple. In Nepal Rudraksh. http://www.nepalrudraksha.com/

Singh, Uma, *Gorakshanath and Patanjali*, Gorakhpur: Gorakhnath Mandir, 2005.

Shree Gorakshanath. In Gorakhnath.org. http://gorakhnath.org/

Shrivastav, Ramlal, *Siddhsiddhant Paddhati*, Gorakhpur: Gorakhnath Mandir, 2000.

Swatmaram, Yogindra, *Hatha Yoga Pradipika*, Gorakhpur: Gorakhnath Mandir.

The Great Natha Siddhas. In Google Sites. https://sites.google.com/site/nathasiddhas/

Tripathy, Ram Prasad, "Taratarini Shrine through the Ages", http://www.orissabarta.com/

White, David Gordon, *The Alchemical Body*, University of Chicago Press, 1996-2006. First Edition India, MunshiramManoharlal Publishers Pvt. Ltd., 2004.

III: The Siddhas and the Buddhist Tradition

Abhayananda, Swami, "Jnaneshvar: The Life and Works ofthe Celebrated Thirteenth Century Indian Mystic Poet", 2012.http://themysticsvision.weebly.com/

Alchemy Symbols. In Ancient Symbols. http://www.ancient-symbols.com/alchemy_symbols.html

Aruna, A.K., "Patanjali Yoga Sutras: Translation and Commentary in the light of Vedanta Scripture", Upasana Yoga Media. Sourced from http://issuu.com/circularcube/docs/sangharakshita_catalogue

Bagchi, P.C. (ed.), Magee, Michael (trans.) *Kaulajnana-nirnaya of the school of Matsyendranath,* Varanasi: Prachya Prakashan, 1986.

Banerjea, Akshay Kumar, *Nath Yoga*, Gorakhpur: Gorakhnath Mandir, 1886.

Banerjea, Akshay Kumar, *Philosophy of Gorakhnath with Goraksa-Vacana-Sangraha*, 6th Reprint, Delhi: Motilal Banarasidass, 2014.

Bhattacharya, Narendra Nath, *History of Researches on Indian Buddhism,* Munshiram Manoharlal Publishers Private Limited, 1981.

Berzin, Alexander, The Berzin Archives: The Buddhist Archives of Dr. Alexander Berzin. http://www.http://www.berzinarchives.com/

Blavatsky, H.P., *The Secret Doctrine: The Synthesis ofScience, Religion and Philosophy*, Theosophical University Press Online Edition.

Brien, Barbara O., "Madhyamika: School of the Middle Way", http://buddhism.about.com/od/mahayanabuddhism/a/madhyamika.html

Briggs, George Weston, *Gorakhnath and the Kanphata Yogis*, Calcutta: Y.M.C.A. Press, 1938; New Delhi: Motilal Banarasidass, 1982.

Buddhist Symbols. In Religion Facts. http://www.ancient-symbols.com/buddhist-symbols.html

Buddhism. In Patheos. http://www.patheos.com/Library/Buddhism. html

Buddhism. Sourced from http://www.buddha101.com/

Chamu, S.V, *Ashtanga Yoga*, Ashtanga Yoga VijnanaMandiram, Mysore, India 2005.

Chu, Joe Hing Kwok, Chapter IV, "The Tibetan Tantra and Qigong", http://alternativehealing.org/TibetFour.htm

Coulter, David, *Anatomy of Hatha Yoga*, Pennsylvania: Body and Breath, 2001.

Dasgupta, Shashibhushan, *Obscure Religious Cults*, Calcutta: Firma KLM Private Limited, 1995.

Dasgupta, Surendranath, *Yoga: As Philosophy and Religion*, Port Washington: Kennikat Press, 1924.

Devananda, Vishnu Swami, *TheComplete Illustrated Book of Yoga*, NY: Three River Press, 1988.

Dwivedi, Bhojraj, *Yantra-Mantra-Tantra and Occult Sciences*, Diamond Books, 2011.

Eliade, Mircea, *Patanjali and Yoga*, Trans. Charles Lam Markman. New York: Schoken Books, 1975.

Feuerstein, Georg, *The Yoga Sutra of Patanjali*, London: Dawson, 1975.

Gopalakrishna, M.K., *Pranayama with Postures*, SAKSIVC, Bangalore, 2003.

Gorakhnath. In Gorakhnath.net. http://gorakhnath.net/

Guru Gorakhnath. In Art of Living Blog. http://artoflivingsblog. com/guru-gorakhnath/

Hsüan Hua, Dhyana Master, *The Diamond Sutra: A General Explanation of the Vajra Prajña Paramita Sutra*, Buddha Dharma Education Association Inc.

www.buddhanet.net International Journal of Tantric Studies. http://www.asiatica.org/publications/ijts/

Krishna, Gopi, "The Role of Prana as the Energy of Consciousness", http://www.icrcanada.org/

Krishananda, Swami, *The Yoga System*, The Divine Life Society, Sivananda Ashram, Rishikesh, India.

Liungman Carl G., *Dictionary of Symbols,* New York: W.W. Norton & Company, 1991.

Mahayana. (n.d.) InWikipedia. 30 April 2014. http://en.wikipedia.

org/wiki/Mahayana

Miller Stoler, Barbara, *Yoga Discipline of Freedom: The Yoga Sutra Attributed to Patanjali,* Berkeley: University of California Press, 1995.

Miranda Bruce-Mitford, *The Illustrated Book of Signs and Symbols,* London: Dorling Kindersley, 1996.

Mitra, S.C., "Cult of Gorakshanatha", *Journal of Anthropological Society of Bombay,* XIV, 1.

Mookerji, Ajit, *The Tantric Way: Art, Science, Ritual.* London: Thames and Hudson. 1977.

Nirvana Sutra. In Nirvana Sutra. http://www.nirvanasutra.net/

Natha Sampradaya. In Google Sites. https://sites.google.com/site/nathasiddhas/natha-sampradaya

Phuntsok, Chöje Lama, *Entering Tantrayana*, Kathmandu: Karma Lekshey LingInstitute, 2007.

Prasad, M.G., "What is Yoga?", Akka Conference Proceedings, Chicago 2008.

Ranganathananda, Swami, Foreword to *Jnaneshvari*, Bharatiya Vidya Bhavan, 1991.

Rinpoche, Gyatrul, *The Generation Stage in Buddhist Tantra*, Snow Lion, 2005.

Rinpoche, Kyabje Trijang, *Various Aspects of Tantra*, Translated by Gavin Kilty. Edited and published by Michael Hellbach, Tushita Editions, 1977.

Shakya, Bahadur Min, "The Iconography of Nepalese Buddhism", Buddha Dharma Education Association Inc., www.buddhanet.net

Shree Gorakshanath. In Gorakhnath.org. http://gorakhnath.org/

Shrivastav, Ramlal, *Siddha Siddhant Paddhati*, Gorakhpur: Gorakhnath Mandir, 2000.

Shiva ShaktiMandalam. http://www.clas.ufl.edu/users/gthursby/tantra/.

Mookerji, Ajit, *The Tantric Way: Art, Science, Ritual.* London: Thames and Hudson, 1977.

Singh, Uma, *Gorakshanath and Patanjali*, Retrieved from Gorakhnath Mandir, Gorakhpur, Printed by The Eureka Printing Works Private Limited, 2005.

Skilton, Andrew, *A Concise History of Buddhism*, Windhorse, 1994.

Srinath, Vijay Kanchi, *The Lesser Known Nath Cult and its Significant*

Philosophy, Vividhata Research &Training Centre, MJ College Campus.

The Great Natha Siddhas. In Google Sites. https://sites.google.com/site/nathasiddhas/

Venkata Ramanan, K., *Nagarjun's Philosophy: As Presented in the Maha-Prajnaparamita-Sastra*, Delhi: Motilal Banarasidass, 1975.

Werner, Karl, *Yoga and Indian Philosophy*, Delhi: Motilal Banarasidass, 1977.

White, David Gordon, *The Alchemical Body*, University of Chicago Press, 1996-2006. First Edition India, Munshiram Manoharlal Publishers Pvt. Ltd., 2004.

Woodroffe, John, (1913/1972), *Mahanirvana Tantra* (Tantra of the Great Liberation). http://www.sacred-texts.com/tantra/maha/

Yantra. In Religion Facts. http://www.religionfacts.com/hinduism/things/yantra.html

Yoga Sutras of Patanjali. In Writings by Paramhansa Yogananda. http://www.yogananda.com.au/patanjali/yoga_sutras00

Appendix

Some well-known (relatively recent) saints belonging to Nath Siddha Parampara (Cult) (Post Jnaneshvar)

Nivrutti Nath	–	Trymbakeshwar, District Nasik, Maharashtra State
Jnana Nath Jnaneshvar	–	Alandi, District–Pune, Maharashtra State
Hatha Yogi Changdev	–	Puntamba, District–Ahmednagar, Maharashtra State
Narayan Tirtha Maharaj	–	Rishikesh, District–Dehradun, Uttarakhand
Vishnu Tirtha Maharaj	–	District–Dewas, Madhya Pradesh
Janardan Swami	–	Devgiri (Daulatabad), District–Aurangabad, Maharashtra State
Eknath	–	Paithan, Aurangabad, Maharashtra State
Visoba Khechara	–	Barshi, District–Solapur, Maharashtra State
Dasopant	–	Ambajogai, District–Beed, Maharashtra State
Niranjan Raghunath	–	Surat, Baroda, Junagadh district of Gujarat State & also at Jhansi, Uttar Pradesh
Mukteshvar	–	Mukteshwar, District–

		Nainital, Uttarakhand State
Shripad Shri Vallabha	–	Kuravpur, Raichur, District–Karnataka State
Narasimha Saraswati	–	Narsobawadi, District–Sangli, Maharashtra State
Akkalkot Swami Samarth	–	Akkalkot, District–Solapur, Maharashtra State
Ramanand Bidkar Maharaj	–	Pune, Maharashtra State
Shankar Maharaj	–	Dhankawadi, District–Pune. Maharashtra State
Manik Prabhu (The Siddha)	– –	Manik Nagar, District–Bidar, Karnataka State
Vasudevanand Saraswati (Tembe Swami)	–	Birth- Mangaon Raigad, Maharashtra State Samadhi at Garudeshwar, Gujarat State.
Nana Maharaj Taranekar	–	Indore, Madhya Pradesh
Sai Nath: Sai Baba	–	Shirdi, District–Ahmednagar, Maharashtra State
Gajanan Maharaj	–	Shegao, District- Akola, Maharashtra State
Tukamai	–	District–Gondhavle, Satara, Maharashtra State
Gondavlekar Maharaj	–	Gondavale, District–Satara, Maharashtra State
Satam Maharaj	–	Danoli, District–Sindhudurg, Maharashtra State
Vidyaranya Swami (13th century)	–	Vijaynagara, Karnataka State
Loknath Teerth Maharaj	–	West Bengal State
Gulvani Maharaj	–	Pune, Maharashtra State
Narayan Maharaj Dekhne	–	Nasik Maharashtra State

Shivom Tirth	–	Rishikesh, District–Dehradun, Uttarakhand State
Bhramanand Maharaj	–	Balewadi, Pune Maharashtra State
Gulabrao Maharaj (Madhura Bhakti)	–	Madhan, District–Amravati, Maharashtra State
Datta Maharaj Kavishwar	–	Pune M.S.
Gagnangiri Maharaj	–	Khopoli, District–Raigad, Maharashtra State
Gajanan Maharaj Pattekar	–	Thane, Maharashtra State
Siddharudh Swami	–	Hubli, Karnataka State
Pednekar Maharaj	–	Laxmibai & Madhukar-Alibaug, Maharashtra State
Bhau Maharaj	–	Lalbugh & Gangapur (samadhi), Maharashtra State
Jambhekar Maharaj	–	Mumbai (Shivaji Park)
Mule Maharaj	–	Satara (Swami Samarth Dikshit), Maharashtra State
Bhagawan Nityananda	–	Ganeshpuri, District–Thane, Maharashtra State
Muktanand Swami	–	Ganeshpuri, District–Thane, Maharashtra State
Ramakrishna Paramhansa	–	Dakshineshwar, Kolkatta, West Bengal State
Ram Krusha Mouni Baba	–	Chikhali, District Buldhana, Maharashtra State
Parnekar Maharaj	–	Parner, District–Ahmednagar,

		Maharashtra State
Nath Bhujang Maharaj	–	Paranda, District–Osmanabad, Maharashtra State
Mouni Maharaj	–	Gargoti Patgaon, District–Kolhapur, Maharashtra State
Raul Maharaj	–	Pinguli, District–Sindhudurg, Maharashtra State
Pant Balekundri	–	Belgaum District–Karnataka State
Appa Maharaj Supekar	–	Vadodara, Gujarat State

Discl: This is a representative list of various known saints, Natha Siddhas and Yogis mainly based in Maharashtra. It is by no means complete. Any names missing may not be taken adversely.

This list may also not be exactly chronological in real time-line.

Some Shaktipat Nath Siddhas

Shaktipat *means instant awakening of the dormant Kundalini Shakti, residing at the Mooladhar Chakra located at the base of human spine, in the form of a serpent.*

Narayankaka Dhekane Maharaj (Shaktipat guru) (Nasik, Maharashtra).

Prakash Bhaskar Prabhune Maharaj (Nasik, Maharashtra)

Anil Gopal Ghodekar Maharaj (Varanasi, Uttar Pradesh)

Vitthalrao Vasudev Barve Maharaj (Rameshwar, Uttarakhand)

Shyamsunder Shesharao Deshpande Maharaj (Thane, Maharashtra)

Govindrao Nagnath Pund Maharaj (Aurangabad, Maharashtra)

Haribhau Niturkar Joshi Maharaj (Hyderabad, Andhra Pradesh)

Shri Swami Samarth

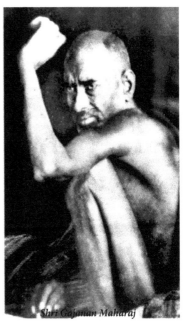

Shri Gajanan Maharaj

Shri Gondavalekar Maharaj

Mukund Vasudeo Thakar Maharaj (Pune, Maharashtra)

Moreshwarbua Nagnath Joshi (Charholikar) Maharaj (Pune, Maharashtra)

Sharad Joshi Maharaj (Barshi, Maharashtra)

Suryakant Rakhe Maharaj (Khamgaon, Maharashtra)

Prof. (Dr.) P. N. Dixit Maharaj (Phaltan, Maharashtra)

Gurumayi Chidvilasananda (Shaktipat guru)

Guru Siyag (Shaktipat guru)

Paramhansa Parivrajakacharya Shri Loknath Tirth Swami Maharaj (Birth: 1892 - samadhi: 1955)

Yogiraj Shri Gulavani Maharaj (Birth: 1889 - samadhi: 1974)

Srinivas (Dada) Nakhate Maharaj (Birth 1920 – samadhi 2001)

Janardan Swami Kher (Vadodara)

Probably the Oldest known Shaktipat initiatation (Diksha) was performed by Guru Vashishta Muni. When he blessed Prabhu Ramachandra (Rama) at his very young age. This story was narrated by Gondavlekar Maharaj when his Guru Tukamai blessed him with a similar Shaktipat Yoga-deeksha

Discl: This is a representative list of some known Skatipath Nath Siddhas it is by no means complete. Any names missing may not be taken adversely.

This list may also not be exactly chronological in real time-line.

The Eighty-four Siddhas in the Varna(na)ratnakara

From the eighty-four Siddhas found in a manuscript (manuscript no 48/34 of the Asiatic Society of Bengal) dated Lakshmana Samvat 388 (AD 1506) of a medieval Maithili work, the Varna(na) ratnākara written by Jyotirishwar Thakur, the court poet of King Harisimhadeva of Mithila (reigned 1300–1321) only 76 are mentioned in this list. An interesting feature of this list is that the names of the most revered Naths are incorporated in this list along with Buddhist siddhacharyas. The names of the Siddhas found in this list are:

Minanātha	Hālipā	Kapāli
Gorakshanātha	Kedāripā	Kamāri
Chauranginātha	Dhongapā	Kānha
Chāmarinātha	Dāripā	Kanakhala
Tantipā	Virupā	Mekhala
Unmana	Bhadra	Sāranga
Kāndali	Pātalibhadra	Vivikadhaja
Dhovi	Palihiha	Magaradhaja
Jālandhara	Bhānu	Achita
Tongi	Mina	Bichita
Mavaha	Nirdaya	Nechaka
Nāgārjuna	Savara	Chātala
Dauli	Sānti	Nāchana
Bhishāla	Bhartrihari	Bhilo
Achiti	Bhishana	Pāhila
Champaka	Bhati	Pāsala
Dhentasa	Gaganapā	Kamalakangāri
Bhumbhari	Gamāra	Chipila
Bākali	Menurā	Govinda
Tuji	Kumāri	Bhima
Charpati	Jivana	Bhairava
Bhāde	Aghosādhava	Bhadra
Chāndana	Girivara	Bhamari
Kāmari	Siyāri	Bhurukuti
Karavat	Nāgavāli	
Dharmapāpatanga	Bibhavat	

The Nath Siddhas in the *Hatha Yoga Pradipika*

In the first upadeśa (chapter) of the Hatha Yoga Pradipika, a fifteenth century text, a list of yogis is found, who are described as the Mahasiddhas. This list has a number of names common with those found in the list of the Varna(na)ratnākara:

Ādinātha	Virupāksa	Kānerī
Matsyendra	Bileśaya	Pūjyapāda
Śāvara	Manthāna	Nityanātha
Ānandabhairava	Bhairava	Nirañjana
Chaurangi	Siddhibuddha	Kapālī
Minanātha	Kanthadi	Bindunātha
Goraksanātha	Koramtaka	Kākachandīśvarā
Jalandharnath*	Surānanda	Allāma
Kanifnath*	Siddhapāda	Prabhudeva
Gahininath*	Charpati	

16 Avatars of Shri Dattatreya

Yogiraaj (Kaartik Shu.15)*	Vishambhar (Chaitra Shu.15) *
Atrivarad (Kaartik Kru.1)*	Maayaamukta (Vaishaakh Shu.15) *
Dattatreya (Kaartik Kru.2)*	Maayaamukta (Jyeshtha Shu.13) *
Kaalaagnishaman (Maargashirsha Shu.14)*	Aadiguru (Aashaadh Shu.15) *
Yogijanvallabh (Maargashirsha Shu.15) *	Shivarup (Shraavan Shu.8) *
Lilaavishambhar (Paush Shu.15) *	Devdev (Bhaadrapad Shu.14)*
Siddharaaj	Digambar (Aashwin Shu.15) *

(Maagh Shu.15) *

Dnyaasaagar   Krishnashyamkamalnayan
(Faalgun Shu.10) *   (Kaartik Shu.12) *

A Few Well-Known Nath Siddhas from Gujarat

Vamanbua Vaidya   Kalavit Swami
Pandurang Maharaj   Rang Avadhut
Bal Avadhut   Maharshi Punitachariji Maharaj
and
Shripad Shrivallabha (Andhra Pradesh)

Some Well-known Muslim *Pir*s (The Nath Siddha Tradition)

Baba Peer Ratannath
Haji Ratannath Ji
Gugga Nath also known as Goganath
Goga Ji
Gugga Veer
Jahar Veer Gugga Peer also known asGugga Peer, Gugga Jaharpee, Gugga Chauhan, Gugga Rana, Guru Shambhujati, Abdu, Quddu, Gangohi, Abdul Quddus Hanafi Ghaznavi Chishti, Gangohi bin, Shaykh Muhaamad Ismail bin Shaykh Safi al-din.
Moinuddin Chishti
Bakhtiyar Kaki
Baba Farid
Nizamuddin Auliya
Gahini Nath (Gaibi Peer)

List of the Eighty-four Mahasiddhas in the Buddhist Tradition of Siddhas

(an asterisk denotes a female Mahasiddha)

Acinta, the "Avaricious Hermit";
Ajogi, the "Rejected Wastrel";
Anangapa, the "Handsome Fool";
Aryadeva (Karnaripa), the "One-Eyed";
Babhaha, the "Free Lover";
Bhadrapa, the "Exclusive Brahmin";
Bhandepa, the "Envious God";
Bhiksanapa, "Siddha Two-Teeth";
Bhusuku (Shantideva), the "Idle Monk";
Camaripa, the "Divine Cobbler";
Champaka, the "Flower King";
Carbaripa (Carpati) "the Petrifyer";
Catrapa, the "Lucky Beggar";
Caurangipa, "the Dismembered Stepson";
Celukapa, the "Revitalized Drone";
Darikapa, the "Slave-King of the Temple Whore";
Dengipa, the "Courtesan's Brahmin Slave";
Dhahulipa, the "Blistered Rope-Maker";
Dharmapa, the "Eternal Student" (c.900 CE);
Dhilipa, the "Epicurean Merchant";
Dhobipa, the "Wise Washerman";
Dhokaripa, the "Bowl-Bearer";
Dombipa Heruka, the "Tiger Rider";
Dukhandi, the "Scavenger";
Ghantapa, the "Celibate Bell-Ringer";
Gharbari or Gharbaripa, the "Contrite Scholar" (Skt., pandita);
Godhuripa, the "Bird Catcher";
Goraksha, the "Immortal Cowherd";
Indrabhuti, the "Enlightened Siddha-King";
Jalandhara, the "Dakini's Chosen One";
Jayananda, the "Crow Master";
Jogipa, the "Siddha-Pilgrim";
Kalapa, the "Handsome Madman";

Kamparipa, the "Blacksmith";
Kambala (Lavapa), the "Black-Blanket-Clad Yogin";
Kanakhala*, the younger Severed-Headed Sister;
Kanhapa (Krishnacharya), the "Dark Siddha";
Kankana, the "Siddha-King";
Kankaripa, the "Lovelorn Widower";
Kantalipa, the "Ragman-Tailor";
Kapalapa, the "Skull Bearer";
Khadgapa, the "Fearless Thief";
Kilakilapa, the "Exiled Loud-Mouth";
Kirapalapa (Kilapa), the "Repentant Conqueror";
Kokilipa, the "Complacent Aesthete";
Kotalipa or Tog tse pa, the "Peasant Guru";
Kucipa, the "Goitre-Necked Yogin";
Kukkuripa, (late 9th/10th Century), the "Dog Lover";
Kumbharipa, "the Potter";
Laksminkara*, "The Mad Princess";
Lilapa, the "Royal Hedonist";
Lucikapa, the "Escapist";
Luipa, the "Fish-Gut Eater";
Mahipa, the "Greatest";
Manibhadra*, the "Happy Housewife";
Medhini, the "Tired Farmer";
Mekhala*, the Elder Severed-Headed Sister;
Mekopa, the "Guru Dread-Stare";
Minapa, the "Fisherman";
Nagabodhi, the "Red-Horned Thief'";
Nagarjun, "Philosopher and Alchemist";
Nalinapa, the "Self-Reliant Prince";
Nirgunapa, the "Enlightened Moron";
Naropa, the "Dauntless";
Pacaripa, the "Pastrycook";
Pankajapa, the "Lotus-Born Brahmin";
Putalipa, the "Mendicant Icon-Bearer";
Rahula, the "Rejuvenated Dotard";
Saraha, the "Great Brahmin";
Sakara or Saroruha; "The Lake-Born"/"The Lotus Child"
Samudra, the "Pearl Diver";
Śāntipa (or Ratnākaraśānti), the "Complacent Missionary";

Sarvabhaksa, the "Glutton");
Savaripa, the "Hunter", held to have incarnated in Drukpa Künleg;
Syalipa, the "Jackal Yogin";
Tantepa, the "Gambler";
Tantipa, the "Senile Weaver";
Thaganapa, the "Compulsive Liar";
Tilopa, the "Great Renunciate"
Udhilipa, the "Bird-Man";
Upanaha, the "Bootmaker";
Vinapa, the "Musician";
Virupa, the "Dakini Master";
Vyalipa, the "Courtesan's Alchemist".

Nath Tradition
Guru-Parampara - Chaurasi-Siddhas

Shri Adabanga Nathji

Guru	:	Shri Shambhujati Guru Gorakshanathji
Panth	:	Pagal
Place	:	Maharashtra, Gujarat.
Tapasya	:	North-eastern highland.
Sadhana	:	Hatha Yoga kriya siddhi, tadasana siddhi.
Deeds	:	Spread of Hatha Yoga, activities for the sake of human beings.

Shri Allama Nathji

Guru	:	Shri Shambhujati Guru Gorakshanathji
Panth	:	Sufi panth
Place	:	Pakistan, Kaikai district.
Sadhana	:	Perfection of pavan-muktasana, vajrasana, virasana, dhyan and gyan yoga siddhi.
Tapasya	:	Highland, Sindhu (Penjab), Pakistan. Nothern areas.
Deeds	:	Preachment of one bhava for Hindu and Muslims, activities for the sake of human beings.

Shri Aughar Nathji

Guru	:	Shri Shambhujati Guru Gorakshanathji
Panth	:	Goraksha-panth (Aughar)

Place	:	Girnarnath, Gujarat.
Sadhana	:	Padmasana siddhi (sitting on the asana can materialise the things (from dhyan), parvat utkatasana siddhi.
Tapasya	:	12 years of tapas on Girnar mountain.
Deeds	:	Own siddhis usage for the sake of society, Nath dharma propagation.

Shri Balagundai Nathji

Guru	:	Shri Shambhujati Guru Gorakshanathji
Panth	:	Aai.
Place	:	Karnal kshetra, Gorakh Tilla, Pakistan.
Sadhana	:	Gorakshasana siddhi, shunya samadhi, Kundalini sadhana, all Yoga siddhis.
Tapasya	:	Gorakh Tilla, Pakistan Himalayan Gadval, Badrinath, Kedarnath, Karnal, Haryana, Rajastan, Punjab
Deeds	:	Guru-seva, tapasya, perfect example of Bhakti Yoga, Hatha Yoga siddhis (miracles), holy life.

Shri Balak Nathji

Guru	:	Shri Shambhujati Guru Gorakshanathji
Panth	:	Bhartrihari Vairag
Place	:	Hamirpur, Shahatalai, Himachal pradesh.
Sadhana	:	Dvipada-vakrasana siddhi, padmasana, gyana-mudra, avadhut tapasvi, yoga siddhis.
Tapasya	:	Kailasa, Manasarovar, Bhadrinath, Kedarnath, Himachal pradesh, Jammu Kashmir, Punjab, Sindu and other places.
Deeds	:	Human society service with

yoga siddhis, parikram and pilgrimage through India, dharma propagation.

Shri Bhadra Nathji

Guru	:	Shri Siddha Yogi Lankanath ji.
Panth	:	Raval yogi.
Place	:	Bhadra-kshetra, Andhra pradesh (southern part)
Sadhana	:	Vajrasana, padmasana, tadasana siddhis, kappar-chimta siddhi, avadhut sadhana.
Tapasya	:	Bhadra area (avadhut sadhana), Shri Shaila mountain, Andhra pradesh, Kadaki-kshetra, Karnataka.
Deeds	:	Tantra siddhi manifestation, service to society, pilgrimage.

Shri Bhagai Nathji

Guru	:	Shri Siddha Yogi Shritainathji
Panth	:	Aai
Place	:	Kurukshetra (Haryana).
Sadhana	:	Yoga mudrasana, tadasana, garudasana, ashva sanchalanasana, hamsasana, pada pranamasana siddhis
Tapasya	:	Dhyan, shunya samadhi.
Deeds	:	Service to humans with yoga siddhis, Nath dharma propagation.

Shri Bhartrihari (Vichar) Nathji

Guru	:	Shri Shambhujati Guru Gorakshanathji
Panth	:	Bhartrihari Vairag (founder).
Place	:	Uijain (Malva), Madhya pradesh.
Sadhana	:	Siddhasana, Kundalini Yoga siddhi, Avadhut Sadhana.
Tapasya	:	Madhya pradesh, Penjab, Haryana, Himalayas, Uttarakhand, Bengalia, Uttar pradesh, Pacistan, Sindh.

| Deeds | : | Helping others with own yoga siddhis, founding of Vairag panth, Nath- dharma propagation. |

Shri Bhuchar Nathji

Guru	:	Shri Siddha Yogi Bhartrihari nathji
Panth	:	Bhartrihari Vairag.
Place	:	Hajara (Punjab).
Sadhana	:	Virasana, siddhasana siddhi, practice of dhyan at snakes area of habitat.
Tapasya	:	Practice under the earth ground, own power over the nature of creation, over the spirit of yogi.
Deeds	:	Defence of all living beings, defence of dharma.

Shri Bhusakai Nathji

Guru	:	Shri Shambhujati Guru Gorakshanathji.
Panth	:	Aai
Place	:	Bengal (Vimala-gufa).
Sadhana	:	Padmasana, brahmacharyasana, yoga mudrasana siddhis.
Tapasya	:	Bengal, Bihar, Orissa, Haryana, forests.
Deeds	:	Dharma propagation, yoga miracles for the sake of society.

Shri Bileshaya Nathji

Guru	:	Shri Siddha Yogi Charpat nathji.
Panth	:	Charpati nathi.
Place	:	Highland, lake Manimahesh (Himachal pradesh)
Sadhana	:	Dvipada-grivasana and padmasana siddhis, rasa-siddhi.
Tapasya	:	Nothern mountains.
Deeds	:	Service to humans through the Yoga, herbal healing.

Shri Birabank Nathji

| Guru | : | Shri Shambhujati Guru |

		Gorakshnathji.
Panth	:	Dhvaj panth (founder).
Place	:	Rishimukh (Mouth of Rishi).
Sadhana	:	Urdhva pada shirshasana siddhi; pavan-hari, Rama bhakta, Gyana Yoga, brahmacharya, endowed with all qualities.
Deeds	:	Defence/safety of all beings, Gyana Vidya transmission.

Shri Brahmanai (Brahmai) Nathji

Guru	:	Shri Siddha Yoga Bhagai nathji.
Panth	:	Aai
Place	:	Haryana (Djind), Hastinapur, Uttar pradesh.
Sadhana	:	Gomukhasana, matsiendrasana, badha padmasana, pavan muktasana siddhis.
Tapasya	:	Jata wearing (Jatadhara), hatha yoga tapasya, Haryana, Uttar pradesh, Penjab, Himalayas.
Deeds	:	Hatha Yoga, karma kanda (Dhuna Yoga), service to humans through yoga siddhis.

Shri Chakra Nathji

Guru	:	Shri Shambhujati Guru Gorakshanathji.
Panth	:	Nateshvari.
Place	:	Northwest area.
Sadhana	:	Svastikasana, chakrasana siddhis, chakri-Tantra sadhana, linga-vakrasana siddhi.
Tapasya	:	Gorakhtilla in Pakistan, Kaikea area, northen mountains.
Deeds	:	Propagated dharma, service to the human well-being, wandering.

Shri Chandra Nathji

Guru	:	Shri Siddha Yogi Kapilnathji.
Panth	:	Kaplani.
Place	:	Bengal, Ganga-sagar, Kolayat

		(Rajasthan).
Sadhana	:	Kapilasana, vajrasana siddhis.
Tapasya	:	Guruseva, tapasya in Kolayat,
		Shiva-bhakta.

Shri Charpat Nathji

Guru	:	Shri Shambhujati Guru Gorakshanathji.
Panth	:	Charpati nathas.
Place	:	Chamba in Himachal Pradesh.
Sadhana	:	Padmasana-siddhi, purna-matsyendrasana siddhi, rasa-siddhi, teaching for Ayurveda (acharya).
Tapasya	:	Himachal Pradesh, Badrinath, Kedarnath, Gangotri, Jammu Kashmir.
Deeds	:	Service to the people by his knowledge in Ayurveda (healing) and showing of yoga-siddhis.

Shri Dariya Nathji

Guru	:	Shri Siddha Yogi Guru Gorakhnath.
Panth	:	Nateshwari (Dariya nathi).
Place	:	Atak Dariya (Pakistan).
Sadhana	:	Gupta-garbhasana siddhi, long being in the water, padmasana-siddhi.
Tapasya	:	Pakistan, Sind Hingalaja, Kabul, Kandhar, Himalayas.
Deeds	:	Yogic miracles for human well-being, wandering around India.

Shri Daya Nathji

Guru	:	Shri Shambhujati Guru Gorakshanathji
Panth	:	Bhartrihari Vairag
Place	:	Mountain Girnar, Gujarat.
Sadhana	:	Gorakshasana siddhi, padmasana, abhaya mudra siddhi.

| Tapasya | : | Dhyan Yoga tapasya at Vindhya mountain, Girnar, Himalayas. |
| Deeds | : | Helping others while pilgrimage all over India. |

Shri Deva Nathji

Guru	:	Shri Siddha Yogi Govindanathji
Panth	:	Varkari (Bhagvat Dharma)
Place	:	Oiyapur (Andjan village), Amaravati (Maharashtra)
Sadhana	:	Hasta-pavan muktasana siddhi, knowledge of Bhagavat Geeta (one of Puranas), Bhaktis Sadhana, poetry, and others.
Tapasya	:	Andjan area, Oliyapur at Maharashtra, Karnataka, Andhra pradesh.
Deeds	:	Bhakti, Bhagvat Dharma propagation, service to the people.

Shri Dharma Nathji

Guru	:	Shri Shambhujati Guru Gorakshanathji
Panth	:	Pav
Place	:	North east of India.
Sadhana	:	Siddhasana, gyan-mudra siddhi, padmasana siddhi, Veda shastra prashna and other
Tapasya	:	Mountain Kailas, Manasarovar, Patal Bhuneshvar.
Deeds	:	Dharma propagation.

Shri Dhir Nathji

Guru	:	Shri Siddha Yogi Allamanathji
Panth	:	Sufi
Placc	:	South eastern part of Bengal.
Tapasya	:	Bengal, Orissa, sea-coast districts.
Deeds	:	Dharma and Nath Siddha knowledge propagation, wandering around all India.

Shri Dhundhakar Nathji

Guru	:	Shri Shambhujati Guru Gorakshanathji
Panth	:	Aai
Place	:	Southeast Assam, Nepal, Nagalend.
Sadhana	:	Padmasana siddhi, atma anubhava, sadhana in a fog, shankha mudra, pavan muktasana.
Deeds	:	Propagation of Jnyana Yoga and samadhi-yoga in Uttarahand, southern east India; impact on people with yogic miracles.

Shri Eka Nathji

Guru	:	Shri Siddha Yogi Jarnadhan nathji
Panth	:	Varkari
Place	:	Paithan, Maharashtra.
Sadhana	:	Siddhasana, padmasana bhakti-rasadhara siddhi.
Tapasya	:	Moutain Shulabhandjan, Trayambakeshvar, Maharashtra, Gangapur, Karnataka, moutain Shri Shaila, Andhra, Malikarjuna, Uttar Pradesh and other places.
Deeds	:	Extraordinary Bhakti Yoga, and through this pure bhakti he showed yogic miracles for the human well-being.

Shri Gahini Nathji

Guru	:	Shri Shambhujati Guru Gorakshanathji
Panth	:	Varkari
Place	:	Trayambakeshvara (Kanaka village) Maharashtra
Sadhana	:	Unmani, Bhakta rasamrita sadhana, hasta kachhavasana perfection.
Tapasya	:	Trayambakeshvar

(Maharashtra), Bengal, Gujarat, Karnataka, Andhra and other

Deeds : Founder of Vaishnavi Varkari Sampradaya, Bhakti Yoga propagation.

Shri Gariba Nathji

Guru : Shri Siddha Yogi Balak nathji
Panth : Bhartrihari Vairag
Place : Kangada (Himachal pradesh), Palampur
Sadhana : Padmasana, utkatasana siddhi, avadhut sadhana, Jnyana Yoga.
Tapasya : Tapasya in jungle and gufa at Unna, Kangada (Himachal pradesh), Sadhora (Penjab), Dafarpur (Haryana), Haidrabad (Andhra), Tuladjapur (Maharashtra), Dhinodhar (Kachha), Hingaladja (Pakistan) and other places.
Deeds : All over India Yoga propagation and service to people with yoga siddhis.

Shri Gaurav Nathji

Guru : Shri Siddha Yogi Matsyendranathji
Panth : Kapalika (Aghor)
Place : Bihar
Tapasya : Himalayas, Assam, Manipuram, Nagalend.
Sadhana : Jnyana-dhyana Yoga, samadhi sadhana, kandharasana siddhi.
Deeds : Siddhi manifestation, dharma propagation.

Shri Gehalla Raval Nathji

Guru : Shri Shambhujati Guru Gorakshanathji
Panth : Raval panth (Kapalika)
Place : Western district of Hangalaj, Sindhu Kshetra
Sadhana : Pavan muktasana, shmashan

sadhana.

Tapasya	:	Hingalaja Parvatia kshetra, Badtinath, Kedarnath.
Deeds	:	Founder of Raval Panth, dharma propagation, perfections in knowledge connected to dharma, artha, Kama and moksha.

Shri Ghora Cholipa Nathji

Guru	:	Shri Shambhujati Guru Gorakshanathji
Panth	:	Aai.
Place	:	Northeast India.
Tapasya	:	Bengal, Gohati (Gauhati), Assam and mountain areas.
Sadhana	:	Siddhasana, virasana siddhi, dhuna karma sadhana, mudrasana siddhi.
Deeds	:	Nath-dharma propagation.

Shri Gopal Nathji

Guru	:	Shri Siddha Yogi Ekanathji
Panth	:	Varkari
Place	:	Tripura kshetra, Kore village.
Sadhana	:	Siddhasana and padmasana siddhi, dhuna karma, Bhakti yoga, divine nectar (amrit) drinking, Nada Brahman realization, gomukhasana siddhi.
Tapasya	:	Maharashtra, Karnataka, Andhra pradesh, Uttar pradesh and other places of tapasya.
Deeds	:	Practice of Bhakti Yoga, amrit usage pleasure, dharma propagation, blessing people.

Shri Gor Nathji

Guru	:	Shri Shambhujati Guru Gorakshanathji
Panth	:	Dharmanathi
Place	:	Kashmir and Sindh areas.

Sadhana	:	Kandharasana siddhi, padmasana siddhi, long living in water siddhi, Jnyana Yoga.
Tapasya	:	In water in padmasana.
Deeds	:	Sadhana, gyana, siddhi manifestation,dharma propagation and care for children.

Shri Havai Nathji

Guru	:	Shri Shambhujati Guru Gorakshanathji
Panth	:	Aai
Place	:	Western area.
Sadhana	:	Moving on the air, perfection in control of pranas, hastapada and padmasana siddhis.
Tapasya	:	Badrinath, Kedarnath.
Deeds	:	Spreading of Nath-dharma.

Shri Jambha Nathji

Guru	:	Shri Shambhujati Guru Gorakshanathji.
Panth	:	Mannathi.
Place	:	Djalapur, Rajastan.
Sadhana	:	Vaishnavi bhakta sadhana, dhyana yoga from hatha yoga, jnyana yoga, urdhva dhanurasana siddhi.
Tapasya	:	Mind and feels control, asketism.
Deeds	:	Bhakti yoga, pravachana.

Shri Jnyaneshvar Nathji

Guru	:	Shri Siddha Yogi Nivritti nathji.
Panth	:	Varkari.
Place	:	Alandi (Maharashtra).
Sadhana	:	Kundalini yoga, padmasana, nitambasana siddhi, Nada Brahman yoga, bhakri yoga and other.
Tapasya	:	Bhakti yoga (in Maharashtra, Uttar pradesh, Gujarat, Karnataka, Andhra pradesh).
Deeds	:	Brahman knowledge

propagation, blessing people
with Yoga siddhi.

Shri Jvalendra Nathji

Guru	:	Omkar Adinathji
Panth	:	Pav (founder)
Place	:	Kalashachala (Djalor).
Sadhana	:	Kapalika and Vajrayana siddhi.
Tapasya	:	kukuttasana and djalandhara bandha perfections.
Deeds	:	Natha samprdaya propagation across India, yoga siddhis, Mantra Yoga.

Shri Kakachandi Nathji

Guru	:	Shri Siddha Yogi Chauranginathji
Panth	:	Palak (Pagal).
Place	:	Kashmir, Kak- bhubhundi tirtha.
Sadhana	:	Kaka-mudra, siddhasana, padmasana perfection, pavan-mukta-mukhasana, linga-bhedasana, linga-bhedi-vakrasana.
Tapasya	:	Jammu, Kashmir, Badrinath, Himalayas, Kakbhub hundi tirtha, Nepal, near Krishna and Kandaki rivers, mountain Sumek, Kailasa, Ujjain and other places of tapasya.
Deeds	:	Bhakti Yoga sadhana and propagation of dharma

Shri Kala Nathji

Guru	:	Shri Siddha Yogi Matsyenrdanathji
Panth	:	Aghora, Kapalika, Kaplani
Place	:	Kullu, Himachal pradesh
Tapasya	:	Kulu, Himachal, Penjab, Eastern India, Assam, Nagalend and other places where he did aghor-tapasya.
Sadhana	:	Utkatasana, pavan-mukta-

| | | karnasana siddhi. |
| Deeds | : | Service to humans, writing of books. |

Shri Kanakai Nathji

Guru	:	Shri Shambhujati Guru Gorakshanathji
Panth	:	Aai
Place	:	Bengal
Sadhana	:	Padmasana siddhi, samadhi-sadhana, yoga mudrasana siddhi.
Tapasya	:	West Bengal, seacost areas, Haryana, Kuru kshetra, Penjab, Gorakh-tilla and other places.
Deeds	:	Yoga miracles for the sake of human beings, pilgrimage across India.

Shri Kanipa Nathji

Guru	:	Shri Siddha Yogi Jalandhar nathji
Panth	:	Pav (Kapalika, hevajra).
Place	:	Pahadpur (Bihar).
Sadhana	:	Urdhva-dhanurasana siddhi, baddha-padmasana.
Tapasya	:	Rajastan, Bihar, Maharashtra, Karnataka, and other places where he practiced shmashan-vairagya.
Deeds	:	Dharma propagation around all India.

Shri Kapil Nathji (Kapila Muni)

Guru	:	Shri Shambhujati Guru Gorakshanathji
Panth	:	Kaplani.
Place	:	Gangasagar, Bengal.
Tapasya	:	East of Nilakantha Kunda, hot water of sunny Ganga, hot rivers, tapasya at Pashupatinath (Rajastan), Kolayat (Bengalia), Kailas, Badrinath.
Sadhana	:	Kapilasana-siddhi.

| Deeds | : | Development of Sankhya shastra, Gyana Yoga pravachana all across India. |

Shri Kaya Nathji

Guru	:	Shri Siddha Yogi Bhartrihari nathji
Panth	:	Bhartrihari Vairag.
Place	:	Penjab kshetra, and Nepal.
Sadhana	:	Svastikasana, Kundalini Yoga siddhi, avadgut tapasya, pavan muktasana siddhi.
Tapasya	:	Nepal, Penjab, Rajastan, Pakistan and others place of tapasya.
Deeds	:	Yoga miracles by power of knowledge and imagi nation, Jnyana Yoga and dharma propagation.

Shri Khechar Nathji

Guru	:	Shri Shambhujati Guru Gorakshanathji
Panth	:	Aai.
Place	:	Punchh, Kashmir district.
Sadhana	:	Padmasana and virasana, khechari mudra siddhi.
Tapasya	:	Powered by prana (pavan hari), levitation.
Deeds	:	various miracles by shakti and yogic siddhis, spreading of Nath-dharma.

Shri Korant Nathji

Guru	:	Shri Siddha Yogi Pir Patannathji
Panth	:	Satnathi.
Place	:	Taksha shila (capital of ancient Gandharvas), Bihar.
Tapasya	:	Mountain areas, Tibet, Nepal (Dang).
Sadhana	:	Shreshtha-utkatasana, padmasana Siddha, Dhyan Yoga, Samadhi Yoga.

Shri Ladhai Nathji

Guru	:	Shri Siddha Yogi Bhusakainathji
Panth	:	Aai.
Place	:	Western and Nothern Punjab, Haryana, Kuru Kshetra, Indraprastha.
Sadhana	:	gomukhasana-siddhi.
Tapasya	:	Punjab, Haryana, Himalayas.
Deeds	:	Ishvara-bhakti propagation which is acquired through the sadhana.

Shri Lanka Nathji

Guru	:	Shri Shambhujati Guru Gorakshanathji
Panth	:	Raval panth.
Place	:	Shri lanka (southern part).
Sadhana	:	Shakti Tantra sadhana, pavan-muktasana, virasana, siddhasana, padmasana, tadasana, vajrasana siddhis.
Tapasya	:	Mountain Kailas, (Rakshas Till lake), Maharashtra (Trayambakeshvar), mountain Shri Shaila, Andhra pradesh, Mallikarjuna in Karnataka, Tamilnadu, Bengal and other places.
Deeds	:	The throne, knowledge of raja yoga, dhyana yoga.

Shri Madra Nathji

Guru	:	Shri Siddha Yogi Lankanathji
Panth	:	Raval yogi.
Place	:	Madra-desha (south of Madhya Pradesh)
Sadhana	:	Siddhi of long-term being in water, siddhasana, raja-yoga, dhuna siddhi, dhyana-gyana yoga, hasta-mukta-utatasana siddhi.
Tapasya	:	Madra-desha, Karnataka, Orissa, Shri Shaila Mountain, Mallikarjuna, Shri Lanka,

		seeacost areas.
Deeds	:	Care for human well-being through the mantra and Tantra, wandering around all India, dharma propagation.

Shri Mallik Nathji

Guru	:	Shri Shambhujati Guru Gorakshanathji
Panth	:	Het nathi (Aghor).
Place	:	Orissa (Nivar district).
Sadhana	:	Ardha-virasana, siddhasana siddhis. Vajrayana-siddhi, shmashan-siddhi.
Tapasya	:	In shmashan of Bengal, Orissa.
Deeds	:	Vajrayana, shmashan siddhi through the yoga, service for human well-being.

Shri Manasai Nathji

Guru	:	Shri Siddha Yogi Bhagai nathji
Panth	:	Aai
Place	:	Mathura, Agra (Uttar Pradesh).
Sadhana	:	Gomukhasana, matsyendrasana, vajrasana siddhi.
Tapasya	:	Avadhoot-tapasvi (jata-sadhana) in Haryana, Uttar Pradesh, Panjab etc.
Deeds	:	Hatha Yoga sadhana, propagated and spreaded dharma through jnyana-yoga tapasya.

Shri Manik Nathji

Guru	:	Shri Shambhujati Guru Gorakshanathji
Panth	:	Varkari
Place	:	Ahmedabad, Gujarat.
Sadhana	:	Padmasana (jnyana-mudra) siddhi, Bhakti Yoga, Hatha Yoga.
Tapasya	:	Asceticism
Deeds	:	Spreading of Bhakti Sadhana.

Shri Manju Nathji

Guru	:	Shri Siddha Yogi Matsyendranathji
Panth	:	Mannathi
Place	:	Kadali, Simhala island (Ceylon)
Tapasya	:	West Bengal, Karnataka, Orissa.
Sadhana	:	Continuous travelling, ardha-virasana siddhi, Tapasthali, Tantra-mantra Yoga, Gyana Yoga siddhi.
Deeds	:	Spreading of dharma around all India.

Shri Markandeya Nathji

Guru	:	Shri Omkar Adinathji
Panth	:	Shiv-yogi.
Place	:	Northeast side of Kaylas mountain.
Sadhana	:	Siddhasana, urdhva kachhavasana siddhis, shankha-mudra.
Tapasya	:	Brahmacharya, service for Guru Adinathji, Agni Brahman; obtained food by begging (bhiksha anna); perfection in strong tapasya to achieve the grace of the gods and goddesses, and thevisions of past, present and future.

Shri Masta Nathji

According to natha-yogis and in particular to yogis ofAai-panth, Siddha Baba Mastanath is recognized by oneof last avatars of Guru Gorakshanath in the humanform that could be approximately in the end of a XVIII-th century.

Shri Meru Nathji

Guru	:	Shri Siddha Yogi Gauravnathji
Panth	:	Kaplani (kapalika)
Place	:	Bihar
Sadhana	:	Virasana and parvat-utkatasana (meru-asana) siddhi.

Deeds	:	Tapasya Sadhana in mountain area, spreading of dharma around all India.

Shri Mina Nathji

Guru	:	Shri Omkar Adinathji
Panth	:	Pav
Place	:	Kashmir kshetra, Assam
Sadhana	:	Vajrasana siddhi.
Tapasya	:	Yoga, dhyana, samadhi-marga, gyana-marga.

Shri Nagarjun Nathji

Guru	:	Shri Shambhujati Guru Gorakshanathji
Panth	:	Parasnathi, Raval-panth
Place	:	Shri Shaila Mountain (south)
Sadhana	:	Knowledge of Rasayana-shastra, Tantra-shastra, worship of Nagadevi, mantra-yoga, gyan-yoga, writing of books, tapasya on Shaila mountain and in Jvalaji, hastapada utkatasana siddhi.
Deeds	:	Spreading doctrine in Malvar, Orissa, Bengal, Tibet, Himalayas, Andhra Pradesh, Shri Shaila Mountain.

Shri Narada Deva Nathji

Guru	:	Shri Siddha Yogi Matsyendranathji.
Panth	:	Satnath
Place	:	Maharashtra (south).
Sadhana	:	Bhakti Yoga siddhi.
Deeds	:	Propagated way of bhakti in Maharashtra, Gujarat, Andhra Pradesh.

Shri Naramai Nathji

Guru	:	Shri Siddha Yogi Brahmainathji
Panth	:	Aai
Place	:	Jinda (Haryana).
Sadhana	:	Avadhoot-tapasya (in naga condition-without clothes), hatha-yoga, padmasana, siddhasana siddhis.
Tapasya	:	Hatha Yoga (in the nude form) in Haryana, Panjab, Rajasthan, Uttar Pradesh.
Deeds	:	Propagated doctrine of Nath and dharma in Haryana, Jammu-Kashmir, Rajasthan, Panjab, Himachal Pradesh and all India.

Shri Nivritti Nathji

Guru	:	Shri Siddha Yogi Gahininathji
Panth	:	Vaishnavi(Varkari)
Place	:	Triambakeshvar (Maharashtra)
Sadhana	:	Pavan-muktasana siddhi, bhakti Yoga sadhana, svastikasana, siddhasana siddhis, Kundalini Sadhana.
Tapasya	:	reached all possible siddhis by Bhakti Yoga.
Deeds	:	Propagated of bhakti-yoga, care for people.

Shri Pippal Nathji

Guru	:	Shri Siddha Yogi Ramnathji
Panth	:	Ramik (Ramnathi)
Place	:	Prayag (Uttar Pradesh)
Tapasya	:	Uttar Pradesh, Uttarakhand, mountains of Nepal.
Sadhana	:	Padmasana, siddhasana, parvat-utkatasana siddhis; courage, mahamudra-siddhi.
Deeds	:	Spreading of Nath Yoga, care for human well-being, showing of yoga-siddhis.

Shri Prabhudeva Nathji

Guru	:	Shri Siddha Yogi Matsyendranathji
Panth	:	Aai
Place	:	Sikkim
Sadhana	:	Tapasya in dandasana.
Tapasya	:	Stay naked in full dispassion.
Deeds	:	Yoga-sadhana, spreading of knowledge.

Shri Prakash Nathji

Guru	:	Shri Shambhujati Guru Gorakshanathji
Panth	:	Bhartrihari Vairag
Place	:	West Bengal, Gujarat.
Tapasya	:	Mountain area.
Sadhana	:	Pada-bhujangasana, siddhasana siddhi, gyan-mudra siddhi, gyan-yoga siddhi, appearance of light volume from body.
Deeds	:	Spreading of Dhyan Yoga, Jnyana Yoga, Laya Yoga.

Shri Praudha Nathji

Guru	:	Shri Siddha Yogi Bhartrihari nathji
Panth	:	Bhartrihari Vairag
Place	:	Ujjain (Madhya Pradesh).
Sadhana	:	Hasta-padangushtha-shirshasana siddhi, siddhasana, avadhoot-sadhana.
Tapasya	:	Avadhoot-tapasya in Madhya Pradesh, Gujarat, Panjab, Rajasthan etc.
Deeds	:	Spreading of dharma of Gorakshanath and Nath Sampraday.

Shri Ratan Nathji

Guru	:	Shri Shambhujati Guru Gorakshanathji
Panth	:	Satnath
Place	:	Bhatinda (Panjab)
Sadhana	:	Raj Yoga, Laya Yoga, Pavanahari Yoga, khanjanasana.
Deeds	:	Working wonders around all India, Kabul, Kandhar, Mecca, Medina.

Shri Sahajai Nathji

Guru	:	Shri Siddha Yogi Kanakainathji
Panth	:	Aai
Place	:	East Bengal.
Sadhana	:	Being in avadhoot state, sadhana in the sea (near the sea or ocean), parvat-utkatasana siddhi.
Tapasya	:	East Bengal, tapasya in eastern seaside areas (avadhoot state).
Deeds	:	Propagated vairadya, gyana, absence of desires.

Shri Sahiroba Nathji

Guru	:	Shri Siddha Yogi Gahininathji.
Panth	:	Varkari.
Place	:	Gova-kshetra.
Sadhana	:	Bhakti Yoga, Kundalini chakra sadhana, Bhunamunasana siddhi.
Tapasya	:	Bhakti Yoga - Maharashtra, Gova, Andhra, Bengal and other places of tapasya.
Deeds	:	Writing of books, spreading of bhakti-yoga.

Shri Sanak Nathji

Guru	:	Shri Omkar Adinathji

Panth	:	Satnath
Place	:	Badrinath in Kashmir, Vaikuntha.
Tapasya	:	Dhyan-Jnyan Yoga, karma-kanda upasana (on the riverbank of Gandaki).
Sadhana	:	Gomukhasana, padmasana siddhis.
Deeds	:	Spreading of dharma and knowledge.

Shri Sananda Nathji

Guru	:	Shri Shambhujati Guru Gorakshanathji.
Panth	:	Satnathi
Place	:	Southeast of Kaylas Mountain.
Tapasya	:	Badrinath, Kedarnath, Gangotri, Yamuna.
Sadhana	:	Dhyan, samadhi, commentation of Vedas, knowledge of Vedas.
Deeds	:	Spreading of Brahma-vidya, svastikasana and hastapada-vakrasana siddhis.

Shri Sanatan Nathji

Guru	:	Shri Omkar Adinathji
Panth	:	Satnath.
Tapasya	:	Badrinath, Kedarnath, Gangotri, yoga-sadhana and gyana-sadhana near Yamuna river, karma-kanda upasana.
Sadhana	:	Padmasana, siddhasana siddhi.
Deeds	:	spreading of dharma and knowledge.

Shri Sanatkumar Nathji

Guru	:	Shri Omkar Adinathji
Panth	:	Satnath.
Place	:	Southwest direction (nairitya)
Sadhana	:	Dharana-Dhyana-Samadhi Yoga, dvipada vatayanasana

siddhi.

Tapasya : Kaylas, Badrinath, Gangotri are the places of tapasya; Brahma-jnyana, Brahma-darshan, commentation of Vedas.

Shri Sarasvatai Nathji

Guru	:	Shri Shambhujati Guru Gorakshanathji
Panth	:	Aai
Place	:	Kaikai (northwest part of India)
Sadhana	:	Pashchimottanasana, siddhasana, virasana siddhis. Spontaneous experience of Shabda-Brahman, also perfect knowledge of music, bhakti-siddhi.
Deeds	:	Spreading of Bhakti Yog.

Shri Shabar Nathji

Guru	:	Shri Siddha Yogi Matsyendranathji
Panth	:	Kapalika.
Place	:	Gauda area in Bengal.
Sadhana	:	mahamudra, shunya-samadhi, antar-mukha sadhana, shmashan-sadhana.
Tapasya	:	Vikram Shila, Magadha (the territory of Bihar and Jarkhand), West Bengal, tapasya on the Shri Shaila Mountain.
Deeds	:	spreading of dharma and care for human well-being.

Shri Shringeri Nathji (Gopichand Nath)

Guru	:	Shri Siddha Yogi Jvalendra nathji.
Panth	:	Pav.
Place	:	Gauda area in Bengal, West

		Bengal (Rangapur).
Sadhana	:	Mulabandha-siddhi in siddhasana, garudasana-siddhi.
Tapasya	:	West Bengal, Rajasthan, Himalayas.
Deeds	:	Wandered around all India and propagated Nath dharma.

Shri Shritai Nathji

Guru	:	Shri Shambhujati Guru Gorakshanathji
Panth	:	Aai
Place	:	Kuru-kshetra (Haryana).
Sadhana	:	Ardhva-pada-hastasana, svastikasana, garudasana siddhis, Kundalini Yoga.
Tapasya	:	Haryana, Panjab, Bengal, Uttar Pradesh, Himalayas etc.
Deeds	:	Spreading of Natha Yoga.

Shri Siddhabuddha Nathji

Guru	:	Shri Siddha Yogi Dariyanathji
Panth	:	Nateshvari (Dariya nathi)
Place	:	Kaikai area, Pakistan.
Tapasya	:	Jammu Kashmir (Amarnath).
Sadhana	:	Padmasana siddhi, gyan-mudra, chandra-ras amrit, , kurmasana siddhi.
Deeds	:	Service for human well-being.

Shri Siddhapad Nath

Guru	:	Shri Siddha Yogi Niranjan nathji
Panth	:	Aai
Place	:	Himachal Pradesh.
Tapasya	:	Uttarakhand, Himachal Pradesh, stood on one foot of 12 years in woods of Badrinath.
Sadhana	:	Padangushtasana siddhi.
Deeds	:	Spreading of Nath dharma around India.

Shri Siddhasan Nathji

Guru	:	Shri Siddha Yogi Matsyendranathji
Panth	:	Aai
Place	:	Southwestern area, Orissa.
Sadhana	:	Tapasya in siddhasana.
Deeds	:	Spreading of yoga around of India and out of it.

Shri Sukadeva Nathji

Guru	:	Shri Shambhujati Guru Gorakshanathji
Panth	:	Ramke
Place	:	On the islands and mountains.
Tapasya	:	Unknown tapasya.
Sadhana	:	Dhruvasana, padmasana siddhis.
Deeds	:	Spreading of Shrimad Bhagavatam, propagating of moksha and mukti.

Shri Surananda Nathji

Guru	:	Shri Siddha Yogi Balaknathji
Panth	:	Bhartrihari Vairag
Place	:	Dungarpur, Rajastan.
Sadhana	:	Gorakshasana siddhi, jnyana-dhyana yoga.
Tapasya	:	Rajasthan, Panjab, Gujarat, Madhya Pradesh.
Deeds	:	Spreading of knowledge and bhakti in Madhya Pradesh, Panjab, Rajasthan.

Shri Surat Nathji

Guru	:	Shri Shambhujati Guru Gorakshanathji
Panth	:	Aai.
Place	:	Panjab, Uttar Pradesh (Shamali).
Sadhana	:	Pavan-muktasana siddhi.

| Tapasya | : | Dhuna-karma sadhana (tapasya near dhuna). |
| Deeds | : | Spreading of yoga siddhanta, showing of the yoga-siddhas in Uttar Pradesh, Panjab, Haryana, Bihar, Rajastan. |

Shri Tara Nathji

Guru	:	Shri Siddha Yogi Matsyendra nathji
Panth	:	Pagal
Place	:	Pancha-janya kshetra (southwestern area).
Tapasya	:	West Bengal, Gauhati (Kamakhya), Himachal, Tibbatia.
Sadhana	:	Padmasana, dvipada-dhruvasana siddhis.
Deeds	:	Kapalika aghora siddhi, care for human well-being.

Shri Tintini Nathji

Guru	:	Shri Siddha Yogi Jalandhar nathji
Panth	:	Pav
Place	:	Southern part of India.
Sadhana	:	Tolasana, lolasana, kukutasana, tripada-ash vasana siddhis.
Deeds	:	Wandered around India, propogated gyan- yoga.

Shri Vakra Nathji

Guru	:	Shri Siddha Yogi Chakra nathji
Panth	:	Nateshvari
Place	:	Kaikei and Jammu district.
Tapasya	:	Himalayas mountains.
Sadhana	:	Svastikasana, vakrasana siddhis, full adherence to Brahman (Brahmacharana).
Deeds	:	Yoga sadhana propagation, yoga

miracles, service to people,
pilgrimage.

Shri Vira Nathji

Guru	:	Shri Shambhujati Guru Gorakshanathji
Panth	:	Dariya nathi.
Place	:	Punjab.
Sadhana	:	Padvirasana siddhi, Shri Hauman upasana.
Tapasya	:	Punjab, Sindh pradesh, Himachal pradesh, Himalayas.
Deeds	:	Propagation of dharma all over the India.

Shri Virupaksha Nathji

Guru	:	Shri Omkar Adinathji.
Panth	:	Sahacharyo (sahajani yog).
Place	:	Shri Parvat Devikot, Orissa.
Sadhana	:	Siddhasana, svastikasana, padmasana, dvipada mastakasana siddhis.
Deeds	:	Support and propagation of Yamari Tantra.

Shri Yajnavalkya Nathji

Guru	:	Shri Siddha Yogi Satyanathji
Panth	:	Satnath
Place	:	Himachal Pradesh, Kanva-kshetra (Kotadvar)
Tapasya	:	Realized siddhis of living on the sun.
Sadhana	:	Dharana-dhyana-samadhi, accent on shunya-samadhi, pavan-muktasana siddhi.
Deeds	:	Propagated JnyanaYoga.

(Source : http://nathas.org/en/parampara/chaurasi)

9 789353 024840